ANZAC NATIONS

Anzac Nations

The legacy of Gallipoli in Australia and New Zealand 1965–2015

ROWAN LIGHT

OTAGO UNIVERSITY PRESS
Te Whare Tā o Te Wānanga o Ōtākou

Published by Otago University Press
Te Whare Tā o Te Wānanga o Ōtākou
533 Castle Street, Dunedin, New Zealand
university.press@otago.ac.nz
www.otago.ac.nz/press

First published 2022

ISBN 978-1-99-004820-3

Editor: Imogen Coxhead
Index: Lee Slater

Printed in China through Asia Pacific Offset

MIX
Paper from responsible sources
FSC® C136333

Contents

Introduction

'We remember'

The Anzac revival 1965–2015

On 25 April 1915 the Australian and New Zealand Army Corps (Anzac) landed in Ottoman Turkey at the beginning of the nine-month Gallipoli campaign, in which hundreds of thousands of men fought and died in the cause of the Great War. A century later and nearly a generation after the death of the last Anzac veteran, a different landing occurred. Ten thousand Australian and New Zealand citizens, their heads of government, members of the British royal family and other international dignitaries gathered for the dawn service at Anzac Cove on the Gallipoli Peninsula, to mark the Anzac Centenary.

The ceremony in 2015 was much more than a memorial to a historic invasion, however. Speaking to the assembled multitude, Australian Prime Minister Tony Abbott declared that the experience of Gallipoli, when the heroes of the two nations came ashore together on that fateful day 100 years earlier, had forged modern Australia and New Zealand: 'Now we gather in the cold and dark before dawn, wondering what to say and how to honour those whose bones rest in the hills and in the valleys above us and whose spirit has moved our people for a century.'[1] New Zealand Prime Minister John Key also celebrated this sense of a joint history, the 'Anzac bond': 'Gallipoli is also a byword for the best characteristics of Australians and New Zealanders,' he said, 'especially when they work side by side in the face of adversity.'[2] The audience shared a connection that transcended the experience of those Anzacs a century ago and linked Australian and New Zealand citizens across the world in a national spirit, founded on the shingle of Anzac Cove. The two prime ministers espoused a shared foundation myth. Australia and New Zealand are Anzac nations and on Anzac Day, as Key intoned, 'we remember'.

This glance at the 2015 dawn service shows that 'Anzac' invokes many things: a place (Anzac Cove), an annual ritual (Anzac Day) and a group of people – the

Anzacs. Anzac symbolises something about what it means to be an Australian or a New Zealander, as well as friendship between the two countries. It suggests a collective existence: a shared story and tradition authorised by the events of 1915, and a legacy of values and attitudes concretised in a heritage of physical sites, relics and monuments.[3] The Anzacs as a corps were precursors to an Anzac citizenship that communicated both social and political relationships. Above all, the shared performance at Anzac Cove in 2015 suggested something fundamentally ahistorical: in invoking the meaning of the past, the centenary inscribed a future that was yet to come.[4]

The 2015 centenary was extraordinary for several reasons. The first was the inconvertible expression of Anzac as a national culture that legitimised a powerful notion of sovereignty – the very basis on which to organise shared society.[5] Remembrance is a site in which social and political consensus is 'forged, manufactured, and maintained'; through this public authority the continuity of statehood is upheld beyond the acts of governments.[6] Nation-states are, of course, particularly invested in shared remembrance, and require myths that provide a distinctive origin story and form the basis for ongoing relationships. The 2015 centenary story obscured the imperial origins of Anzac commemoration, creating a myth that was a break from the past. Historian F.M. Cutlack, writing in 1921, offered his assessment of the word 'Anzac', describing it as a war cry as 'pitiless as a hurled spear': '[Anzac] cuts like a sword … convey[ing] something savagely masculine, ruthless, resolute, clean driven home.' Anthony Asquith's 1931 film *Tell England* depicted the Gallipoli campaign as a Homeric epic of imperial love and loyalty, and there was no contradiction in promoting the film to Australian and New Zealand audiences with the byline 'Out of the mists of Anzac rises a great romance of glorious youth!'[7] No hint of this British militancy or imperial fervour remained in 2015. The centenary evoked Gallipoli as the beginning of the nation: not the arrival of the First Fleet in 1788 or federation in 1901, in the case of Australia, or the 1840 signing of the Treaty of Waitangi in the case of New Zealand, but at Gallipoli in 1915.

The second extraordinary fact of the 2015 centenary was the way it reflected the culmination of a remarkable change in the collective memories of Australians and New Zealanders. Fifty years earlier, the anniversary of the Gallipoli landing in 1965 had been marked by profound anxiety about Anzac Day's imminent demise. The commemoration was intended not for the satisfaction of the public but for those who had experienced the Great War first hand. But the number of ageing veterans was declining. As one famous Australian Anzac ballad goes, 'One day, no one will march here at all.'[8] Like many others, composer Eric Bogle assumed that the tradition of remembering the Anzacs would not survive beyond the death of the last Gallipoli veteran. What was remarkable in 2015, therefore, was not simply the manner in which the Anzacs were remembered, but that they were remembered at all.

Third, the centenary was extraordinary in its presentation of collective histories: an Anzac nationhood shared by Australians and New Zealanders. Anzac itself is, of course, a shared acronym, but a comparison of Anzac commemoration in Australia and New Zealand reveals distinct scripts, practices and constitutional patterns, as the work of Philippa Mein Smith indicates.[9] For example, unlike Indigenous people from other parts of the British Empire, Māori were enlisted as a distinct unit in the New Zealand forces – the Māori Contingent. Indigenous service in Australia, on the other hand, was hidden: although many Indigenous Australians did serve at Gallipoli and in other theatres of war, Aboriginal and Torres Strait Islander communities were officially excluded from recruitment – and, in fact, Australian citizenship – due to racial prescriptions against fighting a 'white man's war'.[10] Australian war memorials tend to celebrate those who volunteered for war service; New Zealand sites honour the fallen.[11] The branding of the centenary programmes is indicative of these differences between the two nations. The Australian logo proudly displayed the acronym 'Anzac'; it is, after all, as Jo Hawkins observes, 'Australia's most powerful brand'.[12] The New Zealand WW100 logo did not use the acronym, suggesting a broader memory of war.

One of the few centenary projects shared between the Anzac nations illustrated further differences. The New Zealand Film Commission and Screen Australia jointly funded a documentary that would illustrate both sides of the Anzac story at Gallipoli. New Zealand distributers opted for the graphic title *Tides of Blood*, whereas in Australia it was called *Why Anzac?* – a title that presumed the myth's pre-eminence in Australian national culture.

These claims invite important questions: why do we remember the Gallipoli campaign, fought over a hundred years ago in a far-flung corner of the world, and see it as an expression of national belonging? What shapes this collective remembrance in Australia and New Zealand? Who has authority over what is – and is not – remembered on 25 April, and why does this national memory focus so heavily on the place and experience of Gallipoli, rather than on other aspects of past violence at home or abroad? And what is its political and cultural function in our societies? Together, Australian and New Zealand commemorations evoke a host of other questions: to what extent do Australia and New Zealand 'share' the meaning of Anzac? Has this shared national focus always existed, and has New Zealand's Anzac commemoration been influenced by Australia and vice-versa?

Anzac Nations examines how this commemoration has evolved since 1965. It draws on evidence and stories from both sides of the Tasman, examining similarities and differences to present a history that is comparative and transnational. It seeks to understand the way in which nation and culture are shaped and enacted across and between imaginative and territorial boundaries; how Gallipoli remembrance has changed in Australia and New Zealand; and how two distinct collective memories have interacted and shaped each other.

The 2015 centenary was part of a wider story of changes to national history, memory and myth in Australia and New Zealand. Since 1965, the story of Gallipoli and the Anzacs has transformed: once understood as a personal and social experience within the British Empire, it now articulates a new nationalism that asserts a distinctive and independent cultural existence for Australians and New Zealanders. In exploring these changes, this book questions the proposition, stated as prima facie in the Anzac Centenary, of an Anzac nationhood shared by Australians and New Zealanders that has motivated us for a century. The connection between Gallipoli as a place and Anzac Day as a national practice is a relatively recent development, and an unfinished story – one that traces how the state has increasingly come to define the way the public sees itself, while interrogating why Anzac heritage is now a chief means of imagining nationhood.

The Anzac revival

The return of Anzac Day – from its decline in the 1960s to its rise as a significant day of commemoration – springs from two decades of political and cultural change around war commemoration in Australia and New Zealand since the 1980s, a phenomenon known as the Anzac revival. Historians, especially in Australia, have debated at length the causes and extent of the ascendancy of Anzac Day in public life.[13] These debates have been shaped by a growing body of scholarship on the cultural, political and social legacies of mass violence in the 'long nineteenth century', and its remembrance and commemoration into the late twentieth century.[14]

Australian historian Ken Inglis was the first to emphasise the sacred qualities of 'the Anzac tradition', arguing that the commemoration provides Australia with a 'national civil religion'.[15] War memorials, he suggests, provide sacred places in which to imagine the connection between the living and the dead.[16] Sociologist Paul Morris speculates that Anzac Day offers a shared spiritual experience for New Zealanders as society becomes more ethnically and religiously diverse in the twenty-first century.[17] Certainly, Christianity provided a shared trans-Tasman language and liturgical practice in 1915 and its aftermath.[18] The original Anzac Day services were modelled on the memorial service for the dead organised by military chaplains, centred on a benediction, and were enhanced by Anzac Day's proximity to Easter Week and the symbolism of Christ's paschal sacrifice.[19] Anzac seems to offer a foundation for guiding principles to re-moralise the past.

The vast cultural trauma of World War I is central to Anzac commemorations. The death and maiming of millions in the course of the Great War produced deep reverberations that continue to echo today.[20] Christina Twomey has added to our understanding of the emotional resonance of modern commemoration. As the complex effects of post-traumatic stress syndrome and other mental wounds of violence have become better understood, the language of remembrance has become more therapeutic, with emphasis on the psychological victimhood of the ordinary soldier who returned from war.[21]

Referring to the cemeteries on the peninsula in his 1956 book *Gallipoli*, Alan Moorehead observed that 'not more than half a dozen visitors arrive from one year's end to the other'.[22] The few who did travel to Gallipoli in those early days, such as those on the *Duchess of Richmond* 'pilgrimage cruise' in 1934 recorded by writer Stanton Hope, were deemed tourists unless they had personally experienced the battle.[23] The number of Australian and New Zealand citizens who attended the dawn service at Gallipoli in 2015 was evidence of the transcendental cachet of Anzac remembrance, the rise of Gallipoli tourism and the commodification of remembrance.[24]

Gallipoli has now become a centre of national attention, depicted in plays, films and books, and thousands of Australians and New Zealanders travel to the peninsula. What began in the 1980s as a trickle of expatriate backpackers over the 2000s became a flood that has turned the landscape into a site of pilgrimage, particularly for young men. Bruce Scates in his study of these Gallipoli 'pilgrims' observes that Anzac Cove appears to be a place through which the 'sordid reality of death' in war is 'ennobled, sanctified, reified, forgotten'.[25] The distinction between tourists and pilgrims has blurred. Walking in the footsteps of the Anzacs, it seems, creates a link between the soldiers of 1915 and New Zealanders and Australians today.[26] Turkish tour guides, eager to embrace the potential commerce offered by tourism, shape this experience of Gallipoli by relating stories of the noble friendship between the Anzac nations and the Republic of Turkey. The sentiment is encapsulated in the apocryphal words of Mustafa Kemal Atatürk, probably the most commonly quoted in Gallipoli remembrance: 'Having lost their lives on this land, [the Anzacs] have become our sons as well.'[27]

The emotional and spiritual appeal of Gallipoli has burgeoned alongside a new political commitment to Anzac commemoration. Mark McKenna notes how, where once military and civic leaders such as the governor-general had pride of place at commemorative ceremonies, prime ministers now take centre stage as 'interpreters of the nation'.[28] Jenny Macleod traces the 'fall and rise' of Anzac Day by contrasting attitudes to Anzac in 1965 with the 75th anniversary of Gallipoli in 1990, when Labor leader Bob Hawke (1983–91) became the first prime minister to attend the Gallipoli dawn service and celebrated a vision of Australia as a modern independent nation, a theme taken up by his successor, Paul Keating (1991–96).[29] This 'commemorative diplomacy' was heightened under the conservative Liberal government of John Howard (1996–2007).[30] New Zealand Prime Minister Helen Clark (1999–2008) embraced a similar vision and aligned closely with the Howard government on cultural and defence policy in her agenda of 'cultural recovery'.[31] As part of this new political rhetoric, public leaders now speak of how the Anzacs died for our values as liberal democracies in the twenty-first century; young and innocent, they were swept away to war by forces beyond their control as heroic victims of arrogant imperialism and the cold machinery of modern violence.[32]

The top-down work of political leaders and policymakers, and public responses through tourism and pilgrimage, are some of the factors that have shaped remembrance. But neither of these strands of the Anzac revival fully explains why Anzac has become such a potent myth, nor why Gallipoli has become a focal point of this myth. After all, the greatest causalities experienced by the Australian and New Zealand forces in World War I were not amid the cliffs of the Ottoman Dardanelles but in the mud of Flanders in Belgium, at battles such as Passchendaele in 1917.[33] Memory has a history; groups and institutions work deliberately to share stories that are necessarily selective.[34] Most of the scholarship on the Anzac revival focuses entirely on the Australian side of the phenomenon; only a few historians have considered the similarities and differences between Anzac in Australia and New Zealand, and no scholarship has yet sought to understand how Australian and New Zealand commemorations have shaped each other.

A third strand of historical writing on the Anzac revival is needed to show how the rise of a national remembrance of Gallipoli rewrites the stories of Australia and New Zealand to remove the legacy of the British Empire. Mark McKenna argues that Australia has a 'history anxiety' owing to European settlement in an ancient landscape; indeed, both Australia and New Zealand inhabit a peculiar cultural and political context as states where 'Indigenous people do not achieve sovereign independence and the settlers do not go "home"', as Miranda Johnson puts it.[35] Monuments, memorials, processions, rituals of social integration, art galleries, museums and official histories have all been a constant part of the meaning-making of settler cultures.[36] If empire was a cultural system that helped to make sense of the first Anzac Day, then any history of change needs to come to terms with the way that Australia and New Zealand are now post-imperial nations.

The 'end' of the British Empire was an extended period of cultural, political and economic crisis. The more than 10-year process of Britain entering the European Economic Community (1961–73) captures some sense of this. During this time Australia and New Zealand had to come up with new markets and defence arrangements on which to base their prosperity and security; and citizens lost the meaning of the imperial language that had circumscribed their worlds. The crucial phase in this process of adjustment was signalled by constitutional upheavals. In Australia, in 1975, the Whitlam Labor government was dismissed by the governor-general in order to end a parliamentary deadlock and undercut the government's radical reform agenda.[37] Nine years later, in 1984, New Zealand experienced its own economic upheaval, which bordered on the constitutional, when the outgoing National Prime Minister Rob Muldoon refused to devalue the New Zealand dollar as requested by the incoming Labour government under David Lange.[38]

In the fragmenting world of empire the governments pursued new strategic alliances and in 1951 signed the Australia, New Zealand, United States Security Treaty (Anzus). Its suspension in 1986, however, suggested an instability that had not managed to plug the gaps left by empire.[39] The period was accompanied by what James Curran and Stuart Ward observe as the linkage between the end of empire and a psychological language of 'identity crisis', itself peculiar to postcolonial nations.[40] In New Zealand, the interminable search for a secure national identity has been dubbed 'the Great Debate'.[41]

The creation of new days of commemoration to celebrate the independence of the nations expressed much of the mixed enthusiasm for a new nationalism after empire. Australia Day, 26 January, which remembers the arrival of the first British penal colonists at Sydney Cove in New South Wales in 1788, emerged in the 1970s to mark the 'beginning' of the nation. In New Zealand, a fragile public consensus suggested that the Treaty of Waitangi/Te Tiriti o Waitangi, signed in 1840 between Māori rangatira (chiefs) and the British Crown, provided a much-needed national foundation.[42] Governments vacillated between calling the 6 February anniversary 'New Zealand Day' or 'Waitangi Day'.[43]

The 1988 bicentenary of British settlement in Australia and the 1990 sesquicentennial of the signing of the Treaty of Waitangi identified parallel fault lines in this process of the end of empire. Both commemorations presented key tropes of national progress. By the late 1980s Australia and New Zealand were multicultural nations who had left behind empire and racial Britishness, but the language and rituals of these celebrations collided with another set of stories: those of Indigenous communities and their survival under the experience of colonisation. The opening of the bicentenary celebrations at Sydney Cove, at which Bob Hawke spoke of 'a commitment to Australia and its future' as the defining characteristic of Australian citizenship, coincided with a growing Indigenous rights movement for whom the bicentenary year was one not of celebration but of mourning. Some 40,000 protesters marched through Sydney demanding public recognition of Australia's colonial past.[44] In New Zealand the 1990 commemoration of the signing of the Treaty was similarly marked by protest. Queen Elizabeth II, invited to oversee the celebrations, arrived at Waitangi to mass demonstrations.[45]

These public debates reflected a decade of massive change. It was impossible for governments to organise national commemorations on home soil that promoted public narratives celebrating contemporary society without stirring up the divisions of the past. Incoherent and commercialist, the commemorations fared poorly. At the bicentenary a Coca-Cola flag was flown above the First Fleet re-enactment regatta, where historically the Union Jack had been raised. Activists laid wreaths at the Australian War Memorial to mourn 'invasion day' and the Aboriginal people who had 'died since white settlement'.[46] In 1990 the New Zealand press accused the Waitangi Commission, tasked with organising the sesquicentennial celebrations of the Treaty signing, of being more interested in inviting international celebrities than fostering a serious reflection of New Zealand history and culture.

History as a practice was central to these constitutional debates. Interpretations of the past, put forward by historians, build on one another to shape how the public view the past, and imbue it with importance. Prominent historians such as Manning Clark, Keith Sinclair and W.H. Oliver saw themselves as prophets searching for national stories of shared identity. Clark's six-volume *The History of Australia* outlined the conflict between imperial loyalties and those who stood for the new nationalism – between 'the Old Dead Tree and the Young Tree Green'.[47] Sinclair and Oliver wove a sense of place, belonging, war experience and pioneering spirit with notions of national identity; Sinclair's 1986 *A Destiny Apart* sought to cut New Zealand history loose from its imperial and trans-Tasman linkages. Ann Curthoys observes how these works focused on 'what is distinctive about the history of the nation, what seems to hold it together', based on the implicit assumption that the task of national history is 'the discovery of what makes a nation, a people distinctive, rather than a focus on 'what is shared with histories and societies elsewhere'.[48]

Decolonisation gave this role of national history a new direction. The Australian 'history wars' conscripted historians into a public debate and asked them to 'justify or condemn the nation', as Richard White put it in 1991.[49] In 1972 historian Henry Reynolds published the first of his seminal works in which he outlined the conflict between Indigenous Australians and European settlers as part of the formative years of the Australian state.[50] Debates raged around whether these books constituted a 'black armband' – brow-beating non-Indigenous Australians about a shameful past – or whether an inability to confront difficult histories was a 'white blindfold'. A nominal ceasefire was declared after Kevin Rudd's federal apology to the Stolen Generation in 2008.

In New Zealand the government established the Waitangi Tribunal in 1975 to adjudicate breaches of the Treaty; its powers were extended in 1985 to include historical claims. Historians were recruited into what became the most significant public hearings of Māori stories of colonisation in New Zealand's constitutional history. This was not without controversy: historian Giselle Byrnes, in her 2004 book *The Waitangi Tribunal and New Zealand History*, argued that the very process of the tribunal created a 'grievance history', one that seriously distorted the understanding of the nation's past.[51]

This whirlwind story of empire and its end covers a period of Australian and New Zealand history that has not been readily integrated into public memory. Scholars refer to the 'amnesia of empire' in the United Kingdom as well as the former dominions – a kind of cultural forgetting of the ways that imperial identity was the sinew that kept the national story in place.[52] Cultural amnesia refers to the loss of the shared stories that bring different elements together in a coherent whole. That Anzac Day was revived precisely at a time when the British heritage of

Australia and New Zealand was called into question is crucial to understanding the spiritual, emotional and political appeal of commemoration in 2015. The fact that Prime Ministers Abbott and Key presided over the Gallipoli dawn service under the auspices of the British Crown shows us that although the empire is gone, its legacies remain.

*

The 2015 centenary offered a mix of family memory and national legend connected to the place of Gallipoli.[53] A drive through small towns in Australia and New Zealand in the lead-up to Anzac Day 2015 revealed many local expressions of Anzac commemoration that were far from the official scripts developed by political leaders. What was powerful about the centenary, however, and especially evident at the Gallipoli dawn service, was the way the rhetoric and ritual rose above these small networks of remembrance and made broad claims about what it means to be an Australian or a New Zealander. The commemoration was an opportunity to remember the past in certain ways. Where Anzac once invoked imperial and martial pride for audiences of the Anzac Day services, today it stands as a metaphor for Australian and New Zealand citizenship and belonging in the twenty-first century; it asserts a powerful sense of permanence and endurance and yet, as this history of Anzac Day since the 1960s shows, remains incomplete and far from certain.

This interaction of official and unofficial commemoration, underpinned by cultures of nationalism after empire, forms the focus of *Anzac Nations*. The Anzac revival was not inevitable, and predictions in the 1960s of the collapse of Anzac Day were not groundless. Cultures of Anzac memory are produced by dedicated groups and networks and the stories they share. Institutions like memorials, archives and government offices might appear to operate in the same way in Australia and New Zealand, but they are shaped by distinct constitutional structures and the needs and demands of memory after colonisation. A recurring tension here is the way in which historians, who frequently cross the line between critiquing remembrance and re-inscribing its meaning, have played a part in the development of cultural myths.[54] Nationalist histories themselves need to be the subject of histories.[55]

A book of this scope cannot possibly cover all aspects of commemoration since 1965. Limited focus is therefore given to the rituals of Anzac Day. The rubrics of the annual commemoration, set during the 1920s, have remained remarkably stable: the last major innovation came in 1939 when the New Zealand Returned and Services Association (RSA) officially adopted the dawn service, first recorded in New South Wales in 1923.[56] In New Zealand the most significant part of Anzac Day services is the laying of wreaths; in Australia the overtly patriotic parade is of central importance.[57]

Since 1965, moves towards a post-imperial remembrance may be placed alongside the search for national foundational myths around Australia Day and Waitangi Day. As well as the Australian Bicentenary in 1988 and the sesquicentennial of the signing of Te Tiriti in 1990, state projects commemorating women's suffrage in New Zealand in 1993 and the centenary of the Boer War in 1999 may also be considered. Most recently, the 250th anniversary of Captain Cook's voyage to the Pacific has provoked discussion about older imperial legacies of European exploration and colonisation in Australia and New Zealand. The commemorations of colonial wars similarly complicate stories of national founding and have been the source of considerable tension: there is ongoing debate, for example, about whether the Australian War Memorial should recognise colonial violence as part of Australia's military heritage.

All of these discussions reflect the way in which growing state investment in war commemoration is an expression of cultural nationalism after empire – a desire to heighten public awareness about history for the purposes of shoring up the claims of the nation. *Anzac Nations* examines how myth-making around Anzac has evolved, and continues to evolve, by exploring 'flashpoints' in the history of Australian and New Zealand commemorations, and the groups, strategies and processes that have contributed to these.

The book focuses on three aspects: the changing and contested meanings of Anzac from the 1960s to the 1980s; the expanded role of the state in commemoration since 1990; and responses to these shifts by Indigenous and non-Indigenous communities. Chapter One explores the role of historians in the changing story of the Anzacs at the 50th anniversary of Gallipoli in 1965, as veterans' groups began to lose their authority over the event. Protests, which redrew the public boundaries of Anzac rituals in the 1960s and 1970s, are the focus of Chapter Two. Chapter Three examines how filmmakers and writers have evoked to a new imaginative engagement with Gallipoli in the 1980s, and in Chapter Four the growing role of the state in commemoration in the 1990s becomes apparent, expressed in particular in the repatriations of the unknown Australian soldier in 1993 and the unknown New Zealand warrior in 2004 – the two repatriations are compared in Chapter Five. Prime ministers take centre stage in Chapter Six as Anzac was woven into a kind of commemorative diplomacy, and Chapter Seven looks at the way Indigenous media have shaped public interaction with the Anzac revival. In the final chapter the book returns to the politics and policies of the Anzac Centenary and considers the future of commemoration in Australia and New Zealand. Each chapter reflects on the power of remembrance to inspire sentiments and stories of the past in order to provide coherence and unity in a changing world, and the cultural and political agendas that underpin the commemoration of the Anzacs.

Anzac Nations is not a definitive narrative of Anzac myth, but offers a fresh perspective to provoke new questions and provide scope for future scholarship. Best historical practice is cautious in its truth-claims and comfortable with its fragmentary narration; otherwise, an account about myth-making simply ends up being another restatement of that myth.[58] Instead, the book places Anzac commemoration in a picture bigger than local and national contexts. At the same time, it shows how remembrance is shaped by the work of dedicated people, working across networks such as museums and memorials, responding to important political and constitutional questions. Because remembrance makes intimate claims on who we are as Australian and New Zealand citizens, so we need to be critically engaged in how these stories are told – and why.

CHAPTER 1

'Between courage and slaughter'

The shifting narratives of Anzac Day, 1965

In many ways, the 50th anniversary of Anzac Day on 25 April 1965 was a typical day of remembrance in Australia and New Zealand. The postwar commemoration was based on shared networks between religious and political hierarchies in Australia and New Zealand, infused with the symbolism of empire. In both countries the commemoration centred on the experience of returned servicemen. Anzac Day and Remembrance Day, the latter commemorating the armistice of the war on 11 November 1918, provided a means to leverage support for elderly soldiers, giving these citizens a special place in the fabric of civil society. 'The spirit of Anzac', which, according to some in the press in 1965, burned 'as brightly as ever', evoked the comradeship of these men.

By 1965, however, Remembrance Day celebrations had more or less disappeared and Anzac Day was showing signs of strain.[1] Attendance rates at ceremonies were declining and there was growing uncertainty as to the meaning of the day. Some 30,000 people had flocked to attend the first Anzac Day ceremony at the Auckland War Memorial in 1946; by 1948 this number had fallen to 5000, and similar drop-offs were recorded in Melbourne and Sydney.[2] This was matched by collapsing membership of ex-servicemen groups. Commemoration, it seemed, was no longer sustained by what author Joan Aspinall-Oglander called 'the pathos of the headstones', when she visited Gallipoli between the world wars.[3]

Changing attitudes towards Anzac Day were reflected in legislation as well. In 1949 the Anzac Day Act 1920 (New Zealand) was repealed to dedicate the day to the dead of both world wars and the Boer War, rather than just World War I, and to discard the ban on 'Mondayising' – the act of moving a statutory holiday to the nearest Monday in order to secure a long weekend. The Act required that 25 April be observed 'as if it were a Sunday', and local councils banned virtually all organised leisure on the day.[4] Other proposals, such as moving Anzac Day observation to the nearest Sunday or limiting the ban on organised recreation to the morning only, were discussed and discounted. By 1965, however, the Dominion Council of the New Zealand RSA was considering further reforms to the day that would free the afternoon of 25 April from its restrictive solemnity. Australian laws differed between states, producing a patchwork of practices.[5]

It is probable that the 50th anniversary of Gallipoli would have been something of a nadir of war remembrance were it not for the decision of the Australian Returned and Services League (RSL), in conjunction with the New Zealand RSA, to organise a three-week pilgrimage to Turkey. Over 300 people registered, 57 of them from New Zealand, most of them elderly males who had served at Gallipoli. The itinerary included a Mediterranean cruise to Malta and Egypt and a restaging of the landing at Anzac Cove on Anzac Day. The landing party – 'first-dayers' (men who had landed on the first day of the Allied invasion of the Gallipoli Peninsula in 1915) and pilgrimage organisers – were met by a ragtag welcoming party: a handful of Turkish veterans and onlookers, a government official and some enthusiastic expatriate backpackers who had made the trip from Istanbul.

The shingle of Anzac Cove was empty, looking more or less as it did when British authorities returned the territory to the newly formed Turkish republic in 1922. The old men shuffled up the beach, shook hands with the locals and exchanged gifts. Over the course of the day they and their fellow pilgrims laid wreaths and mementos on the unkempt graves of Ari Burnu. A small group of RSA members broke away to visit the memorial at Chunuk Bair. By evening the pilgrims had been bustled back on board the ferry to return to their ship, the *Karadeniz*, for the final leg of their journey.

The pilgrimage served to remind the Australian and New Zealand public that 'the war generation' was not long for this world: indeed, three veterans died on the trip.[6] For most Australians members of the party the cost, around £650 per person, was covered by RSL sub-branches and associated clubs, supported through a subsidy of £20,000 from the Australian federal government. The New Zealand government gave the RSA a grant of £5000 to assist with travel costs. Without the federal subsidy, the pilgrimage would likely not have gone ahead on the same scale.

Joining the RSL contingent was Australian historian Ken Inglis, at the time a junior lecturer at the Australian National University. As one of two journalists in the party, he was contracted by the *Canberra Times* to write a series of despatches from the trip. It was, he said, a chance 'to talk … with a large group of veterans and be with them as they returned, most of them for the first time, to old battlefields and the resting places of comrades'.[7] The topic would later form the central theme of Inglis' academic career and several of his essays remain important records of the anniversary.[8]

Inglis' presence highlighted two significant differences between Australia and New Zealand. The first was in funding. Although both governments were reluctant to support the RSL/RSA pilgrimage, seeing it as a private venture and not wanting to single out one particular veterans' group for special treatment, the disparity in funding between the two nations suggested a historical difference in priorities. This was apparent right back in 1914 when the federal government appointed journalist and writer Charles Bean as an official war correspondent to accompany the Australian Imperial Force (AIF) to Europe. After the war Bean brought his wealth of experience to bear in the official histories of 'Australia's War', 12 volumes brimming with the zeal of a writer who had witnessed history unfolding, and which remain among the most popular works of Australian history. In contrast, the New Zealand government refused to pay for a war correspondent to accompany the New Zealand Expeditionary Forces (NZEF). A consortium of New Zealand newspapers eventually funded journalist Malcolm Ross to travel to the front lines. He arrived late at Gallipoli, in May 1915, and, falling ill, relied on his friend Charles Bean to write some of his despatches. Where Bean enjoyed the full support of the federal government, as an unofficial correspondent Ross was reliant on London-based newspapers to telegraph his reports to New Zealand, and his somewhat scrappy reporting was often lost amid the more immediate concerns of his British and Australian counterparts. Delays and poor health eventually led to his recall in 1916. After the war, Ross – a civilian – was sidelined by the government, who instead commissioned military officers to provide an official history.[9]

This leads to the second significant aspect of Inglis' presence on the journey. Historians and other participants in remembrance practices and story-telling can shape the tide of memory. Like a latter-day Bean accompanying the 'second landing' in 1965, Inglis' reports imbued the pilgrimage with special significance. His particularly national emphasis in the story of these Anzac pilgrims came at an important time of change, and suggested how commemoration might provide a story of shared tradition and heritage. Inglis did not create the Anzac revival, but his work would lend a distinctly Australian tone to interpretations of the revival and inaugurate a new historiography of Anzac. Historians have tended to view Inglis' role in writing Anzac history as that of a sideline observer. When RSA veteran Hugh Belliss took photographs of the pilgrims as they landed at Anzac Cove in 1965, however, a young Inglis appears front and centre. The historian was as much a part of the show.

The 50th anniversary occured in an unsettled period in which a variety of narratives vied with one another. The Anzac myth, in 1965, was far from certain. Shared or parallel stories of Anzac Day in Australian and New Zealand Anzac commemoration were about to diverge.

'The old soldiers do not falter': Anzac Day 1965 in Australia and New Zealand

In New Zealand the 50th anniversary of Anzac Day centred on a jubilee service in Wellington. Seven hundred veterans (including 80 Gallipoli veterans), members of the armed forces and school cadets marched in an afternoon parade to the Citizens' War Memorial service, which was conducted by the Roman Catholic Archbishop, Peter McKeefry.[10] Governor-General Sir Bernard Fergusson gave the main address, and Deputy Prime Minister Jack Marshall represented the Holyoake National government. Fergusson called the number of attending veterans 'magnificent', and promised it would be the highlight of his telegram to the Queen. The high turnout was a feature in the wider region too, where hundreds of veterans marched in parades in Lower Hutt and Wainuiomata.

The jubilee service was organised by the Dominion Council of the RSA with the local Wellington RSA branch and the Gallipoli Association, whose members had served in the 1915 campaign. The organisers explicitly sought to avoid a service of 'national character', and instead named it the 'capital city and Wellington district Jubilee Parade and Service'.[11] The Citizens' War Memorial, as well as being accessible, reflected the emphasis on local returned servicemen's networks rather than the public, who were not actively encouraged to participate. The anniversary was for the men who had served in the war and included their next of kin and civic representatives – city councillors, diplomats, and military and church leaders.[12] Australian expatriates, who had formed their own Wellington AIF Association, were also included.

The emphasis was consistent across New Zealand. Some 3000 veterans and members of the public turned out to ceremonies in Christchurch. In Auckland no special events were organised; the dawn service at the Auckland Cenotaph, attended by 2500 people, of whom around 500 were returned servicemen, including a dozen

Gallipoli veterans, was 'smaller than in earlier years and quieter', according to the *New Zealand Herald*.[13] In nearby Ōrākei, a bronze plaque inscribed in te reo Māori and dedicated to Māori servicemen of both world wars was unveiled at the Interdenominational Chapel on the marae grounds.[14]

The largest gathering of Gallipoli veterans occurred in Rotorua, the country's unofficial cultural capital.[15] A parade of almost a thousand returned servicemen from throughout the central North Island marched through the main streets to the sports ground where the mayor, A.M. Linton, conferred on them the freedom of the city. Victoria Cross recipient Cyril Bassett planted a sapling raised from a seed from the forests of Lone Pine on the Gallipoli Peninsula. The ceremony was followed by a prayer service and a reunion dinner. The event was typical of the time: local communities organised reunions for elderly servicemen; the anniversary was not a significant national moment for the wider public.[16]

This was also a feature of Australian commemorations. The major civic ceremony of the anniversary was held in the federal capital, Canberra, where a crowd of 14,000 (one-sixth of the city's population) gathered to hear the Queen's message read by the Duke of Gloucester at the Australian War Memorial service.[17] Some 1600 veterans marched with 1400 active servicemen along the newly opened Anzac Parade, and a special Anzac contingent of 80 men from Gallipoli, including six who had served in the NZEF and one New Guinean, was given prominence. The pageantry reiterated the imperial relationship between Australia and Britain, and newspapers differentiated between the public, who 'witnessed' the ceremony, and the main participants – the ex-servicemen: the *Canberra Times* declared it was about 'the veterans and their day'.[18] Elsewhere, the *Times* reported that a record crowd of more than 16,000 'tourists' attended the Anzac ceremonies.[19]

In Melbourne the dawn service was lightly attended, mainly by veterans, but the afternoon service at the Shrine of Remembrance was host to the largest gathering of ex-servicemen since the interwar period. Some 32,000 marched, compared to around 20,000 the previous year.[20] Four mounted Light Horse Gallipoli veterans led the parade.[21] Officials attributed the size of the crowd – 40,000 lined the streets – to 'the important half-century anniversary' and the perfect weather.[22] Gallipoli veterans were invited to file past the memorial and place a paper flower in remembrance. Local commentators noted the comradeship of the veterans, proclaiming, 'The spirit of Anzac burns as brightly as ever'.[23]

The strong presence of veterans and their prominent place in ceremonies was a common theme across other states. The Adelaide street march and dawn service, conducted by church ministers, drew the largest attendance since the end of the war.[24] Significant numbers turned out in small towns too: in regional New South Wales 400 veterans marched in Bourke and 300 in the Fairfield parade, along with hundreds of schoolchildren.[25] As in New Zealand, reunions were the mainstay of local community commemorations throughout Australia, and the newspapers were filled with pages of details and arrangements.[26]

In both countries, Anzac Day provided a way to leverage government and public support for the welfare of veterans. The New Zealand RSA organised its annual Poppy Day, and the sale of paper poppies was common in workplaces and schools in the early 1960s. Volunteer poppy sellers were becoming harder to find, however, and in 1965 the Department of Veterans' Affairs required staff to take time off work to sell the flowers. Although the poppy was originally associated with Remembrance Day, New Zealanders had promoted sales for Anzac Day since the 1920s. In Australia the poppy remained closely associated with the November anniversary of the armistice, and bunches of rosemary – an imperial tradition – were the main floral tribute on 25 April, sold by volunteers of Legacy, a charity established to support the families of returned servicemen.

The RSL launched its own appeal for donations to support veterans and widows from the world wars. Businesses were encouraged to make cash donations, to purchase laurel wreaths for display, to exhibit posters in support of the appeal, and to promote the sale of Anzac Star badges.[27] Anzac Star donations were directed to the RSL's welfare projects of building accommodation for elderly returned servicemen and war widows.[28] Letters to the editor at this time advocated for greater public support for veterans. One, entitled 'Pittance for old Anzacs', complained of a perceived neglect of veterans' health services.[29] Other forms of support were on offer: Air New South Wales provided free travel for Anzacs wishing to attend the Sydney commemorations; collections for distressed ex-servicemen were taken up at some Anzac services; and a souvenir issue of the *Sunday Telegraph* outlined practical welfare policies for veterans, including guides for 'repatriation benefits' and an RSL-sponsored 'Anzac Tribute'.[30] Meetings of 'the boys of the old unit' – such as a reunion lunch for former prisoners of war (POWs) held in Sydney[31] – was a common trend of the postwar period and an embodiment of the Anzac spirit, as an *Age* editorial mused after Anzac Day in 1954.[32] The role of the Australian public was to observe, respectfully and with gratitude, rather than participate.

The 1965 New Zealand commemorations placed a mixed emphasis on Gallipoli. The Wellington *Evening Post* acknowledged that 'the Gallipoli men' had a special claim on Anzac Day but suggested that, in keeping with the 1949 broadening of the Anzac Day Act to include the war dead of World War II and the Boer War, it should really be a day of 'remembrance of all those who have died in the nation's wars'.[33]

In the week leading up to Anzac Day the media focused on personal experiences of the war. The National Broadcasting Service featured a number of programmes about the anniversary. On the 25th these began in the morning, and ended with the late-night feature *Anzac Plus Fifty*.[34] Although clearly named for the anniversary, *Anzac Plus Fifty* consisted predominantly of stories from World War II and the Korean War interspersed with music and Bible verses. There were interviews – with a former POW of a Japanese camp, German New Zealanders who suffered backlash during the war, the chaplain of a refugee camp, a conscientious objector imprisoned by the New Zealand government during the war and several disabled veterans. The main reference to Gallipoli came from Turkish radio recordings that gave the Turkish perspective on the landing as 'a just cause which ended in the triumph of justice'.[35] Evening television broadcasts featured a Gallipoli segment consisting of footage of local commemorative services and parades. *Te Reo o te Māori*, the evening Māori news segment on radio, included accounts from Māori soldiers who had been at Gallipoli, songs composed in their honour, and stories of the Maori Battalion's service in Italy in World War II.[36]

In Australia there was a stronger emphasis on Gallipoli. The federal council of the RSL promoted the anniversary as 'the birthday of the Anzacs' and paid tribute to the first men to enlist in the AIF.[37] In response, the Australian government announced the issue of commemorative stamps featuring John Simpson Kirkpatrick and his donkey.[38]

In both countries, for the most part, commemoration shared themes and practices and provided a common space for Australian and New Zealand ex-service groups to remember the past. Anzac Day in 1965 was veteran-focused, organised along personal and associative networks, and framed by an expression of imperial loyalties. 'The veterans do not falter,' blazoned the *New Zealand Herald*.[39] The *Canberra Times* quoted the Queen's message: '[By] remembering their courage … we can draw strength to face the problems of our own time.'[40]

'After Anzac': Uncertain meanings of commemoration in 1965

The 50th anniversary also expressed a new sense of melancholy as the war generation continued to decline. The celebrations of these soldier-citizens were illustrated by numerous images of ageing and infirm veterans. In Bourke, New South Wales, Rev N.J. Gough addressed the morning ceremony on 25 April, saying, 'We could count upon the fingers of one hand the number of original Anzacs in our midst today.'[41] In one Australian Broadcasting Corporation (ABC) television news feature, aired in the week leading up to Anzac Day 1965, a journalist interviewing members of the public about the future of Anzac Day asked, 'Should the day continue without the original Anzacs?' While responses ranged from concern for the strain on elderly men marching in parades to complaints that they received too much attention, all focused on the returned servicemen as both the participants and audience of Anzac commemorations.[42] No one was certain that Anzac Day would continue without the old soldiers themselves.

The Australian Capital Territory branch of the RSL proposed to the Menzies Liberal government that a special Anzac medal be created for the 50th anniversary and awarded to surviving Gallipoli veterans. The Labor Party supported the proposal and requested a government bill, but Prime Minister Menzies refused on the basis that there were now too few veterans to justify the exercise. Menzies also asserted that the New Zealand government would not support the creation of a medal, and claimed it was 'not a matter on which Australia should take independent action.'[43] While the chances of Menzies actually consulting the New Zealand government were slim, his response framed Anzac Day as a commemoration united with New Zealand and empire, not as a national remembrance but as a private one which, with the decline of the last veterans, had diminishing contemporary relevance. (The lack of a dedicated Gallipoli honour was later rectified by the Anzac Commemorative Medallion, struck in 1967, which was organised by the Holt Labor government in consultation with the New Zealand government.[44])

There was a small trans-Tasman dimension to Anzac commemoration in New Zealand, where Australian officials were usually given prominent places in ceremonies in major cities and regional centres. This was due in part to the adoption, post-World War II, of the Australian dawn service ceremony as part of New Zealand's Anzac Day ritual.[45] In an established tradition, the Wellington dawn service was usually organised under the auspices of the AIF Ex-Servicemen's Association. In 1965, however, this changed and Australia's Federal Minister for National Development, David Fairbairn, led the official wreath-laying and recited the Anzac dedication.[46] In Auckland, Major-General L.E. Beavis became the first Australian to lead the dawn parade in Auckland. If there was to be an expanded role for political leaders in the commemoration, it would be on account of Australian involvement.

Australian newspapers portrayed New Zealanders as deeply committed to Anzac commemoration in the lead-up to the 50th anniversary. Commentators marvelled at the apparent interest in 1965 as a special remembrance and painted an idyllic picture of a country basking in glorious unity. The *Age* reported that on Anzac Day in New Zealand, 'in the streets of the capital and in cities and towns and lonely country villages, war veterans will march in salute to the men of Anzac and will remember the fallen in religious services'. It noted that Australian veterans were to be special guests and give the address at the Auckland Cenotaph.[47] This inclusiveness was reciprocated in some instances: New Zealand veterans living in Australia were invited to school ceremonies to award Anzac Day essay prizes.[48]

Anzac Day was always an uneasy remembrance. The *Age* noted:

> Gallipoli means either ecstasy or depression to a great many and will continue to do so as long as there are men and women alive who experienced it ... to those who were untouched by it, it has become a legend and one likely to be embodied for all time in the Australian way of life.[49]

The *New Zealand Herald* portrayed the jubilee as a celebration caught between 'courage and slaughter', having earlier editorialised Anzac Day as a symbol 'for fruitless valour, bitter defeat, and unexpected victory'.[50] Newspapers tended to emphasise the successful withdrawal from Gallipoli rather than the failure and tragedy of the landing. The *Radio Listener* dedicated its special issue to the end of the campaign, emphasising the ingenuity of the retreat, the cunning of Allied troops in fooling the Turks and the bombardment by British warships, and described the killing of Turkish soldiers 'with the taste of victory fresh in their mouths' as 'a bitter postscript to defeat'.[51]

Falling on a Sunday, 25 April 1965 had heightened religious significance. In Victoria, where the day was not marked as a state holiday, Anzac services were conducted primarily through the churches. The regular service at St Paul's Cathedral, Melbourne, was remade as an Anzac ceremony, and head of the Victoria RSL Norman Smith and Governor Sir Rohan Delacombe played central roles in the liturgy. Presiding, Archbishop Frank Woods reportedly quipped, 'If you want to see into the heart of Australia now, don't go to Bondi Beach or Hayman Island, but come and spend Anzac Day with us'.[52] Similar messages were articulated elsewhere.

According to Rev Kenneth W. Prentice at Christ Church, Hawthorn, 'Whatever the military value of the Anzac landings, something happened in us as a nation which lives on as an inspiring and unifying spirit.' In Box Hill Methodist Church Rev Trevor Byard contrasted the shameful penal origins of the nation with the 'prideful heritage' of Anzac Day, saying Gallipoli veterans had 'blazoned Australia's name in the world's hall of fame'.[53] In Wellington, where it was the turn of the Catholic Church to lead the service, *Zealandia* editor Fr Ernest Simmons made a similar call to remember the fallen: 'Gallipoli, where no commander won any credit, was a place where the patient endurance of the ordinary soldier stands out, clear and plain.'[54]

Civic and religious leaders lacked a confident message about the significance of Anzac Day beyond a veteran commemoration. Newspaper reports expressed doubt as to whether Anzac Day would continue to be commemorated for much longer, although one *Age* editorial wrote that Anzac would live on despite its apparent abandonment by the younger generation: 'Though the great bulk of the community might not be conscious of it, the spirit that was born at Gallipoli and nurtured through all the long years since then makes its contribution still to the shaping of the character and outlook of our people.'[55]

The term 'spirit of Anzac' evoked a military tradition that seemed to have little bearing on the lives of the majority of Australians, as was widely admitted. The *Mirror* in Sydney questioned whether 'Anzac Day [will] be as meaningless to future generations as Trafalgar and Waterloo, once so cataclysmic, have become today'.[56] The editorial criticised the RSL for making the occasion too narrowly focused on the experience of returned servicemen.

Contemporary commentators understood the declining interest in Anzac Day in varying ways. Some considered it inevitable as old soldiers died and the memory of the war faded; to others it was an expression of ingratitude to the war dead. Suggestions that the 50th anniversary be moved to Monday so that parades and ceremonies would not conflict with churchgoing were perceived as an attack on the RSL. One disgruntled official spoke of 'a large body of unsympathetic feeling against the RSL, much of it inspired by the uncompromising attitude which the League maintains on behalf of the rights of returned men whose claims upon an ungrateful community have been so easily forgotten'.[57] The 'ungrateful community' was a common theme, framed more generally around complaints of lethargy in wider society. The predominant mood was 'one of indifference and even apathy,' warned a *Sydney Morning Herald* editorial; the government had failed to 'arouse the nation as a whole to an awareness of the danger or to a sense that we as a people have reached a most critical stage in our affairs which calls for a united national response'.[58] The unravelling of the personal status of the citizen-soldier, the associative networks of the returned services organisations, and the cultural narrative of imperial unity made for a potent anxiety.

These concerns invariably invoked ignorant youth. Newspapers were filled with veterans decrying how 'the young people have forgotten all that we did', and saying 'the holiday will be the only thing to make them remember the Anzacs now'.[59] Major General Lindsay Inglis, speaking at the Auckland citizens' service the previous year, suggested that Anzac Day was necessary to inform young people of the sacrifices of dutiful citizen-soldiers. RSL national secretary A.G. Keys stated, 'We believe the events at Gallipoli should be impressed on the imaginations of young Australians, so that they will know the sacrifices others have made to keep our country free and independent.'[60] Organisers had hoped the RSA/RSL pilgrimage would inspire young people's interest in Gallipoli.[61] Author George Johnston took a different approach: rather than being a myth of Australian nationhood, Anzac needed to transcend nationalism to become a universal human myth, like Homer's Troy. Observing the various contradictions, debates and 'ambiguities of social misunderstanding' swirling around the 50th anniversary of Gallipoli, Johnston suggested that revision and reassessment were needed 'before it was too late'.[62]

Somehow, Anzac Day needed to be made relevant for the next generation. A new legal framework was sorely needed. In 1965 the RSA Dominion Council proposed that the Anzac Day Act be amended to allow sport and entertainment in the afternoon.[63] This would help to ameliorate what the *Press* as far back as 1933 had called 'the old, dour and inward-looking image that Anzac Day observances have come to assume'.[64] Evening screenings of films relating to Anzac Day in cinemas around the country on 25 April could also be promoted. The mayor of Hamilton, in his speech at the anniversary dinner, suggested that Anzac Day be replaced with a day 'on which all worked and gave their wages for the day to a fighting fund for the eradication of fear, famine, ignorance and evil'.[65] Some suggested that having two war commemorations in the annual national calendar, Anzac Day and Remembrance Day, was excessive. If the dead of both wars were to be mourned, then surely Remembrance Day would suffice. Even as the 1965 anniversary was wrapped around veterans' groups as the arbiters of commemoration, newspapers in Australia and New Zealand argued that Anzac Day needed to be centred less on war experience alone.

The RSL/RSA pilgrimage to Gallipoli

The RSL and RSA's decision to organise a three-week pilgrimage to Turkey to mark the anniversary provided a useful litmus test of contemporary attitudes towards Anzac commemoration. Although both the Australian and New Zealand governments supported the pilgrimage, they did so at a distance. New Zealand Prime Minister Keith Holyoake advocated limited official support. Indeed, it was only after some prompting by Australian Prime Minister Robert Menzies – whose government offered a discount for New Zealanders wishing to travel with the Australians – that New Zealand decided to extend any official support for the pilgrimage at all, and then only through the Ministry of Defence under Dean Eyre.[66] Holyoake approved a government grant of £5000 to the RSA and promised assistance for RSL pilgrims travelling from New Zealand. RSA president Hamilton Mitchell urged Holyoake to make a public statement in support of the pilgrimage.[67]

Complaints were aired that the government's financial support was insufficient – one letter in the *Dominion* stated that the treatment accorded Anzac survivors was 'mean and shabby' when compared with the full government backing given to the contingent sent to the 1954 coronation of Queen Elizabeth, which included 175 ex-servicemen and women.[68] Having handed the grant money to the RSA, however, the government reiterated its determination not to be involved in the pilgrimage. The contribution was a 'starter' only, made to encourage the New Zealand public to 'show their appreciation' to the veterans by contributing also.[69]

The RSA established an application process by which veterans could apply for travel assistance. Although no official comment was made, in a personal memo the Minister of Lands, Ralph Hanan, expressed his unease about the application system, which he described as 'a little odd'. Applicants were asked to indicate how much they themselves could contribute, and applications were then vetted by the local RSA branches to decide whether this was the 'sort of person' who should be helped.[70] On receiving several complaints that the process was leading to uneven assistance, the minister of defence was quick to point out that 'the proposed pilgrimage is not a Government-organised project'. It was a 'private initiative of the Australian RSL, with whom the RSA subsequently associated themselves'. The grant had been given to the RSA to use as they saw fit, 'to enable ex-servicemen … to join the Pilgrimage if they would not otherwise be able to do so'.[71]

Reluctant to intervene in an internal RSA matter, Eyre refused to initiate what he considered would be 'a government takeover of a private initiative' by an organisation of ex-servicemen to 'mark the achievements and sacrifices of former companions'.[72] Exasperated, he pointed out that the New Zealand policy had 'substantially reflected the Australian decision': the government had simply followed the Australians' lead. The federal government in Canberra, it seemed, was writing the agenda on Anzac commemoration.[73] Cabinet was warned by the Prime Minister's Office to limit further government involvement.[74]

The 1965 pilgrimage throws light on government policy and attitudes towards the public role of war commemoration in the 1960s. When considering a possible stance to take in response to the anniversary, foremost among advice given to the prime minister was the concern about setting precedents for government involvement in commemoration. Faced with the prospect of decades of reunions of World War II units and associations, this was not an unfounded fear. The military services were similarly hesitant to contribute to the 50th anniversary.[75] Anzac was about returned servicemen's participation rather than a wider public commemoration. One *Australian* editorial reflected that the government and public attitude was one of indifference.[76]

What might have remained a 'private initiative' of the RSL and RSA, however, was singularly enhanced by the inclusion of historian Ken Inglis as a special correspondent. Inglis represented a new generation of scholars and a new voice in the meaning of Anzac Day; he was not a civic or religious leader nor a veteran, and he encapsulated a new generation of Australians navigating patriotism in the twilight of empire.[77]

In the lead-up to the 50th anniversary, Inglis gathered material from families of RSL members, 'undertaking a most necessary and worthwhile task and an urgent one as the ranks are disappearing and records being destroyed and lost concerning what was the very life of generations of Australians', as he put it.[78] It was precisely this concern for a lost heritage that spurred him to join the pilgrimage.[79] But Inglis crossed the line between history that examines the Anzac myth and its connection to national identity, and history that repeats the myth. He wrote that the dawn of 25 April 1965 became 'uncannily as in 1915'; the pilgrims themselves were the embodiment of 'the Anzac temperament' – laconic, egalitarian, and refusing to tip Turkish barmen because tipping, 'like saluting, belongs to a society divided into masters and servants, not to a land of free men'.[80] Any criticisms of the pilgrimage in his work are muted, although he decried the lack of ceremonies and rituals. At Anzac Cove, 'as at other ceremonies on the journey, some men experienced a sense of flatness, of things having been done inadequately'.[81] *Age* journalist Geoffrey Hutton, on the other hand, writing with little appreciation of Bean's version of the Anzac myth, praised the lack of ritual on the pilgrimage as indicative of a private and personal pilgrimage, without official ceremony or the liturgy of a national civil religion.[82]

Inglis embarked upon a personal mission that would profoundly shape public stories of Anzac in Australia: the recovery of the work of Charles Bean. As Jenny Macleod notes, it was Inglis' work that led to the popularisation of Bean's writing.[83] In 1969 he delivered the John Murtagh Macrossan lecture, in which he asserted that Bean was not only Australia's most prolific historian but also a determining influence in 'the texture of Australian history' itself.[84] Inglis emphasised Bean's role in establishing the Australian War Memorial and the way his work had highlighted the national character of Australia to create 'a new kind of history' that described 'what really happened' from the point of view of the common Australian man.[85] Inglis argued for a new historiography, one that interpreted the relevance of postwar commemoration to national identity. He was not the only writer thinking in terms of a 'national spirit'; over the coming decades he would be greatly assisted by a new generation of military historians supported by the Australian War Memorial. His view of the development of Australian nationhood from the shores of Gallipoli competed for public cachet with the likes of Manning Clark and, later, Henry Reynolds.

In the lead-up to and aftermath of the jubilee, Inglis reconfigured the various meanings of remembrance in national terms. Bean had made war experience integral to the emergence of Australian nationhood, asking in his official history, 'how did this nation react to the supreme test of war?'. Inglis suggested that 25 April 1915 was 'the consummation' of the Australian nation, that is, the place where its nationalism was made.[86] In an eloquent and nuanced ethnography, he rendered the 1965 pilgrimage in sympathetic terms, acting as a key interlocutor of the social networks of the returned services organisations and the changing cultural meanings of Anzac in the postwar world. It appears Inglis, too caught up in Charles Bean's 12-volume account of Gallipoli, could not adequately disentangle his role as chronicler and historian of the 1965 pilgrimage.

Inglis' work in 1965 set up a way of thinking about a foundation myth that was specifically Australian. In 1998 John Lack collated and edited *Anzac Remembered*, a collection of Inglis' key essays published in honour of his contribution to Anzac historiography. In his preface Lack highlighted Inglis' importance in giving credibility to military history in Australia, and the pivotal role of the 50th anniversary in this transformation. 'It was extraordinarily exciting on the eve of Anzac Day,'

Lack noted, 'to find in the feature pages of the Melbourne *Age* Ken Inglis' moving observations on the national day which had been part of my life for as long as I could remember, but whose meaning had been assumed and therefore only imperfectly understood'.[87] The 'meaning' of Anzac Day, in Inglis' work, was the pursuit of Australian nationhood after empire.

Inglis' role as a kind of retrospective historian in the 1965 anniversary revealed much about the differences between Australian and New Zealand attitudes towards Anzac commemoration in 1965. No historian or journalist provided commentary on the pilgrimage from a New Zealand perspective, as part of the official party or otherwise. Despite the journey being an ostensible partnership between the RSA and RSL, Inglis' presence gave weight to the Australian emphasis on the pilgrimage. This was apparent in the content of his despatches, in which New Zealand's role was repeatedly downplayed or left out. The *New Zealand Herald*'s report, likely based on Geoffrey Hutton's despatches, subsequently depicted the pilgrimage as an Australian affair despite the presence of RSA members.

Inglis offered his own comments on the difference between Australia and New Zealand, comparing Bean's official history with the *Official History of the New Zealand Effort in the Great War*, four anodyne volumes written by military staff in the 1920s. In his opinion the Australian history was official; the New Zealand accounts were popular, informal, and written as an accompaniment to the British official history (and therefore with an imperial tone). This, he said, was evidence of 'the lower temperature of nationalism on that side of the Tasman'.[88]

Ken Inglis finished his account of the 1965 pilgrimage with a reflection on a nation not yet fully at ease with how Anzac fitted into a modern Australia: 'For the pilgrims on the *Karadeniz*, Gallipoli is indeed Australia's holy land. How far … they are representative of their countrymen at home is perhaps easier to judge in Sydney or Melbourne or Canberra than on the pilgrim ship.'[89] These words presaged the Anzac revival itself: the shift from the personal experiences and social networks of returned servicemen, unmoored from their imperial origins, to a national story of belonging. The fraying imperial consensus around Anzac Day would continue to unravel after 1965. The hollowed-out commemoration was increasingly ignored or derided, and its dwindling supporters expressed a mixture of sadness, panic and defensiveness about its future.

Chapter 2

'Though I come to lay this wreath / I spit on your stone'

Protest and the remaking of Anzac Day, 1966–87

By the late 1960s Anzac Day in Australia and New Zealand had changed from a site of imperial unity to one of public protest. Over the next two decades growing protest against the 'Anzac myth' would radically reshape how the public perceived the obligations, rights and privileges of citizenship.

The tinderbox of this explosive change was Australia and New Zealand's involvement in the Vietnam War. From 1962 Australia deployed an increasing number of military personnel to Vietnam in support of the American mission to curb communist expansion in Asia. New Zealand followed suit by sending a combat unit in 1965. The Vietnam War was the Tasman nations' first major conflict as Anzus partners, and without their traditional ally, Britain.

Public attitudes to war were changing, and there was increasingly strident opposition to the deployments in Vietnam. New humanitarian movements, which flourished in the wake of World War II and gained impetus during the Cold War, advocated for the recognition of civilian victims of war as much as for military combatants. Without the sentiment of empire that had underpinned wartime politics in 1914 and 1939, politicians, military leaders and the public were divided about their nation's involvement in war. There was no 'commonality of national purpose', as Brian Easton calls it.[1] New questions were asked about the public's appetite for war and the nature of citizenship; and voices, such as those of women and minority groups, began to be heard.

The political and social upheaval around the Vietnam War had implications for the cultural remembrance of violence. The unified politics of the Great War, mobilised through an official script of sacrifice and duty – sometimes to the detriment of conscientious objectors and those who sought a negotiated peace – had created a cohesive scope of remembrance centred on the citizen-soldier.[2] This field of commemoration would gradually be broken open by a new era of contest led by the peace movement, drawn from loose networks of religious, social and political groups.[3] Australian opposition groups, such as Save Our Sons (SOS) and the Youth Campaign Against Conscription, which were closely aligned with the Labor Party, mobilised against the introduction of the National Service Scheme in 1966.[4] In New Zealand, networks of university students in Auckland, Wellington and Christchurch and the radical Marxist-inspired Progressive Youth Movement (PYM) began to rally from 1967.

Contest over Anzac commemoration was renewed by a wave of protests in the 1970s and 1980s energised by 'second-wave' feminism, which reimagined national politics through the mantra of 'the personal is political', and demanded that women be allowed to exercise autonomy over their own bodies. Small but dedicated groups from Rape Crisis centres and women's collectives attended Anzac Day ceremonies to decry sexual violence in wartime. By 1983 all major Australian and New Zealand cities had witnessed these interventions. In Canberra, Sydney and Melbourne, hundreds of marchers were coordinated through Women Against Rape or anti-Anzac Day collectives. In Auckland and Wellington, women's protest groups protested alongside other political causes in the late 1980s, such as Māori and Pasifika groups who, taking their cues from the Black Power Movement in the United States, condemned what they called 'capitalist wars'.[5]

Anzac Day protests over these decades had various objectives. Some used the day as a platform to draw attention to government policy or issues like domestic violence. Others rejected Anzac Day as an institution that valorised jingoistic and patriarchal violence, and called for the day to be a celebration of peace and the end of war. The protesters brought banners, posters, costumes, songs, chants and other performances and mobilised in public spaces such as Melbourne's Shrine of Remembrance and the Australian War Memorial in Canberra. Many made legitimate attempts to be included in the day's events by incorporating traditional rituals like wreath-laying or marching in parades; others were more interested in disrupting proceedings. These sometimes drew angry responses from returned services groups.

The phases of protest contributed to a cultural shift as the ritual and rhetoric of remembrance became an avenue to negotiate and critique society and its values. Commemoration became a litmus test of citizenship in a way never seen before. The fact that many clashes between protest groups and the returned services groups occurred in the capital cities of Canberra and Wellington contributed to Anzac Day's new national significance.

These protest movements have had an awkward place in the history of Anzac Day, and many stories of the day's 'revival' have omitted to mention them. Ken Inglis, for example, had relatively little to say about protest action, and there are no dedicated studies of protest on Anzac Day in New Zealand.[6] Where historians have written about these movements, the protests are commonly interpreted as part of a wider generational clash, typified in Alan Seymour's stage play *The One Day of the Year* (1958), which centres on the conflict between an ex-serviceman father and his postwar son – stand-ins for the domineering politics of the RSL and a growing progressive and urban youth culture.[7] Banned by the Adelaide Festival of Arts board of governors in 1960 for its 'subversive themes' but later produced in London to critical acclaim, Seymour's play heralded the crumbling civic consensus around Anzac Day already under way in the late 1950s.[8] In New Zealand, Ian Cross's novel *After Anzac Day* (1961) shared similar themes of family dysfunction and generational change. Protest was broadly understood as indicative of the slow collapse of the 'postwar consensus' – the shared beliefs and practices about political conduct and values – which gave way to upheaval and anxiety in the late 1960s and 1970s.

The various protests from the 1960s to the 1980s were by movements with vastly different aims, yet all contributed to radically changing the conversation around Anzac Day, which became less about exemplary soldier-citizens, lauded by politicians and religious leaders, and more about the public. Some protests and counter-protests turned violent, adding to the language of confrontation perpetuated in commemoration.[9] The interplay of protest and patriotism opened up public debate about national values and citizenship, and messages of peace diverted Anzac narratives away from military experience and the memory of veterans. The divisions over the Vietnam War, leveraged by the peace movement, created space for a panorama of memory that could accommodate both civilian victims of the war abroad and public participation and ownership of Anzac Day at home.

The protests exposed divisions in Australian and New Zealand society but also emphasised a common space, ritual and language to negotiate those differences on Anzac Day – what Graham Seal calls the 'interplay of official and unofficial'.[10] The rhetoric, symbolism and performances of protests created boundaries that ultimately, irrespective of the protesters' intentions, helped to define what the public was against, rather than for.

The peace movement and Anzac, 1967–71

On Anzac Day 1966 the morning service at the Shrine of Remembrance in Melbourne a dozen women from the anti-war group Save Our Sons made an unauthorised entry into the proceedings.[11] The activists were protesting against the conscription of young Australian men into the Vietnam War, and wore sashes and carried wreaths proclaiming 'Honour the dead with peace'. They joined the queue of people laying tributes at the shrine but were confronted by the memorial's deputy chairman, Colonel A.N. Kemsley, who declared: 'I don't want any wreaths laid … by your organisation; you can go home and take your wreaths with you.'[12] The women withdrew quietly, leaving their wreaths on the memorial forecourt instead.

The peace movement manifested in diverse ways on Anzac Day over the course of the Vietnam War, each protest shaped by the political and ideological motivations of a given group. Reflecting international currents of protest, Australian and New Zealand opposition to the war was often based on moral grounds, such as the impact of military action on innocent civilians.

In Australia the introduction of conscription was a focal point of protests and provoked demonstrations, sit-ins and teach-ins at universities throughout the country. The Moratorium marches, in 1970 and 1971, were the largest demonstrations and aimed to bring an end to Australia's involvement in the war. Broad sections of Australian society took part, from middle- and working-class people to Christian and anarchist groups.[13] In New Zealand the protest movement was significantly smaller and focused on the country's involvement in the war as an unnecessary interference in the domestic affairs of another country. The need for non-alignment was articulated by Jack Hunn, a former New Zealand secretary for defence, as an 'independence of policy' that avoided the rivalries of the Cold War.[14]

By the early 1970s the peace movement had achieved broad acceptance from the Australian and New Zealand public, as first conscription and then the war itself came to an end – symbolised, in New Zealand, by the 1972 election of Norman Kirk and the third Labour government and, in Australia, by the 1975 election of the reformist Gough Whitlam government, in which Jim Cairns, leader of the Moratorium marches, served as deputy prime minister.[15]

Protest on Anzac Day developed in complex ways in this emerging field of public debate. When rival protest groups clashed at the Sydney Cenotaph in the late 1960s, they were using Anzac Day primarily as a shared public place rather than addressing the practice of commemoration itself. Chanting students and trade unionists paraded past the cenotaph carrying placards that read 'End the war in Vietnam'. The arrival of a rival group with placards announcing 'This demonstration is a communist front' and 'Leave Martin Place to Anzacs and boy scouts' resulted in violent clashes and police intervention.[16]

In the days of these early clashes, the press positioned Anzac Day as one of unity and contrasted it with the divisive politics of the wider global protest movement: the *Australian*'s coverage of Anzac Day in 1971, for example, included a front-page photo of a massive anti-Vietnam War rally in Washington DC alongside that of a lone digger at the Australian War Memorial.[17]

Conscription legislation in Australia radicalised anti-war protests.[18] Following their first public action at the Shrine of Remembrance in 1966, SOS organised silent vigils during dawn and morning services on Anzac Day, joined parades, and handed out anti-conscription messages. These drew on the familiar language of peace at Anzac commemoration and the tradition of women attending Anzac Day services as mourners. SOS posters and flyers made the connection between soldier-sons fighting in Vietnam and mothers fighting at home to end the war. In explaining why they chose to protest on Anzac Day, convenor Joyce Golgerth stated, 'Mothers resist all sorts of pressure [in order to] to bring up their children as useful citizens, to look forward to useful careers and to be of service to the community.'[19] Anzac Day, according

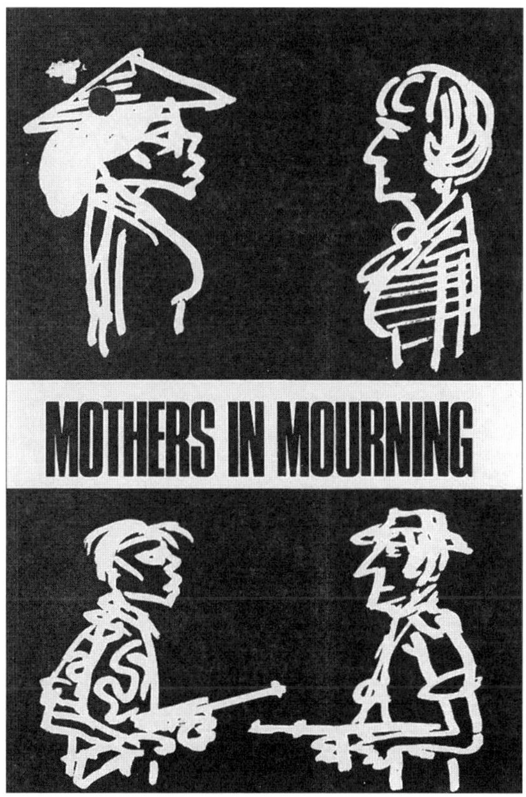

The Australian movement Save Our Sons (SOS) protested against conscription and the Vietnam War. This 1970 poster draws a parallel between mothers waging war at Anzac Day protests and their soldier-sons who were deployed in Vietnam. NAA A6122/2121/1/68, National Archives Australia, Canberra

to SOS, was sustained by the memory and celebration of war; campaigns for financial support for veterans were attempts to shape 'a politics of grief'.[20] Its object was the preparation of youth – through immersion in memory and ritual – for political citizenship. SOS offered a paradigm in which valid citizenship could be achieved through the pursuit of peace.

The SOS strategy of co-opting established modes of ritual and remembrance provided a template for other groups. The New Zealand Peace Council organised a 'war victims remembrance ceremony' in Wellington on 25 April 1972, in which they imitated Anzac Day rituals: activists laid wreaths at the cenotaph, sang hymns of peace and spoke of the importance of peace. The Peace Council actively avoided conflict with the organisers of the official service, however, by waiting until the morning service had been completed.[21]

Peace protests on Anzac Day in the 1960s were part of the political and moral debate around war and recognition of the defenders and civilians of the 'enemy' state. In 1968 members of the Campaign for Vietnam Protest were permitted to join the Adelaide Anzac parade with a placard that read 'Lest we forget the Vietnamese'. The *New Zealand Herald* editorial for Anzac Day 1971 was clear about the line to be drawn here: 'It is not out of keeping with the solemnity of the occasion to allow young people to pay tribute to the dead and dying in Indo-China.' Protest messages could be accommodated as long as they did not attack Anzac Day itself: 'Even to suggest that Anzac services perpetuate a spirit of militarism manifestly distorts the truth.'[22] In Christchurch in the lead-up to Anzac Day, the *Press* commented that a wreath 'To the fallen in Vietnam', respectfully laid alongside wreaths commemorating the dead of two world wars, should cause no offence:

> But a band of placard-carrying demonstrators asserting a 'right' to a place in an Anzac parade would as surely offend any reasonable standards of good manners and good taste, and would justify prompt intervention by the police. There are other occasions and plenty of opportunities for demonstrators to assert their minority views: Anzac Day observances should be spared such indignity.[23]

Many protesters formulated their actions as tributes, expressed with respect and deference to authority, to avoid condemnation and acrimony. The more radical groups, however, were not interested in fitting into the established rubric of solemn remembrance, and attacked narratives that presumed the rightness of national sacrifice. Students for a Democratic Society laid a wreath at the Sydney Cenotaph in 1970 with the message 'Lest we forget people who face war, oppression and injustice'.

In expressing sympathy for victims of the Australian Defence Force, they posited Australia as the enemy.[24]

Protests grew more confrontational towards the end of the war and expressly rejected prevailing Anzac rituals. In 1970 Perth students attempted unsuccessfully to lay a wreath with the emotive message 'To the murdered Vietnamese'.[25] In 1971 protesters painted 'PEACE!' in large letters on the Melbourne Shrine of Remembrance as veterans filed past, and in Sydney in 1972 a carefully timed flare ignited the wreaths at the cenotaph.[26]

New Zealand's Progressive Youth Movement was the most ideologically distinct group to protest on Anzac Day in New Zealand during the period 1967–72. The PYM drew its largely male membership from the communist movement emerging from the Radical Activists Conference political coalition, and autonomous groups sprang up in Auckland, Wellington and Christchurch; there was no counterpart group in Australia. Unlike other predominantly student-led anti-war movements, its members included blue-collar workers. Inspired by the May 1968 riots in Paris, many adopted direct confrontation with police as a chief modus operandi.[27] The movement had considerable influence among radical activists of the early 1970s.[28]

The PYM organised actions in response to the growing awareness of atrocities committed in the Vietnam War. Its members disrupted Anzac Day ceremonies and vandalised war memorials, provoking public opposition. The Christchurch branch distributed pamphlets that called for a 'new militancy – in the streets, in the factories, in the universities, in the schools – everywhere', and described the PYM as 'the vanguard of this country's revolutionary youth', which would unite young people.[29] Their militant rhetoric was matched by a penchant for military costume, especially black trenchcoats and army surplus gear; *Canta*, the Canterbury Students' Association magazine, featured photos of members armed with hunting rifles.[30]

The PYM's Anzac Day actions were part of a wider programme of activism but were by far its most public expression. Much to the group's chagrin, the *Dominion* in Wellington had avoided covering their demonstrations against the Vietnam War, including a protest outside the South Vietnam Embassy in Lambton Quay that attracted 400 activists in late 1969, but its coverage of PYM Anzac Day activities was considerable – a factor that may have influenced the public's perception that this group sought the abolition of the commemoration.[31] Other protest groups explicitly distanced themselves from the PYM. The Victoria University of Wellington student magazine *Salient* complained that the group's actions discredited students, and condemned the PYM as the 'only New Zealand political group whose effective political programme consists entirely of provocation of the police'.[32] The Wellington branch of the PYM was, in fact, the least confrontational of the movement's affiliated groups, and generally opted to avoid official memorial services so as not to legitimise the proceedings. Members there erected a mock cenotaph in central Wellington dedicated to the National Liberation Front in Vietnam.[33]

The Christchurch PYM branch was clear about its style: member Murray Horton stated that their strategy was to 'provoke and shock more than confront'.[34] In a series of dramatic protests in 1970, 1971 and 1972, the group pursued increasingly disruptive tactics. At the morning service at Cathedral Square, 25 April 1971, activists raised an anti-war banner behind the gathering of veterans that declared '35 NZ soldiers killed in Vietnam died for nothing'. An image of the protest, published a few days later in the *Christchurch Star*, provoked outrage.[35]

In 1972, again following the morning ceremony, three PYM members approached the Citizens' War Memorial bearing a placard with the inscription 'To the victims of Fascism in Vietnam' and a small bunch of flowers, which they placed on top of the official mayoral wreath. A fracas ensued. Christchurch mayor and World War II veteran Ron Guthrey ripped up the flowers, and other returned servicemen jostled PYM members who were attempting to erect a second placard. The police intervened. Guthrey was incensed: 'Dumb long-haired louts who have nothing to contribute to our society – who damn everything we have ever fought for – must not be allowed to insult our war dead.'[36] Chair of the Christchurch PYM Ben Rooney feigned innocence, saying the group was 'a little surprised at Mr Guthrey's attempt to instigate a slanging match': 'We would like to make it clear that we acted with as much sincerity as all the other wreath-layers and that we made no attempt to cause any trouble.' The Christchurch PYM subsequently challenged Guthrey to a public debate, an offer he declined.

When the PYM disrupted Christchurch's Remembrance Day commemorations later that year to lay wreaths to 'The dead and dying of Vietnam', its actions were in stark contrast to a silent vigil organised by the Campaign for Nuclear Disarmament (CND), a group which, one newspaper said, stood 'steadfastly by and maintained its dignity'.[37]

The Anzac Day Act 1966, which permitted the incorporation of sport and entertainment into this previously solemn public holiday, brought increased youth participation of a more positive nature. RSA organisers in Wellington went to some lengths to include schoolchildren in the morning service.[38] Speaking

Members of the Christchurch Progressive Youth Movement attempting to lay a wreath to the 'victims of Fascism in Vietnam' during the 1972 Anzac Day ceremony are confronted by members of the RSA. The image accompanying the wreath showed victims of the Mỹ Lai massacre and was subsequently torn up by the Christchurch mayor.
Christchurch Star, 26 April 1972

on Anzac Day 1966, the first under the Act, New Zealand Governor-General Sir Bernard Fergusson dismissed the perception that 'the rising generation does not care about [Anzac Day]', citing as evidence the presence of youth cadets and boy scouts at parades.[39] In Otago the following year the RSA reported that 'vitality was the key impression of the second Anzac Day commemorated in Dunedin in its remodelled form'.[40] Around 12,000 people of all ages had enjoyed an Anzac Day gala that included horseracing, cycling events, gliding displays, musical parades and skydiving demonstrations; 80 percent of the profits from the gala would go to the local RSA retirement home and hospital. Paradoxically, youth were interpreted as a vital concern of Anzac commemoration even as they were presented as its social and political antagonists. Protests during the late 1960s had refocused the language of remembrance around young people, either in support of Anzac Day or against it, and officials and protesters waged a war of rhetoric over who could claim the political loyalty of young people on Anzac Day.

This sense of the growing stakes of commemoration was heightened by political reactions to the protests on Anzac Day. National Prime Minister Keith Holyoake used press coverage of radical groups to leverage electoral support for the war, framing their activities as an affront to decency and a threat to the moral order for which Anzac troops had given their lives. In a meeting of party faithful for a forthcoming by-election in Palmerston North, he singled out the PYM as a 'communist-dominated organisation'.[41] Norman Kirk, then Opposition leader and soon to be prime minister, condemned the Auckland PYM's decision to lay a wreath at the Auckland Cenotaph and march up Queen Street on Anzac Day 'as an impudent affront to decency and a mockery of the sacrifice made by thousands of New Zealanders to preserve the very freedom the PYM delights in abusing':

> There is no need for such a march and, if there is an ounce of decency anywhere in the PYM, they would drop their plans at once … the PYM might as well know that the public is sick and tired of them and their antics. Their behaviour is a fertile seed-bed for disorder and one that should be firmly controlled by the appropriate authorities.[42]

The PYM's actions foreclosed any support from the political left and were deftly used by Holyoake to constrain Labour's critique of the Vietnam War as unpatriotic. The government had been boosted in July 1965 when the only national poll conducted about New Zealand's involvement in the war identified broad public support. Seventy percent of the population believed the level of military aid offered by the government was appropriate or should be increased; just 23 percent thought it too much.[43] When Kirk, as prime minister, outlined the new Labour government's policy on Southeast Asia in 1973, which was focused on building diplomatic relations with individual countries such as China, it was to an audience of ex-servicemen at the Dominion Council annual general meeting.[44]

Protests changed the political message of Anzac commemoration and raised the question of who had authority over this tradition. In New Zealand the RSA remained the central organising body of Anzac Day services, and local and national government deferred to the regional branches for managing interactions with protest groups. The branches also authorised the inscriptions on wreaths, although their approach to this and their dealings with student groups were inconsistent. In its first year of protest action on Anzac Day 1971, the Auckland University Students' Association placed a wreath with the broadly consensual message 'In memory of the dead and dying in Vietnam', which the Auckland RSA deemed acceptable.[45] In the same year, a University of Canterbury students' wreath condemning war as 'an instrument of national policy' was disallowed because the RSA there considered it controversial.[46]

A confrontation before the start of the Anzac service in Wellington, 25 April 1971. The students wished to be part of proceedings but the RSA objected and allowed them to lay their wreath only at the end of the service. Messages on wreaths required the RSA's approval. ATL EP/1971/1799/18-f-c, Alexander Turnbull Library, Wellington

Other student groups considered this requirement for approval as a yielding of the objective of the peace movement – to end the country's participation in the war – to the dictatorial concerns of the RSA. The New Zealand University Students' Association (NZUSA), representing students nationally, unanimously voted to lay a wreath at the 1971 service in Wellington with or without the consent of the RSA – or, as a spokesperson put it, 'whether people were arrested or not'. By holding a protest at the Wellington service the association hoped to draw the attention of the wider public. In a press release the NZUSA expressed its regret for 'the long history of human suffering caused by war … and the continuation of the war in Indo-China'.[47] Wellington's Committee on Vietnam also laid an anti-war wreath at the 1971 Wellington service, with the wording, 'To the dead and the dying in Vietnam'. The committee, which included three ex-servicemen among its members, initially voted for a more pointed message: 'In memory of the victims of Mỹ Lai' – a reference to the massacre of South Vietnamese villagers by American soldiers.[48] However, this would have brought them into conflict with the RSA, which rejected any 'political overtones' in the wording of wreaths.

In 1972 the Wellington Labour Representation Committee suggested that local government could take over organisation of Anzac Day commemorations, but the Wellington RSA rejected the idea, saying that as a 'non-political and non-denominational' organisation, it remained best suited to the task. The Wellington City Council continued to defer to the association's decisions about who could lay wreaths, even when these were not always consistent – one request from the Organisation to Halt Military Service was denied outright. The New Zealand Peace Council's proposal to hold a remembrance ceremony for victims of war was approved after considerable internal debate within the RSA executive. Some were vehemently opposed; others argued that the association needed to engage constructively with 'reasonable' groups wanting to participate in Anzac Day.

The conflict between students and the Wellington RSA intensified after various RSA clubrooms were vandalised with graffiti, but conciliation was eventually reached towards the end of the Vietnam War. RSA officials met with students in the lead-up to Anzac Day and negotiated a compromise: protest groups could attend the morning service but would lay their wreaths after 1pm, when it was deemed the RSA's jurisdiction ended. Victoria University students marched in the city parade behind the ex-servicemen; they carried banners and made clenched-fist salutes during the minute's silence.

By the end of the 1970s a new relationship had evolved between commemoration, its youth audience and the state, and the RSA's authority over Anzac Day had been fundamentally altered as a direct outcome of protest action. Anzac Day anti-war protests raised questions about the purpose of the day. In some ways the RSA's actions enabled change. Their reactions to protesters attracted the interest of the press, strengthened the resolve of some demonstrators, and generally hardened public opinion against the war. This in turn accelerated the states's changing authority in commemoration. Government speeches on and around Anzac Day declaiming the social problems of youth, and direct police interventions at commemorations, contributed to renegotiating the boundaries of inclusion and exclusion.

In 1971 the National Council of Churches in New Zealand organised a survey of public opinion on the meaning of Anzac Day, and specifically invited young people, including members of the PYM, to contribute. In so doing, the council was not only canvassing public interest in Anzac Day – beyond that of veterans – but was also assessing the way in which young people were now invested as participants in remembrance.[49] The voice of 'youth' became a special concern.

'Women died, we care': The rise of feminist voices, 1977–87

Feminist protest on Anzac Day emerged from the broader milieu of the peace movement but quickly took on its own priorities. Many women had been radicalised by their experiences among SOS and student groups, and feminist activists were chafing at the actions and structures of the anti-war movement that often confined women to the back room in support of male activists.[50]

On 25 April 1978 at the morning service at the Auckland Cenotaph, following the example of Australian feminists, seven black-clad women placed a wreath bearing a women's liberation symbol. The group's accompanying press release articulated an ideological departure from the peace movement: 'In war women do not count; women are never remembered as activists or victims of war. The Women's Liberation Movement remembers them today.'[51] The message would dominate Anzac Day protests for the next decade.

University collectives, brought together by issues of violence against women, were vital organisational networks for many feminist actions, such as lobbying for law changes, highlighting the issue of rape within marriage, and demanding justice for victims of rape.[52] Sexual violence, both during wartime and on the 'home front', became a focal point of critiques of society and the assertion of women's rights in public life. Feminist activists wrote poetry, articles and songs that celebrated collectivist actions. Their appropriation of commemorative language and ritual was intended to empower groups against a sometimes hostile public. University of New South Wales student magazine *Tharunka* often compared the actions of the group Women Against Rape (WAR) to a kind of revolutionary warfare.[53]

WAR originated in the United Kingdom, and Australian and New Zealand branches emerged shortly afterwards. Its mission was to draw attention to the issue of rape in society and to develop support systems for women, such as rape crisis centres.[54] The first public WAR actions on Anzac Day occurred in 1977 and 1978. Following the morning ceremony at the Australian War Memorial in Canberra in 1977, a group of women placed a wreath bearing the words 'In memory of women raped in war' at the Australian War Memorial. The following year Sydney activists attended the Martin Place morning service wearing black T-shirts with 'In memory of women raped in war' on the front and 'Women Against Rape' on the back. As they entered the Martin Place plaza the group was stopped by police and forced to move to one side to allow the authorised marchers to pass first.[55] Four representatives were then permitted to place a blank wreath on the cenotaph while the rest of their contingent remained behind barriers.[56] This was a significant change of rules: members of the public were normally allowed to approach and place wreaths or flowers without restriction. A similar event occurred in New Zealand in 1979 at the Wellington morning ceremony, where RSA officials stopped two women from laying a wreath bearing the words 'For our sisters, dead and raped', citing as their reason the message's 'political overtones'. The experiences in Canberra and Sydney indicated that the feminist collectives' central demand – the recognition of rape during war – might eventually be incorporated into public remembrance of Anzac Day, despite the organisers' reluctance.

Silent vigils, wreath-laying and non-confrontational processions were eventually permitted and – to an extent – accepted by participants and spectators, thanks in part to the precedent set by the anti-war movement.[57] The collectives deliberately modelled their actions on the traditional Anzac rituals, such as marching in close formation behind a single identifying banner.[58] Like the SOS groups during the period of anti-Vietnam War protests, the groups' performances, symbols and inscriptions spoke of mourning: they wore black, observed silences and sang laments.[59] When some hundred women protested at the Canberra parade in 1981, WAR spokespeople assured the media that they 'planned to march in a quiet, orderly and dignified fashion' behind a banner that read, in several languages, 'In memory of all women in all countries raped in all wars.'[60]

Public reaction indicated a number of reasons why this particular protest action was tolerated. Few observers could deny the central tenet that women are victims of rape in war, although obfuscations abounded – including the admission by one RSL state president that 'Rape does and will occur in war, but Australian servicemen have a pretty clean record in this regard.'[61] A growing number of scholarly works also acknowledged the reality of rape both in wartime and in Australian society in general – a concession evidenced, ultimately, by the inclusion of rape in the 1987 television mini-series *Vietnam*.[62]

Despite initial antipathy, by 1983 the messages of the Sydney and Canberra collectives would be accepted into the language and practice of Anzac commemoration. One letter to the *Canberra Times* in 1981 suggested that the feminists' actions reinforced the significance of Anzac; another wrote, 'Women do not wish to disrupt the march but to add to this reminder a presentation of the suffering of many women throughout war history.'[63] Others argued that the collectives were participating in a form of mateship and therefore were 'very much in tune with the spirit of Anzac Day'.[64]

Members of Women Against Rape (WAR) march along Anzac Parade to the Australian War Memorial in Canberra to lay a wreath, Anzac Day 1981. The banner reads 'In memory of all women of all countries raped in all wars'. Individual placards carried the same message in various languages. Photo: Martin Jones. ACT Heritage Library, Canberra

In contravening the space of Anzac, protesters more clearly defined the authority of the returned services groups. Some commentators in the press were critical of the RSL's insistence on controlling who could to march in its parades.[65] This control was most pronounced in Canberra, where in 1981 three female activists attempting to take part in the Anzac parade were jailed for a month for police obstruction.[66] As a result, the federal RSL council banned all participation in the national parade in Canberra by women seeking to draw attention to rape in war, a decision given legal clout by the federal police and ACT government through a Public Order Act, which explicitly enacted the parade as an RSL activity and made it unlawful in the territory to give offence to Anzac Day participants. This provoked protests in 1982 as people demanded to be allowed to participate in parades and wreath-laying as a right of

A protester in the Women Against Rape demonstration on Anzac Parade, Canberra, 1981, demands to know the arresting constable's number. Three women were eventually indicted for disturbing the Anzac Day service. ACT Heritage Library, Canberra

citizenship. The issue was resolved when Labor was elected in 1983 and repealed the Act in December of that year.

The civil liberties issues at stake in the Canberra actions attracted other participants to the marches, and feminist collective members worried that this cluttered field of voices 'threatened to swamp the issue of women raped in war'. For this reason, the Sydney collective expressed reservations about combining with peace or anti-nuclear movements.[67] New Zealand feminist groups faced similar challenges. At one Auckland ceremony, police monitoring a feminist protest confiscated a placard reading 'Let East Timor decide' from members of the Campaign for an Independent East Timor; and in Hamilton 'a minority radical group' painted swastikas and obscenities on the local cenotaph.[68]

Any antagonism generated by feminist actions at Anzac Day ceremonies in New Zealand was mostly between police and protesters rather than with the RSA. In 1978 members of the Women's Action Group, dressed in black veils, laid a wreath at the mid-morning Anzac Day service in the Auckland Domain. The attached memorial card read, 'We remember all the forgotten women: all those who died in battle, those raped and mutilated, our sisters who have had their lives destroyed by the wars of this century.' A police constable removed the card from the wreath, and when activists questioned his right to do so, the officer replied that he was acting on a complaint made by a woman. RSA president J.R. Gardiner said he found nothing offensive in the message. The Auckland district chief of police commented: 'Ceremonies at cenotaphs are increasingly becoming the scene of emotional interaction between activist groups ... The police have to do their bit to maintain decorum and the right atmosphere.'[69]

Compared to the federal presence of the RSL in Australia, the RSA in New Zealand was becoming increasingly decentralised, and the direction and maintenance of the boundaries of official and unofficial memory were increasingly defined and directed by the state. Protest actions played a vital, if paradoxical, role in this process.

Unlike the Auckland, Sydney and Canberra WAR protests, the Melbourne Anti-Anzac Day Collective openly celebrated women's interventions as protests. From 1983 onwards their very name – and their banner proclaiming 'Abolish Anzac Day' and chants such as 'What do we want? Anzac Day out' – flagrantly defied proceedings. In 1984 spokesperson Adrian Howe stated, 'We just want our protest to be seen and heard by as many people as possible.'[70] Members deliberately marched *away* from the Shrine of Remembrance in the years 1985–87, and distributed stickers to members of the public calling for abolition of the commemoration.[71] The Melbourne collective's confrontational actions were considered militant and out of step, both with the group's anti-militarist rhetoric and the non-violent tactics adopted in other cities.

A similarly militant form of protest developed in Wellington. In 1980 a 'squad' of women in their early twenties identifying themselves as lesbians disrupted events at Wellington's Cenotaph.[72] Wearing military-style black costumes and berets, the protesters chanted during the minute of silence at the dawn service, 'Women died, we care; women were raped, we are angry.' During the wreath-laying ceremony they appeared with a mock coffin inscribed 'In memory of millions of women raped and killed by soldiers.' Their actions contrasted with those of groups of Wellington peace activists who had been holding an all-night vigil as 'silent, respectful, but prominent observers', and invoked the ire of some.[73] RSA president Sir Hamilton Mitchell stated in his address that in contemporary New Zealand there existed not only an external threat 'which should be brought under our control' but an 'internal threat' as well – by which he meant the subversive politics of protest groups – and called for dedication to its destruction.[74] The squad's tactics and, in the case of the Melbourne group, their declared separation from other WAR actions, further diminished connections of solidarity that had existed across the women's movement and the potential for feminist rhetoric to be incorporated into the reformulation of Anzac Day during this period.

Despite claims by Sydney and Canberra collectives that their aim was to participate rather than demonstrate, feminist protests became progressively more antagonistic. Women carried political placards, distributed polemical flyers, defaced memorials and sang protest songs such as 'We Shall Overcome', or songs with confrontational lyrics such as one chant sung by the Canberra WAR protesters: 'For every hero in his grave/ There's a woman raped living with her pain … Though I come to lay this wreath / I spit on your stone.'[75] This activism sought to diminish the powerful imagery of the heroic soldier-citizen, expressed in stone memorials.[76] Chants were often accompanied by overt militant language and symbolism, including a clenched fist holding the female symbol.[77] The actions were considered attention-seeking, self-obsessed and opposed to sacrifice for the common good, and the press revelled in placing images of this activism alongside those of elderly men. One *New Zealand Herald* editorial suggested that 'memorials have been desecrated, services interrupted, and old soldiers insulted' in order 'to publicise quite incongruous causes'.[78]

In Australia the press went so far as to suggest that confrontational protests could lead to deaths within the thinning ranks of ageing ex-servicemen, a comment that accentuated the victim status of these men. During the 1980s the number of veterans marching declined visibly. The annual installation of war graves for veterans rose from some 2200 to approximately 10,000 at the end of the decade and the number of 'Last Post' notices in the New South Wales RSL's publication, *Reveille*, increased.[79] Protest action on Anzac Day had the cultural cachet of crashing a funeral, and despite the open ructions between the RSL and Vietnam veterans – and the increasing willingness of the political left to embrace veterans as victims – the feminist collectives seem not to have garnered much support during this period.[80]

Broader issues raised by feminist collectives on Anzac Day remained marginalised throughout the decade. Despite eventual recognition of the significance of rape in war, the deeper message that informed feminist actions from the outset – that rape is symptomatic of patriarchy – rarely gained currency.[81] Messages such as 'Rape is war against women' or 'Oppose male power and war for profit', or the graffiti on the Brooklyn War Memorial in Wellington that read, in purple paint, 'Women against male wars', failed to connect with Anzac Day participants and audiences. Arising as it did from existing feminist movements and anti-rape groups, the self-identification as 'Women Against Rape' (and its contraction to WAR) and appeals to universal sisterhood were clearly intended to collide with the prevailing masculine tradition of Anzac Day.[82] Indeed, while ostensibly seeking the inclusion and recognition of women within Anzac Day rites, a significant number of collective materials were directed exclusively at women, and planning meetings were often restricted to 'women only'. *Reveille* in 1983 suggested that International Women's Day might be a more appropriate forum for their protests.[83]

Like the anti-war movement, feminist protest actions were overtaken by the changing political and social landscape of remembrance. Returned servicewomen, most of whom had served during World War II as nurses, had been invited to attend the national RSA conference for the first time in 1960.[84] In an attempt to address shrinking membership, the RSL finally began to allow women's service groups and the War Widows' Guild to march in the Anzac Day parades, and from the late 1970s the number of women participating rose considerably.[85] In its Anzac Day 1986 coverage the Melbourne *Age* ran a sizeable article on the role of women in war.[86] The notion that Anzac Day did not include women was becoming harder to sustain.

By the late 1970s the definition of 'victims of war' had broadened considerably, and the recognition of women as victims of rape during conflict became one of many competing messages. New social histories of the Anzacs, discussed in detail in the next chapter, portrayed World War I soldiers as men broken by the physical and mental stress of conflict. Veterans themselves – particularly those recently returned from Vietnam – began to define themselves as disempowered victims of war.[87]

In contrast to earlier campaigns for welfare for citizen-soldiers, these messages drove the political agenda of returned servicemen and women increasingly towards the left. The Vietnam Veterans' Association of Australia forged political links with the Australian Labor Party, and their agitation for inquiries into the psychological impact of combat and Agent Orange informed wider cultural engagement with war veterans as victims.[88] The development of the concept of the veteran as victim perpetuated the traditional significance of commemoration as the domain of military rather than civilian experience.[89] By the late 1980s sympathy flowed in television mini-series such as *ANZACS*, *Vietnam* and *Sword of Honour*, and in songs by left-leaning musicians such as Hunters & Collectors and Midnight Oil, for these 'ordinary men' affected by war.

Remembrance was shaped by gender. In these 'wars of manoeuvre', masculine voices of co-option or confrontation were more easily incorporated; women's anti-war groups were subsumed into traditional roles as mourners, something the feminist movement explicitly rejected. By the 1980s, feminist interventions were increasingly regarded as shrill acts of aggression, whereas men – both elderly returned servicemen and younger Vietnam veterans – were increasingly positioned as victims of war.

Chapter 3

'The loss of innocence'

Gallipoli and national cinema in the 1980s

The 1980s saw increased interest in stories of war, which were explored in film, television, documentary, theatre, popular writing, school curricula and museum exhibitions. Newspapers began to publish photographs and first-hand accounts of conflicts as war became a key genre for imagining the national past.

'National cinema' emerged in the late 1970s and early 1980s as an industry sponsored by state and private investment for the purpose of producing stories that promoted the origins and collective identity of the nation and would validate 'settled' history.[1] Governments on both sides of the Tasman offered substantial subsidies and tax breaks to the film industry to create local content, and the Australian Film Commission and New Zealand Film Commission were established in 1975 and 1978 respectively.[2] This funding provoked a new wave of cinema as filmmakers drawn to the past began adapting stories from poems, plays and novels.[3] Although it never eclipsed television's established production and programming, national cinema became the state's new cultural flagship.

The emergence of national cinema was central to a new engagement with war memory. Film transforms social remembrance into shared claims about the basis of society, even as it becomes more homogenous and disconnected from reality.[4] It provides an experience of stories that is both individual and collective; a social practice mediated by cinematic image and personal consumption. As well, film achieves coverage that writers and publishers could never hope to equal, and has the ability to magnify – and distort – representations of the past in a way that the written word cannot. National cinema gave new shape to the cultural memory of World War I, and in particular of Gallipoli and the Anzacs.

The 1981 film *Gallipoli*, directed by Australian Peter Weir, was the most successful and influential in Australian New Wave cinema (a resurgence of worldwide popularity of Australian cinema) and was the leading light in a cluster of nationalist war films over the 1980s. *Gallipoli* created a new form of visual remembrance of the Anzacs, and exerted a profound influence on audiences in Australia and New Zealand. Critics quickly celebrated it as *the* Australian film telling 'the Australian story' – the story of the nation itself. Funded by Hollywood and Australian federal government investment, and produced by Associated R&R Films, *Gallipoli* exemplified the economic and cultural impact of national cinema.

Gallipoli provoked a counter-narrative by writers, historians and filmmakers in New Zealand, who attempted to portray New Zealand identity after empire. The 'New Zealand story' of Gallipoli became the catch-cry of a network of scholars, artists and institutions. Among these were the stage play *Once on Chunuk Bair* by Maurice Shadbolt, which asserted a new birthplace of the nation, and the documentary *Gallipoli: The New Zealand Story*, scripted by Shadbolt and produced by TVNZ, which premiered in 1984.

Remembrance is shaped by dedicated groups (in this case, by artists and filmmakers) and texts. Both Weir and Shadbolt set out to tell a national story of the past to satisfy contemporary needs, to portray the Australian and New Zealand experiences of Gallipoli as the end of national innocence; the unmasking, or so it seemed, of old imperial myths to align with the new sense of independence of the 1980s. Both productions drew powerfully on the 'voices from below' approach to social history, incorporating material from soldiers' letters and diaries to bring realism to the script.

Marcia Landy suggests that 'the investment in the past is related to the power to name, to determine what counts as history'.[5] The 1980s was a formative decade for Anzac myth-making. Both Weir and Shadbolt turned to history as a strategy of national memory, searching for a historical basis for their personal experience. The possibilities of recounting tales that fused history, memory and identity appealed to a new generation of creative artists, and a new set of stories, presenting Gallipoli as a place of national founding, filled the vacuum of meaning around Anzac Day.

'An original Anzac memorial': Peter Weir's *Gallipoli* in Australia and New Zealand

The 1980s was an era of expanding audio-visual culture and individual consumption. In Australia the Special Broadcasting Service (SBS) joined the ABC, established in 1932, as Australia's second public broadcaster in 1980. In New Zealand, where there were just two television channels, documentaries and films commanded unprecedented audiences. Television programming around Anzac Day was packed with war-related content, and writers and filmmakers traded on wider social tastes for war content as a new sentimental currency.

New Zealand's evening television schedule in the week prior to Anzac Day 1982 opened with *Dead on Target*, a documentary produced by Ian Johnstone that recounts the story of the Allied attack on an Amiens prison during World War II. Another documentary, *Conflicts*, combined the talents of the New Zealand Army Band and scriptwriter Chris McVeigh to present a musical history of the major wars in the nation's past. Reruns of older films, such as *The Rats of Tobruk* (1944), were part of an earlier generation of war stories on film now getting a second lease of life through television, and the arts series *Kaleidoscope* featured a behind-the-scenes look at Maurice Shadbolt's stage play *Once on Chunuk Bair*, which was to premiere on the eve of Anzac Day. All emphasised war experience as a way of locating the national past, and many recovered stories from obscurity. Johnstone's production was based on archival material showing that New Zealanders led the Amiens attack – a fact Johnstone wanted to turn into a cause for national pride. As prominent figures in what would later be celebrated as New Zealand television's 'golden age', both Johnstone and McVeigh made the war genre a key part of their repertoire of local content for local audiences.

Kaleidoscope received state funding to produce content highlighting New Zealanders' artistic achievements. The 24 April episode reflected this meeting of art, industry and national interest. *Once on Chunuk Bair* is Shadbolt's only stage play; his work to this point had been confined to novels and short stories set in New Zealand. The play dramatised the actions of New Zealand troops, in particular the Wellington Battalion, on the Gallipoli Peninsula at the Battle of Chunuk Bair, a pivotal moment in the campaign's offensive. Describing the play as a 'powerful drama', *Kaleidoscope*'s Jeremy Payne lauded Shadbolt's aim to show 'not only the human cost of war, but also how a sense of nationalism emerged among the New Zealanders who fought there so bravely', contrasting the 'poignant illustration of the futility of war' with 'a tribute to heroism'.[6]

The timing of Shadbolt's premiere – 1982 – and Payne's reference to a national identity were significant. The idea of 'an original Anzac memorial' was familiar to New Zealand audiences in the wake of Peter Weir's *Gallipoli*, released just nine months earlier.[7] It had grossed close to AUD$20m globally and was recognised as 'the Anzac film'.[8] Shadbolt's play now offered New Zealand audiences some claim to the heroism, excitement and tragedy of the Gallipoli campaign.

Weir's *Gallipoli* has become a kind of cliché for accounts of Anzac Day in Australia, and there are literally hundreds of books, articles and websites dedicated to analysing it. Historian Daniel Reynaud suggests that, globally, *Gallipoli* is the most influential war film and 'the most complete rendering of the modern Anzac myth': a cultural landmark of the Anzac revival.[9] Reflecting on changes in Anzac commemoration in 2013, historian Bill Gammage observed that the film represented the stirring of a new hopeful nationalism.[10] Others argue that *Gallipoli* owed its commercial and artistic success to Weir's simple and deft repackaging of old themes for a new audience. His main characters, Archy Hamilton (Mark Lee) and Frank Dunne (Mel Gibson), are young Anglo-Australians who become classic Aussie mates through the shared experience of competitive sport, the rugged landscape of the bush and, eventually, war. The film's blatant anti-British slant also appealed to contemporary anxieties about what it meant to be an Australian after empire.

Gallipoli was the second film produced in Australia to obtain a major release in the United States – the first was *Mad Max* in 1979 – giving it the imprimatur of Hollywood and sealing it as an object of national pride. It was screened in schools as a lesson in patriotism, and came complete with a study guide.[11]

Weir originally intended to tell a story based on the experience of soldiers in battles on the Western Front; Gallipoli was, after all, only one of the many sites of conflict. In a 1981 interview he said his main inspiration for the film – and the decision to focus on Gallipoli – came from a trip to Anzac Cove in 1976. He recounted walking alone on the peninsula and his 'extraordinary experience' of the battlefield, where he experienced a kind of epiphany:

> I saw no one in two days of climbing up and down the slopes and wandering through the trenches, finding all sorts of scraps left by the armies: buttons and bits of old leather, belts, bones of donkeys, even an unbroken Eno's Fruit Salts bottle. I felt somehow I was really touching history ... and it totally altered my perception of Gallipoli. I decided then and there that I'd make the film.[12]

Here was a landscape charged with meaning; empty yet filled with fragments of the past, a connection to the Anzacs that was unfiltered and unbroken by time. To the young filmmaker, Gallipoli simultaneously provided a blank canvas for his own sense of self-identity and a connection to a collective Australian past. Of course the peninsula had been greatly changed since 1915, first by the Commonwealth War Graves Commission and later by the Turkish government, which continued to designate it as a military installation. Rather than discovering powerful emotions amid the trenches, Weir brought these meanings from Australia and 'unpacked' them on site.

Weir returned to Australia to search out like-minded creative artists. Writer David Williamson agreed to collaborate on the script, and the pair undertook extensive research in the late 1970s. Weir initially envisaged a documentary-style film that would capture the broad experience of Gallipoli, beginning with enlistment and ending at the withdrawal of Allied troops at the end of the campaign. This reflected his earlier filmmaking experience, and echoed earlier productions on the Anzacs and Gallipoli in Australian film. In 1961 Channel 7 had produced the series *Anzacs*, 26 half-hour episodes covering both world wars; and in 1965 the ABC had adapted Charles Bean's campaign narratives as *The Anzac Story* in eight half-hour episodes, to coincide with the 50th anniversary.[13] Both emphasised the military prowess and heroism of the Anzacs.[14] *Report from Gallipoli*, produced by the ABC in 1977, captured most of the traditional attitudes towards the Anzac story expressed in commemoration; styled as a news broadcast from 1915, it attempted to combine remembrance and entertainment with objective historical documentary.[15]

Weir quickly departed from this plan, however, and signalled his intention to pursue a new kind of war film, saying a broad, sweeping military narrative would not get to the 'burning centre that had made Gallipoli a legend'.[16] Weir and Williamson crafted a script that spent less time on the battlefield itself and more on getting to the battle, as a way to locate the 'type of Australian largely vanished from the country'. It was the journey, not the destination, that counted. The 'appointment with destiny at Gallipoli' allowed the filmmakers to come 'as close to touching the source of the myth as we could'.[17] The final script, presented to producer Patricia Lovell in 1979, offered a fusion of past, present and future: the film would not portray the experience of Gallipoli so much as Weir's rendition of its meaning to Australians in the 1980s.

Weir's work revealed a number of influences. He drew extensively on Charles Bean's official history, which had been republished in 1979 with a preface by Ken Inglis as part of the latter's strategy to promote Bean as his kind of Australian hero.[18] Reading Bean's account of Gallipoli, especially of the Battle of the Nek, Weir had felt 'respect and admiration for the type of man in the 10th Light Horse', the regiment in which the fictional Archy would enlist.[19]

Alf Rolfe's 1915 film *The Hero of the Dardanelles* was the first cinematic treatment of the Gallipoli campaign.[20] Released to promote enlistment during the war, the film incorporated footage originally shot by British journalist Ellis Ashmead-Bartlett with a broader imperial audience in mind. As part of his mission to carve out a distinct Australian memory of the war, Bean had tracked down Ashmead-Bartlett's negatives to form the heart of the emerging World War I film archive at the Australian War Memorial. Although Weir never publicly stated its influence, the prominence of Ashmead-Bartlett's film in the war memorial's archive and exhibitions – and the myriad visual parallels between *The Hero of the Dardanelles* and *Gallipoli* – make it unlikely that he had not encountered the footage.[21]

Bean also loomed large in Weir's other sources of information. The years leading up to the release of *Gallipoli* had seen a surge in historical writing that engaged with themes of nationhood and identity. One of the most important was *The Broken Years* by Bill Gammage (1974), a landmark work of social history and the most significant scholarship to address Australian war memory since Inglis' writing in 1965. It was the first systematic attempt to explain the war through 'the voices from the trenches', using quotations from thousands of diaries and letters of ordinary soldiers rather than a broad brush centred on the decisions of politicians and military strategists.[22] Gammage drew on the prodigious archive in the Australian War Memorial and dedicated his work to Bean, acknowledging the institution and the extraordinary influence of its founder.[23]

The Broken Years was significant for its success: over 30,000 copies sold in 1974 and a second edition followed in 1975. Gammage had provided a definitive history in a way that other works on the topic had not achieved, and it rippled through Australian culture. He had trimmed Bean's official history of its militarist, imperial and racial underpinnings and delivered an accessible story of the Anzacs that appealed to a new generation of Australians. It was simple and brilliant: the Anzacs were no longer soldiers of empire but victims of mass slaughter – the tragic figures who had featured with increasing prominence in the anti-war rhetoric of Anzac Day protests since the 1960s. Gammage argued that the Great War had not unified

Australia as a nation but introduced a deep division – what he callled 'the broken years'. Although ostensibly a rendition of interwar politics, 'the broken years', for audiences in the late 1970s, was a shibboleth for the contemporary conflict between conservative and liberal forces in Australian society, the fault lines of which were apparent in contests over the ownership of Anzac Day. The transformation of Anzac Day from an exclusive imperial commemoration to an inclusive popular remembrance owned by the public was, in this way, a healing of the wounds of the nation.

Although Gammage's book spanned the whole of the war, it focused on Gallipoli as the place and time where the imperial loyalty of the AIF was broken: 'the light-heartedness' apparent in the early days of the Gallipoli campaign gradually declined in the face of 'a butchery which must be done'.[24] Gallipoli, Gammage suggested, offered a kind of historical threshold in the national story.

On the eve of Anzac Day in 1982, as Shadbolt's *Chunuk Bair* premiered in New Zealand, the Theatre ACT produced and performed a theatrical adaptation of Gammage's book at the Australian War Memorial. The play included extracts from the war memorial collection and from Patsy Adam-Smith's 1978 book *The Anzacs*, the latter a collection of interviews with World War I servicemen in the same vein as Gammage's work.[25] Accompanied by the band of the Royal Military College, Duntroon, and a local youth choir, actors read an anthology of diaries and letters from Anzac soldiers. The backdrop – the war memorial's Roll of Honour – imbued the performance with a powerful sense of connection to the dead, as if the names inscribed there were now being given voice.

The appeal of Gammage's *Broken Years* and its theatrical spin-off lay in the sense of the past coming to life through authentic voices, and appealed to contemporary interest in the possibilities of oral history. Survivors' voices were increasingly at the centre of historical narratives of the Holocaust by the 1980s, and emerging media enabled such stories to be widely shared. In one example, the testimonies of Holocaust survivors were used at the criminal trial of Nazi collaborator John Demjanjuk and were beamed around the world.[26] Historians either celebrated this as a 'democratising' of history or condemned the use of what Patrick O'Farrell called the 'unmediated voices' of the past.[27] It was part of a bigger tussle between traditional history – narrating history rather than analysing or critiquing it – and demands by writers, artists and critics for the past to be made accessible to the public for the emotional, cultural and political needs of the present. New trends in popular consumption gave weight to this reorientation in national historiography and laid the groundwork for an emerging stratum of film auteurs and writers such as Jonathan King and Les Carlyon, whose accounts of the Anzacs would be best-sellers in the early 2000s.[28] These cultural productions foregrounded emotion and drama while claiming to truthfully interpret the past.

This mix of drama and history also saturated the making of *Gallipoli*. Gammage, engaged as the film's historical consultant, was struck by Weir's commitment to historical detail. One of the motivations proposed by Weir and the actors for their involvement in the film was that they hoped it would act as a source of reliable information about the Great War.[29] The film was to be an exercise in history furnished with the scholarly credentials and popular cachet of *The Broken Years* and its author. This was bolstered by a new edition of Gammage's book, published to coincide with the release of *Gallipoli* and advertised alongside reviews of the film.[30]

All of this pointed to a strange alchemy in Weir's film. Having rejected a documentary style as too historical, Weir recognised the unreality of his *Gallipoli* and, indeed, took pride in the film's surrealism, from shimmering salt deserts to the depiction of Anzac Cove as the gates to the underworld. At the same time, he treated the production as a new kind of history. Weir found his archetype, his 'special kind of man' as he called Archy's character, through 'a great deal of research' and conversations with elderly veterans.[31] Before filming battle scenes he drilled his soldiers – some 700 extras – in marching, presenting arms and cleaning weapons. Weir would remind the extras 'of what the original men went through at that moment', and handed out notes on what actually happened.[32] Extras waiting for their scene in the cold and dark shared something of the spirit of the real Anzacs who 'had to … march an hour and a half, then try to sleep with only a thin blanket'.[33] Weir told the story of Gallipoli as if he were 'touching history', even as he engaged in a powerful, conscious and purposeful mythologising.

Gallipoli presented a story drawn from various tropes and archetypes of the war and its memory. The central plot device was taken from Bean's history, in which he described a young Australian soldier at the Battle of the Nek 'last seen running forward like a school-boy in a foot-race, with all the speed he could compass'.[34] Sprinting is a recurring motif in the film, used to represent both youthful enthusiasm and a kind of fatalism – running inexorably to the final destination of mass death at Gallipoli.

The image of Archy being torn apart by Turkish machine-gun fire in the closing scenes of the film was used in promotional posters and the trailer. As Graeme Turner observes, the image functions in much the same way as a war memorial statue and affirms the film as a 'celluloid monument'.[35] This composition is also evident in characterisation. Archy is an archetypal figure – an 18-year-old stockman who is kind-hearted, hardworking and raised on *Boy's Own* and Rudyard Kipling – symbolic of the Australian nation in its imperial youth. Other characters fulfil a similar role: Frank the Irish-Australian rogue loyally follows his mate and enlists; others express their desire to travel, to escape the drudgery of work, and their response to anti-German wartime propaganda. None of the characters have fathers; they are rootless, adrift from family history or genealogy.

The most concrete conflict of the film was not the Great War but the relationship between Australia and Britain. This was a clear dichotomy: the Australian nation was defined by the death of young men fighting an 'English war'. The British officers – snobbish, monocled tea-drinkers – were caricatures representative of the evils of imperial greed and hubris that drove the war. Because the film pivots on the equivocation of the individual with the nation, the Australian nation itself is absolved of the experience of the war in the process of the film; the effect is to expand popular negative images of the British while emphasising the naïve innocence of the Australians, so splitting contemporary Australia from its settler origins after the end of empire. According to Weir, the point of the film was 'not the anti-British viewpoint' but 'the pro-Australian viewpoint' and a 'developing sense of one's Australianness'.[36]

Gallipoli's biggest marker as a fictional work is Archy's inexorable march towards death. The title of the film foreshadows this, and mentor characters convey a profound sense of foreboding. Albinoni's requiem *Adagio in G Minor for Strings and Organ* forms part of the soundtrack and rises to a crescendo at the Battle of the Nek. Archy's death is a result of his own fatalism: when asked to act as a messenger he instead recommends Frank, knowing this will protect his friend from the impending slaughter.

The power of the film lies in its double feint: it offers the feeling of the past without any of the terms and conditions of history. Neither a pro- nor an anti-war film, as Jane Freebury notes, *Gallipoli* is a celebration of national ideology and conflates the Anzacs and the nation in a way that was unprecedented in the history of Anzac commemoration.[37] Until now, Anzacs had been referred to as the epitome of an imperial citizenship, founders of a military tradition, models to live by for future generations. Never had their experience been so literally equated with the identity of contemporary Australians. In identifying with the soldiers as Australians, the audience were able to claim their heroism and their identity.

Gallipoli was quickly celebrated as an affirmation of Australian nationhood. Reviewer Evan Williams in the *Australian* proclaimed that Weir's purpose was more original, daring and important than a great battlefield epic: 'It is to explain what Gallipoli and the First World War meant to Australia's history and our understanding of ourselves.' Elsewhere Weir's film was interpreted as depicting 'the appalling slaughter of fine youth' and as 'the war message that stunned a nation'.[38] Philip Adams celebrated the film as a vindication of public investment in national cinema: 'The story gives us back our history. This is what having a film industry is all about.'[39] *Gallipoli*'s international success ensured its position as *the* national film.[40]

Even critical reviews confirmed the film's cultural significance. Sylvia Lawson complained that the equation of Australia with 'images of innocent youth, opposed by repressive Authority and doomed by forces beyond any visible source of control' would not be conducive to the mature cultural nationalism or political independence that Australians so craved.[41] John Carroll suggested the film's focus on individuals was a consequence of the upheaval of the previous decades. Weir was representative of 'the present younger generation' with 'little sense of purpose' who had 'lost confidence in the values of their fathers and failed to kindle a sense of community for the new generation': 'Here was *Gallipoli*'s telling insight – on the role of fathers. When there are no fathers worth emulating the culture becomes negative, turning against all values and especially those of the immediate past.'[42]

The film offered an abridgement of the shift from imperial to post-imperial war commemoration that centred on new relationships of individual and nation. The idea that on Anzac Day Australians should 'praise famous men, and our fathers that begat us', as expressed in the social memory of Anzac a generation earlier, was disconnected from this new landscape of myth.[43] *Gallipoli* was a historical film stripped of all but the most elemental historical context.

David Williamson observed, 'In a country with a short history, the few high points become inflated into mythical proportions.'[44] *Gallipoli* certainly became a key settler story of the 1980s. Weir himself recognised the new focus on films in national cultures, saying, 'a great deal of unnecessary focus is placed on films and filmmakers today. They have become public commodities. They are endlessly discussed.'[45] Critiques of the film affirmed the role of cinema in forging new mythologies of nationhood – in this case, Gallipoli as the birthplace of the nation – and Weir's role as a kind of interlocutor of the public and national past. In an interview following the release of the film in the United States, Weir opined that Australia 'had no Wilfred Owen, no Robert Graves, no Sassoon, no Great War poets who could tell us about the lost generation'. There had been 'no films made in Australia about Gallipoli, no great novels, no great poems or paintings'.[46] His film would finally provide the definitive story.

Weir was an emerging prophet of a new Australian nationalism – a project reinforced by subsequent publications from those connected with the film. To coincide with its release, Bill Gammage published *The Story of Gallipoli*, a dossier of nationalist texts that included the film's screenplay and chapters from *The Broken Years*.[47] With a preface by Weir, the book reflected the broader historical project of *Gallipoli*: 'Our story became more about the journey than the destination, about people rather than events,' Weir wrote. He quoted Soviet director Serge Eisenstein's line, 'It was no longer stones that appealed to us and told us their history, but the people who had laid them.'[48] Weir's Anzacs were not martial warriors of imperial tradition but were akin to the veterans returning from the Vietnam War: injured, ostracised and psychologically damaged, these were the Anzacs who laid the foundation for the reconciliation of Australian nationhood in the 1980s. The Anzacs in *Gallipoli* would provide the platform for coming to terms with the fragmentation and divisions in Australia since the 1960s, when 'our country was torn in half … [by] the moratoriums, the passions round the family dinner table, with father and son shouting at each other,' Weir told his American audience. *Gallipoli* and other films of national cinema were 'giving Australians a view of themselves they've never had before, a feeling of context and of separateness'.[49]

The entwining of collective-national and personal-individual innocence into a consumer product through *Gallipoli* shaped the film's audiences in a number of ways. Gallipoli tourism became increasingly popular over the 1980s, especially among young New Zealanders and Australians who identified with the fresh-faced youth of Archy and Frank. Newspaper reviews portraying the film as an adventure story were common; travelling to Turkey was like taking part in the action. According to one *TV Listener* review, the film was 'a tale of friendship and adventure, the story of young Australians who find excitement and death'. *Movie* magazine called it 'an everlasting tribute to the likes of Frank and Archy and to the courage of the human spirit'.[50]

The early 1980s saw an explosion of media coverage, in both Australia and New Zealand, of first-person experiences and detailed accounts of the campaign, in which Gallipoli the place, *Gallipoli* the film and Anzac Day became synonymous.

Alistair Thompson, in his seminal oral history *Anzac Memories*, observed that World War I veterans' recollections were re-scripted over the 1980s in line with this shift. National cinema, the media's focus on war experiences, new public sympathies for the soldier-as-victim and the sense of elders sharing their wisdom at the end of their lives all helped ex-servicemen to compose their memories for a public audience that was hungry for stories of war.[51]

Gallipoli also provided a shared reference point for veterans whose war experience took place outside the AIF or the NZEF in subsequent conflicts of the twentieth century. An *Evening Post* interview with Cecil Manson, who fought at Gallipoli with the British army, demonstrated this.[52] Though Manson had landed at Suvla Bay, he described at length the 'utter confusion at Anzac Cove', as shown in 'the recent film *Gallipoli*'. Manson referred to 'runners' between commands and units on the front line – the central dramatic device of Weir's film. In a way that became typical of depictions of the campaign throughout the 1980s, *Gallipoli* framed Manson's experience. World War II veteran Buzz Kennedy in his column in the *Australian* described the 'incredibly young Australians' who were his comrades during the war as 'carbon copies of Archy and his mates … good-natured, remarkably naïve, not very well informed about why we were going to war'. He applauded the film for portraying 'participation in war by not preaching about the war', saying it did not condemn anyone except 'a thousand politicians on their platforms or parsons in their pulpits'.[53] This cliché of veterans' memories was a cultural formulation of war experience, redacted and folded into the film, so that at the premiere, as one press report claimed, 'memories of the battle at Gallipoli … came flooding back for older members of the crowd milling around the theatre'.[54] The triumph of Weir's spectacle was the historical film collapsing into history itself. Reviews interwove the film's imagery with biographical accounts and a cathartic process by which Manson, Kennedy and others authors would come to terms with their experience as soldiers.[55]

Gallipoli as a place was increasingly invoked as a national totem rather than a set of actual experiences; a feeling rather than an event. The film emerged from a frenzied mix of innovation and debate in the late 1970s, and provided a cultural text through which the paradoxes and tensions between history and memory, historiography and dramaturgy would play out in national cinema. Preceded by *Breaker Morant* (1980) and followed by *The Lighthorsemen* (1987), films that shared the theme of the Anzacs as innocent victims hoodwinked by empire, only Weir's film offered the complete abridgement of past and present encapsulated in Gammage's 'broken years'. Remembering 'the old days [that] never will come again' was one way to make sense of Australian society after empire.[56] The film would demand homage from all productions about Gallipoli and World War I in Australia and New Zealand, if not the world. War memory would never be the same.

'Our place': Chunuk Bair and *The New Zealand Story*, 1984

Engagement with the landscape of Gallipoli continued to spiral outwards over the 1980s. Observers in 1982 drew connections between increased attendances at Anzac Day and the success of the film on both sides of the Tasman, and images of Mark Lee and Mel Gibson appeared alongside New Zealand editorials, supplements and articles commemorating Anzac Day. To coincide with this newfound interest, John Wadham, curator of Auckland Museum's war collection, arranged a display of artefacts associated with the Gallipoli campaign.[57] Newspapers and magazines published personal accounts that emphasised the horrors of the campaign and reproduced the film's central theme: the innocence of a nation struck down by British incompetence.

Gallipoli's strongly Australian emphasis provoked an editorial in Wellington's *Evening Post* in the lead-up to Anzac Day 1982: 'Many of the younger people in the audience could have been forgiven for gaining the impression that Australia fought the Gallipoli campaign by themselves, but of course, the NZ in the middle of Anzac stands for New Zealand.'[58] It was precisely this challenge, of asserting the 'NZ' in Anzac, that shaped a new generation of creative artists and scholars in search of a post-imperial New Zealand identity. When Maurice Shadbolt's stage play *Once on Chunuk Bair* was performed for the first time at the Mercury Theatre in 1982, the cinematic spectacle of Weir's *Gallipoli* was large in the audience's minds.

Shadbolt was a seminal figure in the pursuit of a New Zealand perspective of Gallipoli.[59] *Once on Chunuk Bair* centred on the experience of the New Zealand Infantry Brigade in the disastrous August offensive.[60] Shadbolt dramatised the death of Lt-Col. William Malone (renamed Connolly in the play) as a heroic sacrifice in the face of impossible odds on the one hand and a callous British command on the other.

Shadbolt's play shared many of the Australian filmmaker's priorities. Like Weir and Williamson's script, it was imbued with a nationalist agenda and shaped by history. In a *Kaleidoscope* interview, Shadbolt showed a similar commitment to historical accuracy: his characters were all 'in some way based on men who fought at Gallipoli', drawn from soldiers' diaries, letters, autobiographical accounts, military documents and the many books about the campaign.[61] Echoing Weir's presentation of his own work, Shadbolt claimed, 'If the play makes a statement, it is one from all the materials I've explored.' Like *Gallipoli*, *Chunuk Bair* was neither pro- nor anti-war but a nationalist production. Shadbolt considered it a direct response to *Gallipoli*, a kind of historiographical corpus in which competing interpretations of the campaign were acted out. *Chunuk Bair* was his answer to 'the Australians' magnificent debacle at Lone Pine and the Nek'.[62]

In choosing Chunuk Bair as the site of his nationalist revolt, Shadbolt connected with a component of the military tradition of Anzac Day in New Zealand that had drawn attention to this hilltop as a place of significance for the NZEF. Ormond Burton's 1935 book *The Silent Division: New Zealanders at the Front, 1914–1919* described the way in which 'every man on that ridge knew that the thin line of New Zealand men was holding wide the door to victory'.[63] Burton wrote, 'How men were to die on Chunuk [Bair] was determined largely by how men and women lived on the farms and in the towns of New Zealand.'[64] This was Shadbolt's counter-myth: Chunuk Bair was 'New Zealand's cruellest, and finest, hour', and 8 August 'the day that New Zealanders lost their innocence'.[65]

The underlying assumption was that an assertion of a New Zealand perspective would recover an obscure history. This had echoes of 'the broken years' of Gammage's narrative, with the added need – of which Shadbolt was all too aware – to resonate with a distinctive New Zealand nationalism.[66] In the introduction to the play's programme Shadbolt stated that he found writing about the campaign 'a very painful and tragic process of self-discovery'. He observed that 'there was nothing in our national culture about Gallipoli'.[67]

> No poem, no song, no novel, no symphony – nothing in our national culture – enshrines the experience of Gallipoli; and this despite the fact that Anzac Day remains conspicuous in our calendars. Was the experience just too traumatic? Or is it that we still lack a Homer to process tribal memory? It was in that theatre in Troy that *Once on Chunuk Bair* was conceived.[68]

Shadbolt wrote his play to fill a gap in the national memory of Gallipoli. Like Weir, he was inspired by a visit to the peninsula, in 1977. Shadbolt, too, drew a parallel between his personal search for identity and that of the nation itself; he repeated the fallacy of Gallipoli being imbued with meaning and claimed Gallipoli

A scene from Maurice Shadbolt's play, *Once on Chunuk Bair*, during the first production at Auckland's Mercury Theatre, 1982. The set conveyed the feeling of a cramped landscape in which the Anzacs desperately tried to find shelter from gunfire and the harsh climate. NZMS873, Sir George Grey Special Collections, Auckland City Libraries – Tāmaki Pātaka Kōrero

as a sacred space. Anzac Cove was an extension of home, a sentiment expressed in Shadbolt's script when the character Connolly renames Chunuk Bair 'New Zealand'.[69]

Shadbolt drew heavily on Robert James Rhodes' book *Gallipoli* (1965), which claimed 'the Australian mythology about Gallipoli has often been neither objective nor fair'.[70] This bias, Shadbolt argued, was fuelled by Australian writers' 'deeply flawed and grievously over-praised account' of the campaign.[71] *Once on Chunuk Bair* was to be not only nationalist but revisionist, a historiographical foray into the story of Gallipoli, 'a living memorial'.[72]

The play's success owed much to some heavy editorial work by Mercury Theatre director and acclaimed writer Ian Mune, and his account of the work's first reading provides insight into *Once on Chunuk Bair*'s appealing mix of drama and history and the intentions that underpinned its production. Mune told of how Shadbolt presented the assembled cast with three relics wrapped in a handkerchief: a bullet, a piece of artillery metal and a bone fragment, apparently recovered on his journey to Gallipoli in 1977. Although the actors struggled with the 'dense and long-winded prose', the end of the reading was met with a 'heavy silence'; in a kind of epiphany, Mune, Shadbolt and the cast stood, filled with a 'sense of oneness'. 'These are our forebears,' Mune wrote. 'Their heroism and struggle, their suffering, their achievement is part of us, of what made us.'[73] This striking sense of a personal connection – between the cast of young male actors and the Anzacs – was evidence of the power of a re-enactment of the past offered by theatre or film. In a subsequent rehearsal Shadbolt told the actors, 'You are not doing this for the Mercury Theatre, not for Maurice Shadbolt or Ian Mune, and not, I hope, for yourselves; you are doing it for the New Zealanders who remain on Gallipoli.'[74] This language of memory – the reference to those who remain forever at Gallipoli as the national fallen – both reimagined the Anzacs in national terms and asserted a history distinct from that offered in Weir's film.

In parallel to Weir's reflections of contemporary Australian anxieties, Shadbolt's promotion of a heroic nationalism mapped onto New Zealand's newly independent, post-imperial position in global politics.[75] Shadbolt commented that *Once on Chunuk Bair* was 'only ostensibly about New Zealand's fatal day on Chunuk Bair on 8 August 1915. It was really about New Zealanders – and New Zealand – seventy years on.'[76] This meant shearing the Anzac story of its fundamentally imperial and racial orientation – common features of cultural productions of war remembrance since the end of World War II.[77] The equating of national innocence with the individual innocence of the soldier would be made through the experience of Chunuk Bair as 'one that had long since been erased from national consciousness through a collective amnesia'.[78]

'National innocence' was a key part of this new script of memory because it resolved any tensions that, historically, Pākehā New Zealanders were active participants in colonial settlement; rather than perpetrators, they were victims of empire as much as the Anzacs were victims at Gallipoli. Moreover, despite the play being an explicit reaction to Australian claims on Gallipoli, Shadbolt claimed to be telling history 'like it was' – the implication being that Weir had not.[79] Where *Gallipoli* was an example of romantic myth-making, according to Shadbolt *Chunuk Bair* was about historical reality in all its gritty detail.[80] Shadbolt had drawn on Malone's diaries and letters and oral interviews with Gallipoli veterans. They were the unmediated 'voices of Gallipoli' that would speak again through the work of the playwright and author and were eventually published as *Voices of Gallipoli* in 1988.[81]

Shadbolt was part of a new generation of creative artists who would act as prophets of memory detached from historical critique.

Once on Chunuk Bair resonated with the emerging New Zealand-centred commemoration of Gallipoli in the 1980s. Over the space of several years, New Zealanders were saturated with a cluster of works related to 'the New Zealand story' that spanned films, books and museum exhibitions, all heavily framed by Shadbolt's 'tribal memory'. The centrepiece of these productions was the television documentary *Gallipoli: The New Zealand story*, produced with state funding through Television New Zealand (TVNZ) and released on 22 April 1984.[82] Shadbolt wrote the script, Doc Williams was director, former Chief of Defence Leonard Thornton was narrator and TVNZ director general Allan Martin, formerly of the Australian ABC, drove the project and ensured its funding.[83] What *Once on Chunuk Bair* had begun, *Gallipoli: The New Zealand story* would finish – an ambition expressed in the seminal line of the documentary, spoken by Thornton: 'For a time, it was as if the whole balance of the war was in the hands of these men.'[84]

Military historian Christopher Pugsley, who had supported Shadbolt in preparing and staging *Once on Chunuk Bair*, now acted as military adviser to the TVNZ documentary team. Shadbolt had met Pugsley when they were both delving into the Waiōuru Army Museum archives, and had become a mentor to the young scholar. Both shared a passion for 'filling the silences of New Zealand history', as Pugsley later recounted.[85] As a young army officer Pugsley had also visited Gallipoli, and his book, with the same name as the documentary, was published in the year *Gallipoli: The New Zealand story* was released. It was the first critical work on the campaign to be written from 'a New Zealand viewpoint'.[86] Pugsley's scholarship introduced a new historiography of the campaign and initiated a much-needed New Zealand slant.[87] In his introduction he wrote that he owed much to Shadbolt – 'the catalyst who made it happen and gave me the confidence to complete the task'.[88]

The title of Pugsley's book paired it with the documentary, and their releases coincided with a third strand of a wider commemorative strategy: a museum exhibition of the same name that opened at Waiōuru Army Museum in 1984. Among other things the exhibition contained the diorama of the Gallipoli Peninsula and Chunuk Bair originally produced for the TVNZ documentary, as well as the only Victoria Cross won by a New Zealander at Gallipoli, awarded to Cyril Bassett for 'his extreme bravery under fire on the slopes of Chunuk Bair'.[89] The exhibition asserted New Zealand's role in the campaign and centred on Chunuk Bair.[90] In 1983, in an update to museum staff on the progress of the documentary *Gallipoli: The New*

Zealand story, researcher Colleen Hodge wrote that 'our film, like the Australian feature *Gallipoli*, is proving to be a slow and expensive project. However, we've great faith in our sources.'[91] Hodge's research provided a shared knowledge base for the book, the documentary and the exhibition.

The researchers ran into the same problem Shadbolt had faced earlier: the lack of a centralised New Zealand archive. The Waiōuru exhibition would build this national resource. Over eight months, Hodge and other researchers gathered a large collection of diaries, letters and official records relating to Gallipoli and deposited these with Waiōuru Army Museum.[92] TVNZ, the documentary's producer, advertised for stories and input from the public in local and national newspapers, including the RSA *Review*, and contacted Gallipoli returned services groups in Australia and the United Kingdom.[93] Speaking to the ambition that the project would shape public commemoration in much the same way as Weir's *Gallipoli*, in a press release Allan Martin stated, 'Our aim is to produce a film which will be referred to again and again in years to come.'[94] The exhibition *Gallipoli: The New Zealand story* was an unprecedented nationalisation of war memory in New Zealand as soldiers' personal and family records were transcribed and repackaged within an institutional and textual framework.

The project focused on New Zealand-recruited troops and intentionally excluded Australian soldiers; offers of help from AIF returned servicemen or their families were politely declined as 'falling outside of the scope of the documentary'.[95] J.O.C. Smith was probably the first New Zealand-born soldier to land at Anzac Cove as part of the AIF dawn landing, but even he was not included in the documentary.[96] This was a conscious attempt to provide an alternative story to Weir's *Gallipoli*.[97] Shadbolt and Pugsley hoped to provide the framework for a new national structure of memory in the same way that Weir's film had contributed to the re-scripting of Australian veterans' memories.

These challenges highlighted the lack of institutional frameworks of remembrance that had enabled Australian productions around Gallipoli. The archive of the Australian War Memorial, collected by Bean and established by the memorial's first director, John Treloar, to promote Australia's national war experience, provided Australian artists and scholars with a curated national memory.[98] Ken Inglis suggested that the absence of any such institutional infrastructure in New Zealand was a sign of a lower temperature of nationalism among New Zealanders – a comment that highlighted the novelty of the project being undertaken by the creators of the documentary *Gallipoli: The New Zealand story*.[99]

The lack of resources was acutely felt in the production of the documentary. Researchers relied on returned servicemen and their families to provide interviews, diaries, letters and manuscripts, many of which were in private hands. One important resource was a series of World War II radio programmes called *The Diggers Sessions*, rediscovered in the early 1970s, which included interviews with broadcaster Rod Talbot recounting a history of the campaign; footage sourced from the Australian War Memorial archive and the Imperial War Museum in London was also useful.[100] But even as the research drew from archives and resources in Australia and Britain, it rejected the notion that this was anything but a specifically national story.

Pugsley called for the government to replace Anzac Day with 'Chunuk Bair Day' on 8 August.[101] Like Shadbolt, he argued that a New Zealand perspective of Gallipoli would be more authentic than piggybacking on the Australian version.[102] Modern New Zealand society had been irrevocably shaped by this experience of war; Pugsley suggested that New Zealanders were 'the sum of what they did, what they found and what they lost'. He evoked Shadbolt's creative rationale and this nationalist project, saying, '[Chunuk Bair] was the loss of innocence.'[103] Pugsley's contrast between Australia's 'myth-making' and the 'authentic' experience of the New Zealanders at Gallipoli was strategic: it allowed him to obscure the myth-making at the heart of his own scholarship.

The exhibition *Gallipoli: The New Zealand story* ran from 1984 to 1985 and was a multi-media project that loosely connected the museum, public history, theatre and cinema in a spectacle of memory. The revisionist scholarship, the reinvestigation of military history and the publication of soldiers' experiences did not, however, provide a strong enough infrastructure to consolidate a consistent national remembrance. The documentary had some popular success and resulted in a public petition to the government to award a posthumous VC to William Malone, a 'born and bred New Zealander and true-blue', as one letter to the editor put it.[104] The apotheosis of the exhibition could have been the film adaptation of Shadbolt's play as *Chunuk Bair* in 1992 – the final counter-move to Weir's 'Australian' film – but the film failed as a result of insufficient funding and its execution by first-time director Dale Bradley, who struggled to transpose Shadbolt's theatre script to the cinematic screen.[105] There were no further attempts to create *the* New Zealand war film.

The film's failure signalled a wider state and public disengagement from the New Zealand Anzac story. New Zealand film and television in the 1980s had been preoccupied with revisionist histories of colonial New Zealand. *The Governor* was a landmark television show that depicted the outbreak of the Waikato War, the seminal conflict in the New Zealand Wars overseen by Governor George Grey. Whereas traditional histories had celebrated Grey as a kind of founding father of New Zealand society, *The Governor* revised him as a villain in much the same way that Weir and Shadbolt's works had depicted British imperial figures.

Geoff Murphy's 1983 film *Utu* was similarly ambitious and was the first feature film based on the New Zealand Wars. Unlike the documentary styles of other war films, *Utu*, like *Gallipoli*, is a historical mythology that presents composite characters and approximations of real events. Both films were essentially westerns, that quintessential American genre, given local form in their respective national cinemas.

Colonial stories as histories that played out contemporary politics were evident in literature too, not least in the work of Shadbolt himself. *Chunuk Bair* was published in the middle of Shadbolt's New Zealand Wars trilogy, the most famous of which, *Season of the Jew*, dramatised the history of the Māori prophet Te Kooti Arikirangi Te Tūruki. Across film, writing and television, the examination and exploration of the New Zealand Wars signalled a shift under way in New Zealand's national memory of war, as artists and their audiences grappled with early imperial myths of violence.[106]

This thread of national production reflected the long tail of empire and its legacies, still felt towards the end of the 1980s. It seemed that, despite Shadbolt's dream, a break with the imperial past was never quite complete. The interest in Māori histories of New Zealand pointed to the Māori renaissance as another crucial cultural movement under way in New Zealand society.[107] As a different language of cultural resurgence, this renaissance contested the primacy that might have been held by the Anzac revival.

In explicitly rejecting imperial loyalties, Weir's *Gallipoli* and, to a lesser extent, its New Zealand response in Shadbolt's *Chunuk Bair* and the search for a wider 'New Zealand story', sought to salve contemporary anxieties reverberating throughout the 1980s. It was all very much in tune with the deliberate search for new stories and symbols to define the nation in the wake of empire. By 1990, a fresh story of World War I had emerged from the boom and bust of national cinema; this, in turn, shaped Anzac commemoration. The Anzacs were now young men who had given their lives in a national sacrifice; Gallipoli was an emotional spectacle, melancholic but also epic and heroic. In the subsequent decades, Anzac commemoration would become increasingly focused on this space and its emotional registers.

Weir's *Gallipoli* was not simply an expression of the change from the old exclusive imperial Anzac Day to a new inclusive form: it provided its narrative form. *Gallipoli* refracted these elements for new audiences in the 1980s, and its influence extended to New Zealanders. Although historians have tended to compare *Once on Chunuk Bair* and *Gallipoli* as contrasting approaches to the dramaturgy and historiography of World War I, the texts are more similar than different. Both pivot on young male individuals and friendships forged through shared experience.

The fact that *Gallipoli* became celebrated as *the* Anzac film while *Gallipoli: The New Zealand story* languished shows how national cinema in Australia and New Zealand differed. Both productions were intended to translate personal experience to a national memory. In Australia, however, Weir's project was able to build on the groundwork of historians such as Inglis and Gammage, the recovery of Bean's official history, and the archives of the Australian War Memorial. The lack of such institutions in New Zealand undercut *Gallipoli: The New Zealand story*, and Shadbolt and Pugsley's commitment to a historical documentary form over cinematic spectacle diffused the myth-making around Chunuk Bair. New Zealand's cultural memory of World War I would continue to take its cues from the Australian film, setting up the next stage in the transformation of Anzac: the expansion of commemoration by the Australian state.

Chapter 4

'The birthplace of the nation'

Gallipoli and Waitangi, 1990

Anniversaries carry symbolic importance in cultural remembrance, and function as milestones to consolidate changes in patterns of memory and myth. In 1946, on the first Anzac Day after World War II, the war was still strongly linked with the British Empire. In 1965, efforts to commemorate the 50th anniversary of Gallipoli showed up a clear ebbing of social memory, apparent in the decline of the returned services organisations, the reluctance of governments to prop up the commemoration, and public disagreement about the future of the day.

Anzac Day 1990, the 75th anniversary of the landing at Gallipoli, was different again. The Hawke government in Australia orchestrated an official pilgrimage to the commemorations at Gallipoli, and to execute this they established the Gallipoli 75 Task Force. Although Australian governments had invested in various kinds of commemoration over the twentieth century, this was the first federal body dedicated to remembering war that proposed a framework of national cultural identity. Gallipoli 75 was an example of a state cultural project – an initiative that aims to create shared understandings for the purpose of citizenship, bounded, affected and located through negotiation and a recognition of cultural relationships.[1] It presented an opportunity to break away from imperial relationships and make new claims on the place of Gallipoli in 1990. This political investment transformed Gallipoli Anzac Day commemorations into an event dominated by Australian prerogatives and priorities.[2]

In New Zealand a commemoration of a different sort took priority. The year 1990 marked the 150th anniversary of the first signing of the Treaty of Waitangi/Te Tiriti o Waitangi, an agreement in te reo Māori and English that was made in 1840 between the British Crown and, eventually, around 540 rangatira (Māori chiefs). The government prioritised this landmark event and left the RSA, with some government funding, to promote the 75th Anzac commemorations. The Labour government of David Lange established its own state cultural project, the Waitangi 1990 Commission, to forge a public narrative of national unity that reflected New Zealand's role in the international community. This 'internationalising' of New Zealand national identity would be carried out at Waitangi, the location of the signing of the Treaty. Like the controversial 1988 Australian Bicentenary, the sesquicentennial would provoke a flashpoint for fundamental challenges to the constitutional basis of the New Zealand state.

The commemorative year opened the door to the shaping of national identity in both Australia and New Zealand, but the success of the Gallipoli 75 Task Force contrasted acutely with the limited impact of the Waitangi 1990 Commission. The comparison provides valuable insight into the divergence of state policy around Anzac commemoration between Australia and New Zealand since the 1980s.

'An Australian corner of Turkey': 1990 and the Gallipoli 75 Task Force

In February 1990 Australian Prime Minister Bob Hawke confirmed his intention to attend the dawn service at Anzac Cove on 25 April. He looked forward to the special commemoration, 'where Australian survivors will join British comrades and their former Turkish foes'.[3] In his speech at the dawn service Hawke would declare that, because of the courage, devotion and ingenuity of the Anzacs in 1915, 'this place Gallipoli is, in one sense, a part of Australia'.[4] His claim was supported by the nearly 10,000 Australians who joined him at the service. For the young expats sporting green and gold and draped in Australian flags, this Gallipoli experience meant belonging to Australia.

Hawke's simple February announcement belied the significant diplomatic and logistical efforts that had already taken place under the aegis of the Gallipoli 75 Task Force. Formed in 1988, the task force was the fruit of the Gallipoli 1990 Steering Committee led by Ed Attridge and John Quinn and overseen by Minister for Veterans' Affairs Ben Humphreys.[5] Its mission was to bring together interested parties – youth, the media, veterans, stakeholders, government departments and the Prime Minister's Office – and coordinate them in a triumphant political project. As Humphreys stressed to the federal Cabinet, 'Government support for the Gallipoli visit should be commensurate with the importance of Anzac in the minds of Australians.'[6] In Humphreys' formula, Anzac and the state would be synonymous.

In order to secure international recognition for the commemoration, Humphreys travelled to Turkey to discuss arrangements and engaged in discussions with the governments of the United Kingdom and New Zealand. Both the UK and New Zealand downplayed their participation. The UK Foreign Office had no plans for the Prime Minister Margaret Thatcher to attend, or for sending veterans groups to Gallipoli. As one British attaché said, 'The Gallipoli campaign did not loom as large in British history as it did in … [that of] New Zealand, Australia or Turkey.'[7] The New Zealand government had not planned any official representations at the 75th anniversary until Humphreys proposed a suite of bilateral activities and offered the services of the task force to coordinate political, military and veteran representation.[8] In the end, New Zealand sent Governor-General Sir Paul Reeves to the event.

By far the most enthusiastic partner in the 1990 anniversary was the Turkish government. The task force was crucial to connecting the commemoration with Turkish economic ambitions. Over the 1980s Turkey had sought to expand its diplomatic relationships with Australia and New Zealand. The Turkish government formally recognised Ari Burnu and renamed it Anzac Cove in 1985; in return the New Zealand government created a memorial to Atatürk at Moa Point in Wellington 'to honour the spirit of Anzac born at Gallipoli' and 'the heroism and self-sacrifice' of the Turkish forces. In Canberra a promontory on Lake Burley Griffin was renamed Gallipoli Reach in recognition that 'victory in the campaign belonged to Turkey, the valiant defenders.'[9] The first official visit to New Zealand and Australia by a Turkish government minister occured in 1987, when a memorandum of intent to form closer economic relations was signed with New Zealand.[10] Joint meetings of New Zealand, Australian and Turkish trade and defence delegations also took place in 1988 and 1989, accompanied by state commemorative projects.[11]

The Gallipoli commemorations also offered a chance for an international rehabilitation of Turkey and a revision of its own post-imperial remembrance of World War I. Turkish experience of the conflict was defined on the one hand by the Ottoman Empire, from the rubble of which the Turkish Republic emerged in the 1920s. On the other hand, the invasion of the Gallipoli Peninsula by Allied forces had coincided with the beginning of the relocation of millions of Armenians by Ottoman authorities, a process that became known as the Armenian Genocide. The 1990 celebrations provided a means to rewrite the scripts of the Ottoman Empire, with Kemal Atatürk at the centre of a new national account of Turkish nationalism that emphasised a noble friendship between former foes, rather than the legacy of genocide.[12] The Australian and New Zealand governments were complicit in this politically mandated forgetting.

Australia's Gallipoli 75 Task Force was also entrusted with creating and executing the elaborate state ceremonies to be held at Anzac Cove and Lone Pine, and ensuring that the 1990 commemoration would be a significant international event led by the Australian government. Prime Minister Hawke was given pride of place and was joined by an array of international leaders, including Turkish President Turgut Özal. Australia would take centre stage.

Weir's *Gallipoli* had changed the way audiences viewed the landscape of Gallipoli, and was followed by a boom in Turkish tourism in the 1980s. Young Australians, and to a lesser extent young New Zealanders, had begun to travel to the region in pursuit of the emotional adventure they had seen on the screen, and expatriates living in Europe increasingly made Gallipoli a site of personal pilgrimage: in 1987 around 450 Australian expatriates attended the dawn service at Anzac Cove; in 1989 there were 3000. Turkish entrepreneurs provided guidebooks and tour packages that affirmed the emerging Australian readings of the landscape and its history.[13]

The task force sought to include young people in the commemorations. Legacy, a charity established in 1925 to support the families of deceased war veterans, funded an Australian youth contingent as well as a number of other representatives, including war widows and nurses.[14] Hawke's youth contingent was later joined by a smaller New Zealand one. As well, school teaching resources were disseminated through the Australian War Memorial and were also used in New Zealand. There was also a wide programme of events and activities.

It was the veterans, however, who were the most important symbol in the 1990 pilgrimage. The 75th anniversary is interesting precisely because the veterans played a new role: supporting Hawke as the central figure. The inclusion of veterans was central to the task force's successful emphasis on the state's expanded role – even as parliamentary opposition criticised the government's scaling back of veterans' welfare.[15] In 1989 the task force organised a nationwide search for Australian World War I veterans to join the pilgrimage.[16] Out of 300 applicants, 60 were chosen to be part of the official delegation, announced with great fanfare by the Department of Veterans' Affairs. It was to be a national group with every state represented.[17] Artists Clifton Pugh and Bryan Westwood were appointed to accompany the veterans. During the war the federal government had sent official artists to capture the experiences of the AIF; Pugh and Westwood would now paint 'the same subjects' 75 years later.[18]

The task force worked closely with the media to achieve this political synthesis in the 1990 celebrations. The Department of Veterans' Affairs produced a monthly newsletter dedicated to Gallipoli 75 that provided media talking points and culminated in a souvenir edition recording the activities of those veterans selected to travel to Turkey.[19] In the months leading up to the anniversary, Gallipoli veterans' stories dominated Australian newspaper coverage. The *Melbourne Herald* ran a regular four-page spread on preparations, and other print media ran feature articles in the two weeks preceding Anzac Day. Newspaper accounts published broadly on two themes: stories of colourful, heroic war experiences featured widely, as did macabre depictions of the campaign portraying the Anzacs as victims of a futile campaign.[20] 'The hero was the victim,' as one *Age* journalist wrote.[21]

Seven media groups travelled with Hawke, including some hundred print and electronic media representatives. The ABC planned a half-hour documentary on the pilgrims and their journey to Anzac Cove, to be called *The Boys Who Came Home*, the title reflecting the popular imagery of the Anzacs that Weir's *Gallipoli* had generated. The ABC also covered the service at Anzac Cove and other events for all Australian and New Zealand networks, and this coverage doubled for Indian and Turkish television networks. Interest from the Indian media reflected the roughly 15,000 Indian troops who were present at Gallipoli as part of imperial forces, and the way the Australian-led commemoration provided a space for international interests.[22]

Comparisons between the 50th and 75th anniversaries were inevitable. Some of the veterans in the official delegation had attended the 50th anniversary pilgrimage, and a few felt the celebratory tone of 1990 stripped away the quiet dignity of the 1965 event. New Zealand-born journalist Frank Devine suggested that 'The only way the significance of the ... Gallipoli festivities can possibly be useful is if they contribute to the final exorcism of a debilitating myth.'[23] Devine challenged heroic narratives of the Anzacs, especially Ken Inglis' representation of stoic veterans attending the 50th anniversary pilgrimage, and quoted Maurice Shadbolt's line from *Voices of Gallipoli* about 'unlocking terrible nightmares and unvarying bitterness'. Devine was conflicted, however; elsewhere he asserted that in spite of the state's 'myth-making', the 75th anniversary was not a day for 'abandoning the men around whom ... the myth was woven'. National RSL secretary Ian Gollings denounced Devine's comments as a 'cruel assault on the facts', suggesting the journalist had allowed 'his cynicism to influence his objectivity'.[24] Gollings believed that the majority of ex-servicemen were as supportive of the Gallipoli 75 Task Force as they had been of the earlier pilgrimage.

This episode highlights the shifting politics of remembrance around veterans in the 75th anniversary. The 1990 commemorations saw a consolidation of political authority over the history of commemoration itself, a rewriting of the story of the 50th anniversary in the government's favour. The image of veterans formed a central rhetorical device in this revision. Those accompanying Hawke provided important legitimacy for the task force; celebratory rhetoric could play out during the commemoration because, as media commentary around Devine's comments suggests, the presence of the veterans obscured the distinct political change taking place. As one commentator put it, the fact that the prime minister was accompanied by 'a group of old-timers on their last chance to visit the place of their youthful blooding' provided 'hefty insurance' politically, as well as being an object of extraordinary national emotion.[25]

Media stories amplified the historical significance of Hawke's presence at the 1990 commemoration. The *Australian* called the dawn service at Anzac Cove the 'event of the decade'. Channel Seven planned to beam a live two-hour presentation from Gallipoli as Hawke and the official contingent arrived, saying it would be 'a moving and an unforgettable experience'.[26] It would be a national spectacle with unprecedented international attention.

The live coverage was accompanied by a two-hour evening programme on the history of the Gallipoli campaign and Australia's involvement in the 1990 commemoration.[27] This was a telling conflation: the Australian federal government's involvement in 1990 was imagined as equivalent to a re-enactment and extension of Australian involvement during the campaign, and rewrote the 'Australian experience' in war and remembrance in the performance of the state.

The central focus on the nation of Australia was supported through collaboration – not with old allies such as New Zealand or the United Kingdom but with the 'noble enemy'. The extensive Australian media coverage was made possible through a joint arrangement with Turkish Television (TRT), for whom the celebrations were the biggest media undertaking in Turkish history.[28] TRT's involvement inserted a significant Turkish voice into the celebrations. Support came also from the Turkish government and the 'respect for Australia that runs through the Turkish people themselves'.[29] As one pilgrim stated, 'No matter where you are in Turkey, if you're

Australian Prime Minister Bob Hawke greets veterans after the dawn service at Anzac Cove, 25 April 1990. This and other similar oft-captured moments were widely circulated by government media to emphasise the commemoration as a pilgrimage of fading national heroes, led by the indefatigable Hawke himself. John Curtin, Prime Ministerial Library, Perth

Australian you are on a higher level than most.' Another commented, 'The Turks like us: they feel they have some bond.'[30]

Turkish stories were aired in Australia, too. The *Melbourne Herald* featured stories from both Australian and Turkish veterans. One article described an interview with Adil Özşahin, the last living Turkish veteran of the Gallipoli invasion. Özşahin is depicted as grappling 'with the question of how he felt about killing Anzac soldiers and answers that his duty was to fight for Turkey'. In a dramatic finish, as the veteran recalls the memories of bloody battles, 'he slowly stands up and bent with age walks from the room – too tired for more, or too disturbed'.[31] This scene came to form a repeated trope of Australian media coverage in 1990: a veteran celebrating the relationship between Australia and Turkey, alluding to the violence before falling silent, presumably in the face of trauma for which remembrance offered redress. The violence of war was implied without disturbing the national celebration. Invariably, these articles finished with Kemal Atatürk's ode to the dead. 'The Turkish eyes that saw the Anzacs land,' as one editorial put it, were now witnessing Anzac remembrance in 1990.[32]

This Australian–Turkish dialogue reinforced the cultural remembrance under way through the Gallipoli 75 Task Force, and conflated Hawke's actions in 1990 with those of the Anzacs in 1915. The 75th anniversary was 'another Australian invasion on its way to Turkey', in the words of one Turkish commentator, with 'the most Australians gathered on the now silent Gallipoli battlefields since the landing in 1915'.[33] The image of a Turkish and an Australian veteran saluting each other in a gesture of brotherhood formed the iconic photo of the pilgrimage and was framed as laying to rest a war that claimed 100,000 Turkish and Allied lives. This image, along with others of Hawke greeting elderly veterans, were promoted by the task force and published through the Department of Veterans' Affairs.

In its commemorative newsletter, the task force also promoted the voices of Turkish Australians, in particular, who were able to personify the symbolic performance taking place in 1990. Sydney-based Turkish filmmaker and actress Ayten Kuyululu was interviewed and described her experience at the dawn service in spiritual terms:

> When I heard the bugle notes, I felt goose-bumps down my arms. It was my first dawn service and the experience of all the Australians singing together and praying together and praising the courage of the Turks – I felt very proud to have been born Turkish and very proud to be Australian ... I felt so near to all the dead, as though I was there with them.[34]

Turkish travel agents and tour companies sought to turn this spiritual connection into business. Ocean Tours travel agency, 'conscious of a common respect between the Australian and Turkish people that grew from the mutual tragedy of Gallipoli', used 'the special relationship between the two countries to spearhead a drive to attract Australian tourists to Turkey for Anzac Day'.[35] Yilmaz Tours offered accommodation in Gallipoli township, transportation to Anzac Cove, a complementary dinner and a screening of Weir's *Gallipoli*.[36] Similar tour packages were offered by Australian travel agencies. One included an 'Anzac tour of Vietnam', pitched 'not just for ex-servicemen but also for families or other interested people'.[37]

Thousands of Australian tourists joined the official delegation for the 1990 dawn service. Some media intimated that these were mostly young people, standing 'shoulder to shoulder with the surviving diggers who created the Anzac legend'.[38] This vision of young Australians and elderly veterans completed the powerful image of the 1990 commemoration. In a radio interview following the dawn service, Hawke talked about the emotional meetings between '20-something' Australians and 90-year-old veterans, and 'the bonding that took place between them'. This 'outpouring of affection from the youngsters for the old veterans,' he said, was like 'all the generations of this century coming together and recognising what the young owed to the old and the way in which the old were proud of the young'.[39] The generational bonds of nationhood had been disrupted by disagreement at home in 1988; now the international space of Gallipoli in 1990 would forge new connections between Australians.

There had been a significant shift in young people's participation at Anzac over the 1980s. Queensland RSL president Bruce Ruxton noted that 'young people are showing more interest than ever' and commented on the 'volume of inquiries from families about a grand- or great-grandfather'. On the growing tourism to Turkey, Ruxton observed that 'what affects most Australians who visit Gallipoli is that it is part of Australia. You get a feeling that what you are walking on is yours ... It is an eerie quietness that draws young people.'[40] Far from being a quiet and empty place, however, Gallipoli became an international site filled with a range of assertions about the meaning of Anzac as the task force, veterans and the media all clamoured to make claims about the anniversary and its significance.

The tourism packages, media coverage and state press strategies all emphasised the 75th anniversary as a celebration of the founding of Australia. The battle of Gallipoli was, according to one *Daily Telegraph* reporter, 'the making of Australia as a nation'.[41] The campaign was variously a 'day written in blood', the 'saga of epic courage', 'a day in Australian history that will never be forgotten' – all 'binding a young nation called Australia forever'.[42] The journey made by Hawke and the official delegation would redress the trauma of the past, 'purging the nightmare with comradeship'. The 'eerie quietness' of Gallipoli was broken by an extraordinary public conversation made possible by the Gallipoli 75 Task Force. As commentator John Stevens observed, 'the veneration of the old' allayed 'any suspicion of political advantage or the manufacture of cultural cement'.[43]

The 'noise' of this commemoration heightened the contrast between New Zealand and Australian approaches to Anzac Day 1990. As the Waitangi 1990 Commission attempted to negotiate public commemoration of the 150th anniversary of the signing of the Treaty, the New Zealand government's response to the 75th anniversary was similar to the approach to Anzac Day 1965: it would be a broadly civic commemoration organised by veterans.

The RSA organised a school essay competition and produced a 15-minute video and classroom resource, *Gallipoli: The muddle that moulded a nation*, which essentially reworked the themes of the 1984 documentary *Gallipoli: The New Zealand story*. In this sense, 1990 was a redux of national cinema in the 1980s: 'the Australian film' versus the muted, multifaceted 'New Zealand story'. Other 1990 events in New Zealand included festivals, concerts and exhibitions, the installation of the sculpture *The Man with the Donkey* on the forecourt of the National War Memorial, and veterans' reunions in Rotorua and Gisborne.

New Zealand's state involvement in the Gallipoli events was limited to organising Governor-General Sir Paul Reeves' part in the official delegation. There were no New Zealand representatives in either the Australian task force or the Turkish steering group, and this lack of collaboration was apparent in the sidelining of functions organised by New Zealand's Ministry of Foreign Affairs in Gallipoli and Istanbul: the governor-general's official diplomatic function, for example, was accidentally scheduled at the same time as a dinner in honour of Hawke in Istanbul.[44] The services at Lone Pine and Chunuk Bair were also held at the same time – ostensibly to avoid overcrowding, but further emphasising the differences between Australia and New Zealand.

Australian claims to Gallipoli – that the landscape, in Ruxton's terms, belonged to Australia – and the eclipse of the New Zealand story may be summed up in the Gallipoli 1990 Plaques Project: the installation of 10 bronze information plaques at key sites on the peninsula. These were the brainchild of Melburnian Ross J. Bastiaan, who remarked on the lack of interpretive signage in his book *Images of Gallipoli* (1988).[45] Touted to media as 'a voluntary two-year task to enable visitors to understand the significance of the Anzac National Park at Gallipoli', it is an example of a project dedicated to the new imaginative geography of Gallipoli, and reflects the visual engagement with Anzac over the 1980s and the political investiture offered by the task force. Bastiaan said his intention was 'to help others understand the importance of this small part of Australia in Turkey'.[46] The text of the plaques, in English, Turkish, French and German, emphasised the Australian experience in the campaign: French and British Allies were mentioned only in joint actions. The decidedly Australian content – and the claims being made on the landscape of Gallipoli – quickly became a source of contention, as many felt the 'Australian geography' obscured New Zealand stories around sites such as Chunuk Bair.

Each plaque received corporate sponsorship – Coca-Cola, for example, sponsored the one for the Hill 971 battlefield site – and Bastiaan belatedly contacted the New Zealand High Commission in Canberra about organising third-party sponsorship of another plaque. The High Commission, in turn, hastily sought sponsorship from the New Zealand government for the Chunuk Bair plaque, which would have the New Zealand coat of arms cast in the bronze rather than the logo of the major sponsor, Qantas. The initial response was positive: it was hoped that Qantas would swap with the plaque at Quinn's Post, since this site had connections for both Australians and New Zealanders.[47] When Qantas reneged on the agreement, however, the New Zealand government withdrew its interest.[48] The imbroglio became public when Hawke unveiled the Lone Pine plaque at the wreath-laying ceremony: there was no official unveiling at Chunuk Bair. The New Zealand government press secretary diverted media queries by saying the existing monument was sufficient and stating tersely, 'there has been no government involvement in the project'.[49] It was a telling, if discordant, note on which to end the commemorative celebrations.

'Belonging Here – Toi Taketake': The Treaty of Waitangi and the 1990 Commission

For the New Zealand government, 1990 was a challenging year: a wealth of commemorative celebrations, a general election and the Auckland-hosted Commonwealth Games all took place against a backdrop of political upheaval, economic uncertainty and increasingly tense race relations. With its busy schedule of state events and projects, the government relegated the 75th anniversary of Gallipoli to the back seat.[50]

Over the 1970s, 6 February had tentatively evolved as a day on which to celebrate the nation's racial partnership between Māori and Pākehā. Most Pākehā viewed Waitangi Day as an occasion to celebrate harmonious race relations; Māori, however, were beginning to view it as a day to draw attention to breaches of Te Tiriti. Commemoration of the Treaty signing always took place at the Treaty grounds at Waitangi, but protests had become commonplace and disruptive. In 1984, in the face of a renaissance in Māori political opposition, the Lange government had instigated a 'policy of retreat' from the Treaty grounds, and moved official Waitangi celebrations to Wellington. Māori protest had moved into the courtrooms and the negotiations of the Waitangi Tribunal, the standing committee of inquiry set up in 1975 'to make recommendations on claims brought by Māori relating to legislation, policies, actions or omissions of the Crown' that were alleged to 'breach the promises made in the Treaty of Waitangi', with its powers later expanded to explore historical claims since 1840.[51]

Against this backdrop the Lange Labour government established the New Zealand 1990 Commission in 1988 to encourage participation in events and activities to celebrate the 150th anniversary of the nation of New Zealand. It invested $20m of state funding into the project; an additional $2m came from the New Zealand Lottery Grants Board. The commission was intended to be both an advisory body and responsible for the distribution of funding for celebrations, and had a broad brief: to 'increase understanding and awareness of the Treaty' and of 'alternative points of view and differing cultural backgrounds', and to encourage planning in order to lay 'a better foundation for the future'.[52]

At the launch of the commission the chair, Minister of Internal Affairs Michael Bassett, expressed optimism for the 1990 project, saying, 'A sense of national pride and community spirit will re-emerge.' He cited a recent survey that showed three-quarters of New Zealanders thought the commemorations would have a positive effect on the country. 'There's a strong groundswell out there of people who are tired of stress and conflict, and of listening to prophets of doom saying that the country is going down the gurgler.'[53] The anniversary would, however, be more modest and community-focused than Australia's 1988 bicentenary 'razzmatazz', as Bassett put it.[54] The minister tried to avoid politicisation of the commission, declaring its work 'apolitical'. Given the nature of the Treaty as a founding document, however, it is hard to imagine how its 150th commemoration could be anything *but* political.[55]

The first nationwide promotion, launched in April 1989, featured the commission's four patrons – Governor-General Sir Paul Reeves, Prime Minister David Lange, leader of the Opposition Jim Bolger and the Māori queen Te Arikinui, Dame Te Atairangikaahu – in a national television, newspaper and radio campaign and a tour of regional towns.[56] Clearly the commemoration was to have bipartisan and bicultural support. The central focus was the historical signing of Te Tiriti.[57] This was despite the fact that Lange, in a speech to the Labour Party two months earlier, had declared that the Treaty was not a unifying symbol but 'one that was being dragged through political or legal arguments' – a reference to the efforts of the Waitangi Tribunal, which at the time was facing a growing number of claims. The Treaty, in Lange's thinking, was at risk of becoming reduced to a symbol of injustice or guilt that Māori and Pākehā 'wished they'd never heard of'.[58]

The commission's approach to the place of the Treaty reflected considerable public uncertainty about what to emphasise in what was intended as 'a year of nationhood'. In one interview, Bassett expressed amazement at 'the number of definitions and perceptions around the Treaty', stating that the commission's job was to 'ensure that the Treaty is made clear'. The wrongs of the past would be left behind through a process of 'harmony and healing'.[59]

Like Australia's Gallipoli 75 project, the New Zealand 1990 Commission had a strong educational focus. The commission encouraged schools to plan studies of New Zealand culture and heritage over the course of the year, appointed teacher and student coordinators and distributed an educational resource kit.[60] Entitled *Belonging Here – Toi Taketake*, the resource outlined possible curriculum topics and suggested projects for the 150th celebrations, such as the staging of mini-Commonwealth Games, Treaty studies and re-enactments, marae visits, native tree planting and speech contests. Promotional material explained: '1990 provides the potential for students, teachers, parents and caregivers to come together as a school community to explore and appreciate our cultures and heritage, and to discuss issues such as the place of the Treaty of Waitangi in schools.'[61]

There were other initiatives for young people. A government-funded Youth Treaty Summit was gazetted by youth advocates to promote bicultural understandings of the nation and to demonstrate a united front among Māori and Pākehā 'committed to a Treaty-based future'.[62] Among the images of the commemoration was one of two boys playing together, one blond and fair-skinned and the other dark-haired and brown-skinned – embodying 'the spirit of two peoples in one nation', as Claudia Orange wrote.[63]

In an attempt to present New Zealand nationhood at the international level, the commission initiated the Living Treasures project, in which it asked various European countries, Japan and the United States to send citizens of cultural importance to New Zealand during the sesquicentennial.[64] These 'living gifts' would be honoured guests in a calendar of national and local events. American author Alex Haley, for example, represented the United States and travelled across New Zealand during March 1990. Haley delivered talks to the New Zealand Writers' Guild, worked with Māori writers and artists, and took part in community events. Each Living Treasure would be the subject of a half-hour TVNZ documentary, which the government hoped could later be used to promote tourism in New Zealand.[65] The project was intended to enhance the country's cultural life, and was lauded by Deputy Prime Minister Geoffrey Palmer as the first venture of its type in the world, intended 'to stimulate young New Zealand talent'.[66] The commission also asked the public to nominate friends and relatives living overseas to be invited to New Zealand by the prime minister for 1990, and received some 38,000 responses. These visits would culminate in the attendance by Queen Elizabeth II at the 1990 celebrations at Waitangi where she would meet with descendants of rangatira (chiefs) who had signed Te Tiriti in 1840.

The cast of *Living Treasures* soon came under public criticism. The majority of invitees were from Europe, and critics were quick to point out the project's hackneyed Eurocentrism. When the Chinese ambassador to New Zealand approached the commission with a number of potential candidates from China, Bassett admitted the programme had room for only 12 guests: all places were filled.[67] In an editorial titled 'Treasuring the obscure', the *Evening Post* criticised the choice of candidates and questioned 'their relevance to this young country's attempts to come to terms with its history and place in the South Pacific'.[68] Others criticised the programme as 'too highbrow' and portrayed Michael Bassett as an élitist, out-of-touch 'culture vulture'.[69] Some pointed out that Māori had already successfully provided a model of international cultural branding through the immensely successful *Te Māori* exhibition (1984–87) in New York's Metropolitan Museum of Art. Anthropologist Hirini Moko Mead was critical of the commission's emphasis on projects of international significance and suggested they might obscure local stories such as that offered by *Te Māori*.[70]

In an effort to shape a media narrative and quash public criticism of its international focus, the 1990 Commission introduced Radio New Zealand (RNZ) as the principal sponsor of the anniversary, saying, 'Given the enormity of our role in encouraging every New Zealander to take part in [Waitangi Day] and to contribute to the year's objectives, the role of Radio New Zealand is paramount to our success.'[71] RNZ was, in the words of the *New Zealand Herald*, 'part of the country's history' with a responsibility 'to reflect the New Zealand identity'. One RNZ producer expressed hope that the debate about the sesquicentennial would at least lead to more people listening to ordinary Māori voices.[72]

Other aspects of the commission's work came under fire. In his editorial for the *Listener* in February 1990, Andrew Mason questioned the language of celebration being used. In light of debates surrounding the Treaty, could New Zealanders actually 'celebrate' Waitangi Day? 'Sacred covenant or fraud?' Mason asked. 'Founding document or Victorian relic? Pact of partnership or symbol of disunity?' He noted that 'in the confused and divided public of 1990 … these conflicting views could all be regarded as valid interpretations … The debate is intense and often angry.' Mason concluded: 'The treaty is certainly a major thread in the fabric of the nation but at times it almost seems the fabric cannot hold.'[73] The social fabric, damaged by trenchant media criticism, was certainly fraying around the Waitangi project.

One of the images from the 1990 Commission's Treaty of Waitangi 150th anniversary campaign, September 1989. The boys represented 'the Treaty's original spirit of goodwill, unity and honesty which can continue to be its symbolism and hope for the future'.
EP-Ethnology-Māori Land from 1976-02, Alexander Turnbull Library, Wellington

One writer asked whether '1990 [would] be a year of celebration or a year of deep division in New Zealand? ... a massive birthday party, or a troubled episode in New Zealand's race relations?'[74]

The growing ambivalence among Pākehā over the commission's narrative was apparent also in Māori reactions to the 1990 project. Historian Keith Sinclair, acting as historical adviser to Bassett, suggested the commission offer funding for iwi (extended tribal groups) to build waka taua (war canoes) to form a massive fleet for the Queen's arrival at Waitangi.[75] The source of Sinclair's inspiration was a similar spectacle at the 1940 Waitangi centenary celebrations, promoted at the time by Māori statesman Sir Āpirana Ngata. The funding would enable the revitalisation of traditional carving skills, and the waka would remain iwi property and therefore represented investment in local communities.[76] The symbolism of these waka, funded by the government and built by iwi, was intended to be one of unity, and aligned with calls to 'paddle one canoe' during the 1990 anniversary.[77] The commission's funding fell short, however, and additional fundraising was required.

Enthusiasm for the waka project differed among the regions. A joint

Māori–Pākehā committee was formed in Hawke's Bay to organise donations to support the carving of Ngāti Kahungunu's canoe, which would be the largest in the fleet.[78] The confederation of nine Nelson and Marlborough tribes, Te Runanganui o Te Tau Ihu o Te Waka a Maui, sought Nelson City Council sponsorship of $40,000 to build a twin-hulled waka, noting in their application that this was 'not designed to be an exclusively Māori project' and would involve training young Pākehā and Māori in the construction and crewing of the vessel.[79] The council refused, however, preferring 'a project that improves harmony, that involves everyone [and] which is going to last for the next 150 years'.[80]

The commission's attempts to create national unity began to fracture under the tensions of regional claims. Manawatū Museum director Mina McKenzie argued that 'biculturalism and the Treaty still need to be sorted out properly before we can celebrate 1990'. In her opinion, local identities and histories were more important than grand national myths. McKenzie cited Rangitāne rangatira Te Peeti Te Awe Awe as one historical example – a chief who wanted to bring Pākehā and Māori together to establish a new settlement in what became Palmerston North. In a letter to the editor, another Rangitāne woman wrote, 'What we want to celebrate or not is a personal matter, and we certainly don't want 1990 to be full of controversy.' She agreed that the commemorations should be at community level.[81]

In July 1989 the Waiariki District Māori Council announced it would boycott the 1990 celebrations, and called on other district councils and the New Zealand Māori Council to join the protest. Chair of the New Zealand Māori Council Sir Graham Latimer was asked to lead a group of rangatira in presenting a protest to the Queen regarding the lengthy delays in resolving Treaty disputes. The government needed to honour its obligations, or it would 'continue to drag Aotearoa down in history, as the oppressors'.[82] Latimer rejected the boycott, however, saying that it would jeopardise tribunal negotiations.[83]

Waikato-Tainui's acceptance of the 1990 Commission, evidenced by the Māori Queen's patronage, was a significant shift in this group's position, from one of standing apart from the Crown to a kind of accord. There was an element of political strategy here as the iwi entered negotiations with the Crown over its land claims. For many iwi, the sesquicentenary was an opportunity to shore up community support for Waitangi Tribunal claims. Taranaki iwi Te Ātiawa, whose claims were soon to be heard by the tribunal, held meetings or hui to discuss how to mark the anniversary; and a national hui of Māori leaders was held at Rātana Pā in 1989 to discuss the anniversary and Māori aims.[84]

The commission's work was further complicated by the government's marked ambiguity about its own role in Waitangi. Legislative changes over the past two decades suggested the state's uncertainty: the Waitangi Day Act of 1960 had established 6 February as a national day, in 1973 the Kirk Labour government had renamed it New Zealand Day and made it a public holiday, and three years later the incoming National government had changed it back to Waitangi Day.[85] The site of Waitangi itself had not been maintained, and work on the Waitangi Treaty House to prevent deterioration and restore its historical authenticity had been kickstarted in 1987 by a Lottery Board grant. The neglect of the house was perhaps symbolic of the national attitude towards Waitangi and the Treaty, an irony not lost on commentators.[86]

There was considerable debate as to who would foot the bill for the Waitangi Day commemorations. The 1990 Commission was adamant that events at Waitangi were not within its purview, and refused to fund anything related to the Northland commemorations. Instead, Northland iwi covered the costs of the celebrations at the Treaty grounds and catered for 6000 guests over the four days in the lead-up to 6 February. Latimer was concerned that iwi would be blamed if the commemorations failed, saying 'it makes things very difficult when you can't even put a deposit on an order because there is no money'.[87] These and similar comments were repeated widely in both Māori and mainstream media.

The narrative of the 1990 Commission began to splinter. Chief executive Don Hutchings claimed the Treaty events were a commemoration, not a celebration, saying, 'We are not yet in the position with the Treaty to say that we can celebrate it.'[88] He suggested the commission should leave Waitangi Day activities to local iwi.

The commission's attempted retreat from Māori opposition and the politics of place was unsuccessful. Growing political agitation began to intersect with the broader context of the Auckland Commonwealth Games, scheduled for the fortnight leading up to Waitangi Day.[89] Māori activists had already mobilised in protest against the Games; they now threatened to extend their protest to Waitangi, arguing that in both cases 'Māori should not be involved in any party to celebrate 150 years of oppression.'[90] In a *Metro* article titled 'Te Karanga o Te Iwi: What the Treaty means to me', activist Syd Jackson wrote that 1990 would mark the fact 'that for a century and a half we have suffered the degradation and indignity of gross exploitation and oppression by whites'. Jackson targeted the Lange government's failure to accept the Treaty, rejected conciliatory language of 'Treaty principles' as a political feint, and reiterated calls from Māori to boycott the commission's 1990 programme.[91] In a salient critique, Jackson claimed the failing project of the commemoration had resulted in 'the government getting the worst of both worlds'. 'Many Māori have been antagonised,' he concluded, 'because they have gained little of tangible benefit [and] many Pākehā have been antagonised by all the bicultural rhetoric.'[92]

The 1990 Commission and the Auckland Commonwealth Games were part of a wider framework of creative reinvention by the New Zealand government. In both cases, these state cultural projects entailed reaching back into the comforts of a disintegrating imperial past in a post-imperial rendering of Commonwealth networks. This nostalgia was vividly captured in the promotional campaign for the Games, which centred on an epic television advertisement directed by Māori filmmaker Lee Tamahori. 'Join Together' imagined the stirrings of the spirit of the Games in the mud of the Western Front in 1917. The language of joining together also alluded to the aims of the 1990 commemoration as a project of nationalism. Neither the Games nor the 1990 Commission escaped historical tensions, however. Writing in *Metro* in March 1989, Māori activist Matiu Tarawa condemned what he called the 'Empire Games' and referred to the 150th anniversary as indication that New Zealand society was 'a corrupt system loaded with injustices that destroy the family structures and deprive us from true democracy and a better way of life'.[93]

In this storm of controversy, the 1990 Commission failed also to escape the historical legacy of empire evident in contemporary Pākehā myth-making. Māori media suggested that the $2m in community grants was an attempt to sway Māori to support the anniversary. The editor of *Te Iwi o Aotearoa* mused that, rather than controlling an official version of the anniversary, the 1990 Commission needed to step back and 'let the celebrations or non-celebrations bring us closer together'.[94] Hakatere Māori leader Coral Jones argued similarly: 'People have been sucked in by the publicity of the 1990 Commission: because they have a lot of money, a lot of people are going for it – they see it as a form of advertising for the things they are doing.' Unless there was a debate on Te Tiriti with good facilitators, Jones concluded, the commission would simply continue to aggravate Māori groups.[95]

The tension around the 150th commemoration was exacerbated by the commission's failure to respond adequately to Māori voices. Commentators argued that one way to avoid the prospect of large-scale protest would be for the commission to come out with a strong position on the Treaty rather than focusing on international visitors.[96] Instead, the commission attempted to continue the pantomime of an 'apolitical' commemoration, with Don Hutchings arguing that '1990 should not become bogged down in the past' and criticising the 1980s as a 'divisive decade'.[97]

His comments only spurred opposition, and two Auckland coalitions – the Māori He Taua and non-Māori Auckland Treaty Action Coalition – were mobilised in response. The Treaty Action Coalition called on the government to state its Treaty commitments clearly and start implementing some of the Waitangi Tribunal's recommendations, citing the 'huge number in New Zealand who support the Treaty' and arguing that the government needed to listen to the people.[98]

In July 1989 the commission announced it would seek Māori representation on its Community Committee, responsible for allocating the $2m of local project grants, to ensure 'a wider understanding of what 1990 meant to the community'. No Māori had been represented before now because the committee had not understood the protocols for inviting iwi to send a delegate to meetings.[99] The commission pointed out ways that Māori had benefited from the funding, such as the 21 waka taua that had been constructed and many other projects relating to iwi and Māori history, including the publication of the first volume of *Ngā Mōteatea*, a collection of Māori literature, Sir Āpirana Ngata's poetry, maps, compilations of Māori travels, whakapapa (genealogy) and whaikōrero (speeches).[100] The language of the commission's reaction to its critics only underlined the state's difficulty in controlling the various interpretations of the 1990 anniversary.

Academics increasingly abandoned the 1990 Commission and the debate it provoked. The growing sense of unease and uncertainty came to a head in a structured debate on national radio between retired Pākehā academics C.K. Stead, emeritus professor of English from the University of Auckland, and Margaret Orbell, an expert in classical Māori language and literature at the University of Canterbury. The debate, which centred on questions of cultural heritage and identity, reflected the way in which contestation of the 1990 Commission had eroded its celebratory language and its authority as a state project. In a sometimes acrimonious exchange, Stead stated, 'Pākehā society is becoming resistant to a lot of things Māori because they're having them forced on them all the time, and they feel a kind of artificiality, a kind of insincerity is being asked of them, and they resent it.' He suggested that because the imperial basis of New Zealand identity was gone, 'the old binding alignment to the parent culture' having been 'gradually stretched and broken and set aside', 1990 might promote 'a new independent consciousness' among Pākehā New Zealanders.[101]

Orbell agreed that Pākehā discussion around the 1990 anniversary had been marked by ambiguity and silence, and suggested this contributed to 'a subtle apartheid in many areas of New Zealand life … an unconscious feeling that Europeans

– Pākehā – represent culture, civilisation, and that Māori represent nature – the opposite of civilisation'. She argued that there was 'no conflict between the two traditions', and suggested that the expansion of Māori literature in the school curriculum, for example, would be a way to resolve Pākehā anxiety through an 'increased understanding of culture identification with the country itself'. The silence from Pākehā about engaging with Māori was the source of 'a terrible insecurity, one much deeper than people would normally admit to or realise'; the notion that New Zealand was a 'young country' without a national identity was an erasure of Māori history.[102]

The debate between Stead and Orbell over the need for a 'New Zealand consciousness' and its uncertain foundations reveals the paradoxes and fault lines running through the 1990 project. Stead's position reflected the approach of Pākehā academics of an older generation. Keith Sinclair, invited by the *Times Literary Supplement* to write an explanation of the anniversary and its controversy for a British audience, repeated his old argument that although 'far from perfect', New Zealand's race relations were 'much happier than in Australia, South Africa, or Canada', and argued that biculturalism was being eclipsed by the new multiculturalism of the 1980s.[103]

New Zealand was still very much a Pākehā-dominated society at the end of the 1980s; if public debate began to make room for Māori rights, it remained focused on an anxious search for the foundations of a shared Pākehā myth. This presented something of a catch-22 for the New Zealand government heading into 1990. The Stead–Orbell debate was framed as having been between 'those who say [the government has] gone too far on the Māori thing' and 'those who say the government was doing so little'.[104] Somewhat lamely, the commission tried to deflect this fundamental division. Bassett admitted that, as with the Australian Bicentenary, which had highlighted the plight of Aboriginal peoples, 'so New Zealand's commemoration will put the spotlight on our race relations record'.[105] In an interview a few days later he affirmed, 'I think the opportunity for Māori here is so much greater, because of the Treaty itself. It's a binding document, our founding document.'[106]

*

The 1990 Commission failed, however, even in the initial language of remembrance. Despite seeking to promote a sense of citizenship, participation and belonging within the community, the intended celebration of 150 years of European settlement in Aotearoa simply highlighted the nation's racial, legal and political divisions. Questions of whether Pākehā should embrace Māori customs and culture challenged the very basis of Pākehā cultural authority and belonging. This ambiguity felt towards pioneer and multicultural threads in public culture reflected the changing face of the country.

In this way 1990 was something of an *annus horribilis* of New Zealand national commemoration. The attempts to establish a national mythology after empire foundered on the realities of a burgeoning Treaty claims process in which the worlds of hapū and iwi (kinship groups and tribes) would only take on more public prominence. New Zealand remained a Pākehā-dominated public culture, but one that increasingly had to take account of alternative readings of the state and its moral foundations. The year was, however, significant as a cultural turning point, when Pākehā New Zealand acknowledged the Treaty of Waitangi as a foundational document and narrative.

The contrast with the activities of the Gallipoli 75 Task Force could not have been more pronounced. The task force achieved a unified international commemoration. This place-making project operated in the emerging cultural geography of Gallipoli, supported by the Turkish government and shaped by the symbolic interactions of veterans and youth pilgrims. It was enabled by a unified political narrative, supported by media, and premised on a new Australian 'colonisation' of Anzac Cove and the wider peninsula in which Turkish political and economic partnership was crucial in the construction of a new international space for Australian myth-making.

A number of positive public history projects came out of the 1990s in New Zealand, including the first volume of the *Dictionary of New Zealand Biography*, which built on the work of the Waitangi Tribunal and suggested that a positive portrayal of the Treaty and nation was possible.[107] Other projects included a festival of Indigenous film supported by the New Zealand Film Commission and the Council for Māori and Pacific Arts.[108] The 1990 Commission funded the restoration of Māori Land Court records, thereby making the recovery of these aspects of iwi history public and accessible.[109] The advocacy group 1990 Coalition called for further revisions of public history, including to public monuments marking the New Zealand Wars.[110]

In December 1991 a new area opened in the National Archives in Wellington. The Constitution Room would hold the founding documents of the state: the Declaration of Independence/He Whakaputanga and the Treaty of Waitangi/Te Tiriti.[111] A public story of Waitangi, in which Waitangi was a messy but determining foundation of political relationships from 1840 to the new millennium, was gradually being institutionalised. Despite its difficulties, 1990 was an important step towards greater recognition of Te Tiriti in the history and public life of New Zealand.

The year had important implications for the trajectory of Anzac commemoration. In New Zealand the 1990 Commission suggested that the Department of Internal Affairs was an ineffective vehicle for carrying out cultural policy; nine years later, the department's public history functions would be removed to form part of a new Ministry of Culture and Heritage. Furthermore, the divisive 150th anniversary enhanced the effectiveness of war commemoration as a diplomatic and political project, to the point that some advocated for Anzac Day to become 'New Zealand Day' in place of 6 February.[112] Although ultimately rejected by the RSA and the government, the proposal suggested the potential for a commemorative mythology of war centred on the state. Finally, 1990 sent a clear message to government: any future state cultural project would need the discipline and authority of the Prime Minister's Office over official remembrance.

In both countries, 1990 was a seminal year in which the state became more invested in the production of national myth-making – an investment that would intensify over the coming decades.

Chapter 5

'To serve his country once more'

Repatriating the unknown Anzacs, 1993 and 2004

In 1993 the remains of an unknown Australian soldier killed during the Great War were exhumed from a French cemetery and transported to Australia. On the morning of 11 November 1993, on the 75th anniversary of the armistice, the remains of the unknown soldier, flanked by Great War veterans and a full military guard, were borne on a gun carriage through Canberra to the Australian War Memorial, where a tomb had been cut in the Hall of Memory.

In 2004 the New Zealand government undertook a campaign to repatriate a New Zealand World War I soldier from a European battlefield. After lying in state at Parliament House – as his Australian counterpart did in the Old Parliament of the federal capital – the unknown warrior was paraded through the streets of Wellington to a tomb in the forecourt of the National War Memorial.

At the funeral of the unknown Australian soldier, Prime Minister Paul Keating declared, 'He is all of them; and he is one of us.' Prime Minister Helen Clark echoed his words at the funeral of the unknown New Zealand Warrior, saying 'He was one of us.'[1] Keating and Clark presented the repatriations as a way of stimulating cultural renewal following periods of seismic economic reform and social change.[2] They were a way of coming to terms with the grief of war, and a cathartic act to heal the wounds of the nation. The national war experience would come to rest in these tombs.

There are few things more intimate than the exhumation and re-burial of human remains, and the act carries a profound sense of responsibility and authority.[3] In 1993 and 2004 respectively, both states reached back into a remembered past. Although the soldiers of World War I might have considered themselves to be of British descent rather than Australian or New Zealand nationals, the war dead were

The funeral procession for the unknown Australian soldier, Anzac Parade, Canberra, 11 November 1993. Australian Broadcasting Corporation

now reimagined in terms of modern nationhood for a new century. A repatriation would create a new national memory.

The practices, performance and language of the repatriations in Australia and New Zealand were part of a continuum of change in the commemoration of Anzac. The naming of the unknowns –'soldier' in Australia and 'warrior' in New Zealand – reflected deeper textual, institutional and constitutional patterns, evinced also in the sites in which they were entombed.

Institutions such as war memorials convey languages of memory that are rhetorical, spatial and embodied. The Australian War Memorial proposed and directed the repatriation of the unknown soldier. Celebrated as 'the most significant commemorative event in the history of the memorial', the burial marked its transformation into the most influential cultural institution in Australia and justified the director's 2013 declaration that the institution was 'the heart and soul of the Australian nation'.[4]

The Australian precedent was vital in securing Helen Clark's support for the repatriation of the unknown New Zealand warrior. The National War Memorial in Wellington was, however, a very different site of national memory to the Australian

The unknown New Zealand warrior was borne on a gun carriage along Lambton Quay, Wellington, on 11 November 2004. Over 100,000 people lined the streets to watch the funeral procession.
Photo: Rob Kitchin

War Memorial, and a number of institutional and constitutional matters disrupted what was suppose to be a strictly national performance. The New Zealand memorial would come to represent a bicultural nation in which the memorial was but part of a network of cultural institutions.

The practice of repatriation shapes cultural remembrance and allows the state to produce a self-legitimising vision of the past by validating certain public stories. The memorial spaces in which these unknown Anzacs were laid provided powerful ideological statements about the past and present visions of these two nations.[5]

'He is all of them; and he is one of us': The unknown Australian soldier, 1993

The unknown soldier was not the first body of an Australian World War I soldier to be repatriated: the remains of Major-General Sir William Throsby Bridges, killed in the first few days of the campaign, were brought home and buried in Canberra in 1915. Bridges' tomb quickly fell out of public view, however, and did not become 'an enduring focus for the grief of individual Australians'.[6] Discussions in the 1920s about the possibility of establishing a memorial tomb akin to those in Britain and France were evidence of the way grief continued to be understood in terms of local and imperial identity. The states of New South Wales, Victoria and Queensland each proposed establishing a tomb, and in 1933 the Paddington-Woollahra RSL sub-branch resolved that a body be brought from Gallipoli and buried in Sydney.[7] In the end, however, the federal RSL decided against a national tomb, saying 'the sentiment of the Empire was expressed in the burial in London of the unknown Warrior'.[8] The decision was reinforced by the practical challenges in exhuming and transporting human remains, and a complete lack of political will and state support.

In 1970 the 55th national RSL congress moved to seek federal government approval for the interment of the remains of 'an Australian unknown warrior' within the precinct of the Australian War Memorial.[9] The government was reluctant to be involved, however, and the idea languished.[10]

The lack of interest in a national tomb was evident at the Australian War Memorial itself. Although its tour guidebooks, since the 1950s, had celebrated Bridges as the 'father of the AIF' who was 'mortally wounded' at Anzac Cove, the fact that he had been repatriated was not mentioned.[11] This reflected a deeper institutional ambiguity: the war memorial's first director, John Treloar, had publicly argued against the exhumation of an unknown Australian soldier from a European battlefield, ostensibly on the basis of imperial sentiment. However, as Inglis pointed out, Treloar's argument was in fact an act of self-preservation on behalf of the war memorial. In a private note to Charles Bean, Treloar explained: 'The big danger in my opinion is that if the proposal to bury an unknown warrior at Canberra be considered … it may become the basis of the Commonwealth memorial.'[12] Politicians would make the unknown soldier a substitute for the memorial, something Treloar felt would be disastrous to its future.[13] Treloar's argument was a truism: there was nothing inevitable about the repatriation, let alone that any remains would be laid to rest at the Australian War Memorial. This uncertainty partly reflected the paradoxical place the war memorial held in the federal capital: at once prominent and yet in constant need of reiteration.[14]

Bean had originally envisioned the war memorial as a combined monument, museum, library and art gallery, 'far grander and more sacred' than any European memorial.[15] After the inevitable public debate about expense, the foundation stone was laid in 1925 and the memorial was eventually completed in 1941. Sited on the slopes of Mount Ainslie opposite the old Parliament buildings, it would come to have a more symbolic connection to Canberra as the seat of federal power than any other cultural institution. It was 1975 before the idea of a national museum for the Indigenous and settler history of Australia was formally mooted.[16]

During the 1980s, with political and financial support from the federal government, war memorial director Brendan Kelson and deputy director Michael McKernan transformed the institution.[17] Legislated as a corporation in 1980, the memorial was restructured as an expression of Australia's newly confident creative cultural sector.[18] It became a statutory authority within the Department of Veterans' Affairs, with the director responsible to the minister. A governing council presided over the war memorial's three arms: the national collection, public programmes and corporate services. Funding expanded, and there was a modest increase in staff.

Like the state cultural project of the Gallipoli 75 Task Force, the war memorial's reinvention was part of an agenda to promote a new, confident national identity. Thanks to the precedent set in 1990, this identity would increasingly focus on military heritage in an international network of commemorative practices. The Hawke government's decision to transfer responsibility from the Minister for Arts, Heritage and Environment to the Minister for Veterans' Affairs was one step in this process. It was also globally unprecedented. Never before had a nation's institutional tribute to its war dead been incorporated into a government department the equivalent of Veterans' Affairs. The International Council of Museums considered it an infringement of the independence of the war memorial as a library and research facility, and contested the decision. The chair of the Australian Council of Museums, N.J. Flanagan, conceded that 'there might be a case that the maintenance of such a symbol could be with the Prime Minister's Department, the Department of Defence, or the Department of Veterans' Affairs', but only if 'the memorial to the nation's fallen was simply a cenotaph, a shrine or a tomb of an unknown soldier, as is the case in all other countries'.[19] If this were to happen under the war memorial's current structure, Flanagan argued, it would become 'the outsider' among Australia's cultural institutions, as matters of common concern such as future developments would then be decided in Parliament House rather that internally. Although retaining its independent statutory authority, the war memorial staff's day-to-day work with Canberra's wider cultural sector took place within a totally different ideological framework.

Flanagan's concerns were prescient. The interment of the unknown Soldier in 1993 completed the reinvention of the war memorial. Far from becoming an institutional 'outsider', however, as the shrine of the national dead the Australian War Memorial would be celebrated as the spiritual heart of the nation itself. Any loss of autonomy was smoothed over by the prospect of increased government funding and aided by the endorsement of the RSL, who hoped the war memorial's closer institutional relationship with the prime minister would have positive flow-on effects for veterans' interests.[20]

The new status of the war memorial gave impetus to an emerging network of historians in support of a national commemoration centred on Canberra. The establishment of an annual military history conference and launch of the *Journal of the Australian War Memorial* in the 1970s encouraged scholarly debates on military history in Australia and provided a career pathway for an emerging generation of historians.[21] When war memorial leadership sought proposals from staff in 1990 about how best to mark the 50th anniversary of its opening, a solid body of experts was able to lend authority to any redevelopment.

Among a number of suggested initiatives, war memorial chief historian Ashley Ekins proposed that the unveiling of a tomb of an unknown soldier be made central to the anniversary celebrations.[22] Ekins supported his proposal with several sources of scholarly authority. The first of these was Bill Gammage, author of *The Broken Years*, who had already expressed his interest.[23] The second was preeminent Anzac scholar Ken Inglis, whose work had imagined Charles Bean's establishment of the war memorial as a way of turning imperial loyalty into Australian patriotism.[24] Ekins also referred to McKernan's institutional history of the war memorial, *Here Is Their Spirit*, the title of which drew on Bean's famous line: 'Here is their spirit in the heart of the land they loved; and here we guard the record they themselves made.'[25] According to Ekins, while the second clause of Bean's statement was true, the first was not: 'Many feel that the Australian War Memorial is devoid of the spirit of the 102,000 Australians who have died in wars … The tomb of an unknown soldier would provide a solemn and inspirational focal point for visitors to the Hall of Memory while also giving physical substance to that "spirit".' It was a bold claim: the spirit of the national dead would be centred not on their families, churches or local communities but on Canberra, the federal capital and the Australian War Memorial.

Ekins felt the memorial lacked a symbolic point of significance, 'a place which tangibly eflects the spirit of sacrifice commemorated in its museum galleries and on the Roll of Honour'.[26] The inclusion of a tomb for an unknown soldier would form part of the war memorial's broader strategy of self-preservation laid down by Treloar as its first director; after all, the institution needed to evolve 'in order to remain relevant to successive generations in a multicultural society'.[27] The scheme would enrich the significance of the Hall of Memory and promote the memorial as a whole. Visitors would be encouraged to venerate the dead and imagine their deaths as a national sacrifice.

Support for Ekins' proposal for repatriation of an unknown soldier was the fruit of collaboration among historians keen to situate the war memorial at the heart of the Australian nation. Inglis would complete the circle in 1999 with his account of the repatriation, in which he applauded Ekins as a kind of prophet of the national mood.[28]

The idea that the Hall of Memory was a neutral 'empty space', as Gammage called it in 1990, mirrored the idea that the landscape of Gallipoli was a *tabula rasa* on which to project a new vision of the nation on Anzac Day.[29] It was not entirely true, however: since 1951 the statue of a male soldier, an assertion of the powerful citizen-soldier of both world wars, had stood as the centrepiece in the Hall of Memory. Sculpted by Raymond Ewers, the statue had long baffled historians invested in a national memory of war, including Inglis: it was 'not an embodiment of the nation at large,' he wrote, 'not a symbol of mourning or sacrifice, but a representation of the serviceman himself'.[30] Ewers' statue was a hierarchical and imperial obstacle to the concept, emerging in the 1990s, of Anzac Day as an inclusive event, and to the repatriation of an unknown soldier as a democratic state project designed to assert a new image of Australian citizenship. In 1994, reflecting on the first Anzac Day after the repatriation, Inglis celebrated the way the custodians of the war memorial made a 'profoundly significant gesture when they removed from the Hall of Memory the huge overbearing statue of a serviceman'.[31]

Inglis was hardly an outside observer to this process. By early 1993 he was chief historical adviser to the repatriation Directing Group, which consisted of the Australian War Memorial directors and representatives of federal government (including the Australian War Graves office) and the defence forces. It was chaired by war memorial staffer Richard Reid.[32] These different vested interests reflected the

Ray Ewers' statue of an Australian infantryman, originally in the apse of the Hall of Memory and now situated in the gardens of the Australian War Museum, Canberra. The defiant, masculine posture – monumentalising the social authority of the RSL citizen-soldier – obstructed efforts by war memorial leadership to transform the Anzacs into national victims, embodied in the Unknown Australian Soldier. Photo: Russell Byers. Monument Australia

'why' of the repatriation: the changes in the nature of the Australian War Memorial itself; the generational work of national historians; and the shift towards a cultural memory of war centred on the post-imperial state, expressed in the antagonism towards Ewers' statue and all it stood for. The networks present in the Directing Group would shape the commemoration in particular ways.

The reinvention of the war memorial was not without its own internal critics, and the first challenge faced by the Directing Group was to ensure the repatriation was promoted as a national commemoration rather than a military funeral. Kelson invited Inglis to introduce the proposed repatriation to war memorial staff through a lecture on the history of similar tombs, with an emphasis on national symbolism.[33] Kelson prefaced the lecture with a brief statement justifying the tomb: it would enhance the memorial and ensure 'the ongoing relevance of the commemoration of war into the twenty-first century'.[34] Kelson's speech, as Reid wrote in a briefing to the director, recognised that some staff 'have difficulties in understanding why we have decided to embark on this project'.[35] Inglis' lecture would allay the fears of staff whose views of the war memorial were defined by understandings of war memory that centred on civic networks such as the RSL or the armed forces, rather than the nation.

Inglis' contribution to the Directing Group was also key to giving the project a focused public narrative and shaping the repatriation. Rather than a small military funeral limited to civic leaders, the repatriation would consist of a series of grand national ceremonies.[36] The role of the Australian Defence Force would be downplayed to ensure 'the public mood feels more like that sense of national community spirit'.[37] Considerable emphasis was placed on directing the public's response: the tomb inscription should be simple, and a moment of silence would be annotated in the official programme to provide people with 'information about how to use the silence'. A narrator was 'essential'.[38] Inglis advocated that Bean's writing, so popular and well known, be incorporated as much as possible. The event was to be a seamless experience so that 'all sense of stage management should be lost in the minds of participants and beholders'.[39] In a 'spectacle of such dignity and apparent simplicity', the significance of the repatriation would be clear.[40] The act of entombing the unknown soldier must stand alone in the 75th commemoration of the armistice.

Following a request by the Directing Group, a pilgrimage for a large group of veterans planned for Armistice Day 1993 and organised through the Department of Veterans' Affairs was rescheduled to take place a month earlier. The media picked up on this apparently fussy government intervention, and commentators argued that the decision was surely up to the veterans, not the Minister of Veterans' Affairs. In an interview with radio host Alan Jones, Minister Humphreys defended the decision and claimed it was made to protect the health of the elderly men who would otherwise have to face the cold European November.[41] When pressed by Jones as to whether anything would be arranged at home for veterans on 11 November, Humphrey revealed the proposal for the repatriation of an unknown soldier. It was the government's first public confirmation of the project.

The Directing Group was concerned about how the public would receive the plan, since the war memorial's role was far from assured. McKernan himself had suggested caution in presenting the idea to the public.[42] In asserting authority over the project, the war memorial might find itself having to fend off competing narratives to the claim for a national tomb, which would delay the project and reduce its emotional and political impact. Any negative publicity could undercut the plan to showcase the institution to the national public.

Following Humphreys' radio interview, returned services groups wrote to Kelson reminding him that RSL members had raised the idea of a tomb in the

1960s and 1970s, the implication being that the RSL wanted to be included in the decision-making process.[43] Kelson replied that, unlike the earlier RSL proposals, the proposed tomb was a distinctly 'national project'.[44] In a show of institutional strength, he added that while he was aware of earlier arguments by the RSL against repatriation of an unknown soldier, 'times and circumstances have changed': 'Arguments that were once advanced against a tomb … have been completely overtaken or have lost any strength they might [once] have had.'[45] His comment – implicitly referencing the dwindling imperial sentiment that had underpinned earlier opposition – shut down the likelihood of a challenge by RSL authority: the plan was not simply an entrepreneurial initiative.

RSL involvement in the project was constrained. There was no formal veteran representation on the Directing Group, and the war memorial council approached a number of veterans to seek their support, thus further curtailing the RSL's influence. This was on the recommendation of Inglis, who argued to limit RSL input. He similarly advised that the committee seek the support of sculptor Ray Ewers in order to reduce the likelihood that the removal of his statue should become a point of public criticism.

Like Hawke's pilgrimage to Gallipoli in 1990, the planned repatriation also required some delicate international diplomacy. The graves of AIF soldiers from World War I were under the custodianship of the Commonwealth War Graves Commission (CWGC), originally established in 1917 as the Imperial War Graves Commission to establish and maintain Allied war cemeteries. The commission had a history of rejecting repatriation requests – enquiries by the Canadian, South African and Fijian governments a decade earlier had been unsuccessful – and its cooperation was vital. This old imperial relationship irked the project managers; the Australian High Commissioner in London, R.J. Smith, wrote to Kelson complaining that it was 'inconceivable that the Australian government would be approaching the commission cap in hand to ask its approval to carry out this proposal'. In his view, it was 'the commission's job to work out a basis on which this could be done'.[46]

Initial conversations between the CWGC and the Directing Group were tentative. In an attempt to dissuade the Australian government from pursuing the project, the commission chair cited the fact that the Westminster Unknown Warrior had not been in the custodianship of the commission; the repatriation in 1918 was, rather, a unilateral decision by the British and dominion governments to remove a body not yet placed in a final cemetery.[47] It was entirely different to the exhumation and transportation proposed by the Australian state. The Australian government's riposte was to secure Canadian and South African support on the commission's representative committee: a successful Australian repatriation would set a precedent for those nations to pursue their own projects. Kelson himself had already embarked on an informal mission to Germany, France, Belgium, the United Kingdom and Israel to talk with authorities about the possibility of the return to Australia of the remains of an unknown soldier from a French battlefield.[48]

This manoeuvring inside and outside the CWGC was indicative of the political and diplomatic implications of the project. Any repatriation would be a national act that removed the unknown soldier not only from European soil but also from the historical lineage of empire itself. Negotiation of the project meant sifting through imperial relationships to create a national state claim against a backdrop of international relations in which the British Empire was, at best, a distant memory.

The emotional rationale for this domestic and international *realpolitik* on the part of the war memorial's Directing Group was expressed in the language of cultural trauma. When Michael McKernan appeared on the 2CN morning radio show in May 1993 to promote the repatriation, the announcer asked him whether the removal of Ray Ewers' statue was controversial. McKernan was emphatic: the war memorial had always intended to repatriate an unknown soldier to that site; Ewers' statue had simply been a placeholder.[49] Australians had 'lost the sense of their own history,' McKernan suggested; the war memorial would now become the nation's central cultural institution, the 'focus and heart of commemoration', and the Tomb of the Unknown Soldier would 'be a suitable and dramatic climax to the experience of the memorial's whole commemorative area'.[50] Repeating these comments at the interment six months later, McKernan claimed that the war memorial was now 'very much in touch with Australia's own history'. In previous decades the idea of repatriating an unknown soldier had threatened to disturb the trauma of the past; now the tomb offered a way to bury not only the ruptures of the war but also the connection with empire.

The repatriation was a gambit in a wider struggle to determine the foundations of national history in Australia, and came at a time of growing public debate about colonial violence in Australia's past, triggered in part by the 1988 bicentenary and Henry Reynolds' 1989 book, *Dispossession: Black Australians and white invaders*. Indigenous perspectives that might have questioned the construct of national unity were completely absent from the funeral of the unknown Australian soldier. The Australian Aboriginal Flag, officially recognised by the federal government in 1995, was not included in the collection of standards raised at the war memorial and throughout Canberra for the occasion. The public assumption, implicit in the ritual and language of the entombment, was that the unknown soldier was a descendant of a British Australian. McKernan could argue that the repatriation was a 'healing of the nation' only because Indigenous voices were still treated as irrelevant. In 1993, 'Australia's own history' continued to mean the story of settler Australia, a story in which Indigenous Australia appeared simply as prologue.

The national healing offered by the repatriation was part of a longer history of colonisation, one in which the Australian landscape was depicted as a blank slate on which to establish a national identity. Hawke's 'colonisation' of Anzac Cove in 1990 was mirrored in the Canberra landscape. There were constitutional implications too, which Kelson had successfully obscured. Suspicions that the tomb was a pro-republican statement swirled around the war memorial in the lead-up to 11 November.[51] Several prominent RSL members questioned the decision to exhume a body in the first place: surely, 75 years later, such a disturbance amounted to a kind of sacrilege.

The closest the Directing Group came to losing this sense of national unity was around the issue of naming the Unknown himself. At the outset, war memorial leadership and their supporters in government and the academy had settled on the word 'soldier'. In early discussions between interest groups and the public, however, various other names had been suggested. The navy objected to the use of 'soldier', saying the term represented the army and excluded war casualties at sea and in the air. Kelson could see no alternative: 'warrior' did not resonate, as Australia had never been a warrior nation; 'soldier', on the other hand, conveyed a sense of the national character – ordinary, simple and honest.[52] Various alternatives – 'Tomb of the Unknown Australian' and the wording 'An Australian son is resting, returned to the land of his birth' – were voted down, although some resistance continued.[53] The Tomb of the Unknown Australian Soldier it would be.

The debate reflected the deeper reality of a military funeral overtaken by national commemoration, a shift that began under the 1990 Hawke project. In denying the use of 'warrior', the war memorial was foreclosing the possibility of alternative histories of remembrance that invoked both imperial and local ways of understanding the war experience. This was underscored by the exclusion from the repatriation ceremony of those old custodians of Anzac Day, the returned services organisations and the church, though the RSL national executive 'expressed strongly' its desire that the pallbearers be the national presidents of the RSL and the Naval Association, VC winners and other men of military rank.[54] There were also complaints about the secular nature of the commemoration: although military chaplains would be involved, the ceremonies would take place between Old Parliament and the Hall of Memory rather than in any church or cathedral.[55]

The RSL made various overtures to empire in the lead-up to the repatriation. The national executive requested that the tomb slab be engraved with the Australian flag because this incorporated the British Union Jack.[56] ACT RSL president James Cullen argued that 'God Save the Queen' should be included in the ceremony as 'the only Anthem [the Unknown's] spirit will recognise';[57] and the RSL petitioned the prime minister to invite the Queen, which Keating politely declined to do.[58] Disputes over the language, symbolism and rites extended to the funeral procession: the RSL was included only as a 'national organisation' and requests from sub-branches to be included in the formal ceremony were denied.[59] The Directing Group also refused requests for members to be allowed to place objects of local significance in the tomb, saying items must have 'national significance'. In this containment of the RSL we can see the thematic claims of the Unknown project, situating social remembrance of war as cultural memory within the state, an arrangement made possible by the transformation of the war memorial as a key interlocutor of statehood.

The war memorial did not consult local heritage agencies regarding the removal of Ewers' statue or its replacement with a sarcophagus.[60] Once McKernan and Kelson had secured Ewers' support and promised to move the sculpture to a new location in the war memorial grounds, there were few objections.[61] The statue was eventually unveiled two years later for the 50th anniversary of the end of World War II. The fact that it had once been part of a trinity of statues that included an airman and a sailor, which still stood at the ends of the side galleries of the war memorial, was not mentioned. The RSL did propose that a new statue be commissioned of a soldier standing in a guard posture in the Hall of Memory to watch over the tomb of his fallen comrade, but it was too late: the exorcism was complete.[62] The citizen-soldier, that emblem of Anzac Day in 1965, had been banished from the Hall of Memory.

The Directing Group held a competition for the design of the tomb to hold the remains of the unknown soldier. The brief contained a number of stipulations: the tomb should neither glorify nor denigrate war, it should echo existing features of the Hall of Memory, and religious symbolism was to be avoided. One entry proposed to site the tomb in the floor between the Hall of Memory and the Hall of Valour below, to create a connection between valour and memory. The concept was rejected: it was precisely this connection between the valour of soldiers and the national memory of the war that the repatriation was intended to sever.

The group chose a proposal by architecture firm Tonkin Zulaikha Harford. Where the Ewers statue once stood would be four pillars, of wood, steel, marble and glass, to represent the elements earth, air, fire and water. These would align with the 'four freedoms': of speech and religious practice, and from want and fear. The sculpture was envisioned as 'a row of totems' invoking the heat of the sun, the souls of the dead, change and transfiguration, and the life-force of God.

The 'four freedoms' symbolism introduced an American inflection to the language of commemoration in the newly entrepreneurial war memorial. Part of the classic idiom of liberal democratic citizenship, the four freedoms were articulated in Roosevelt's 1941 justification for ending American isolationism in the lead-up to the nation's entry into the Pacific war.[63] The translocation of this language to the Australian War Memorial was evidence of the economic and military alignment of the Hawke–Keating government and the United States, and the reconceptualisation of Australian military experience. Narratives of war were now to be associated with freedom and liberal democracy. This also resonated with the use of 'soldier', a nomenclature shared with the United States' own national tombs.

Tonkin's design for the tomb itself was simple: it would be a marble slab set at floor height with a sloping border to mark 'a physical division between the living and the resting place of sacred sacrifice'.[64] The gold-leaf inscription read, 'An unknown Australian soldier killed in the war of 1914–1918'.[65] The overall effect was such that a visitor, standing at the door to the Hall of Memory, would first see the tomb before their eyes were led to the pillars and then to the dome above.

The tomb's installation marked a triumph of war memorial leadership, and the government's support, so lacking in previous attempts to install a national tomb, was fundamental to the 1993 project. The imprimatur of the Prime Minister's Office enabled Kelson, McKernan and others to negotiate with the likes of the Commonwealth War Graves Commission, the navy and the RSL. Keating was kept closely informed of developments, and invited the state premiers to be official mourners at the funeral and to call for two minutes' silence at 11am on Armistice Day as a way of uniting the nation. As historian Jacqui Rees observed at the time, the entombment was 'an event of great national significance' that turned the eyes of the nation to Canberra.[66]

The government's price for this collaboration was the central role that the prime minister would play in the repatriation ceremonies. Keating's place was unambiguous.[67] He was the chief pallbearer and eulogiser, and was centre stage throughout the ceremony as the voice of the nation and narrator of its new foundation myth. Keating's now-famous eulogy at the funeral of the unknown soldier spoke of the heroes of the war – 'not the generals or politicians' but 'the soldiers and sailors and nurses' whose service taught ordinary Australians the importance of endurance, courage, boldness and resilience, and 'to believe in ourselves, to stick together'. The Anzacs 'proved that real nobility and grandeur belongs not to empires and nations but to the people on whom they, in the last resort, always depend'. Keating transformed the Anzac legend into a summary of political citizenship and 'what it means to be Australian'.[68] His language drew powerfully on the idea that identity could be forged through war and grief.

The few remaining citizen-soldiers who might have contested this reinterpretation of war commemoration were rendered once again as heroic victims, their position overshadowed by the prime minister. Called upon by media to articulate, 'one last time', the place of the Anzacs in the national story, one veteran dutifully responded, 'We have had our time. We are finished. But it is important that the kids know that they are living in the best place there is in the world.'[69]

The sense that 1993 marked a watershed in state authority over Anzac commemoration was increasingly apparent, and the repatriation provided a firm foundation for this. Two years later Keating launched the campaign *Australia Remembers 1945–1995*, a programme of activities to commemorate the end of World War II. As historian Liz Reed notes, *Australia Remembers* was the most comprehensive state management of national mythology in Australian history; through a range of educational materials and state ceremonies it evoked the memory of the past as crucial to imagining the nation.[70] University of Sydney historian Richard White's cynical summary of the campaign could have applied to the repatriation of the unknown soldier: it 'exploited nostalgia, turned memory into spectacle, marginalised women and indigenous Australians in the very act of recognising them, and brilliantly appropriated the memories of "ordinary people".'

The repatriation of the unknown soldier became a kind of marker of the progress of Australia's military heritage. Every Remembrance Day Keating's eulogy is read aloud, each time reiterating the significance of the event and, in turn, the central role of the Australian War Memorial in the life of the nation. On the 10th anniversary of the interment, Kelson stated that the unknown soldier was 'part of Australia becoming a nation in its own right'. The tomb 'changed the character of the memorial', Kelson reflected, and provided a focus for the Hall of Memory:

World War I veteran Robert Comb sprinkles soil from the Pozières windmill site in the Somme, France, over the coffin of Australia's unknown soldier, 11 November 1993. Audiences related to the image of the frail Comb being supported by a younger officer.
Photo: Kerry Alchin. Australian War Memorial, Canberra

> He's somewhere on that Roll of Honour in the cloisters. He ties it all together – the events, the exhibitions, the whole story of remembrance of that war – and of course he stands for Australians who have fallen in subsequent wars and will fall in future wars.[71]

The entombment of the unknown soldier was presented as the embodiment of Australia, offering healing to the nation mourning its fallen dead and giving coherence to the very structure of the war memorial itself. It was the ultimate conflation of those who had died in war with the 'story of remembrance'. Anzac had truly become the founding mythology of the Australian state.

Subsequent controversies have only emphasised this practice of state mythology around the unknown soldier. In 2013, 20 years after the repatriation, Liberal Prime Minister Tony Abbott intervened to prevent war memorial staff from covering up the tomb's inscription 'Known unto God' – ostensibly because of its Christian language.[72] In the same year, Paul Keating was invited to speak at the Remembrance Day service. The former prime minister recapitulated some themes from his 1993 speech and sought to broaden its emphasis on war as a foundational experience of Australian nationhood. Keating celebrated a progressive national history that valued, among other things, equality, fairness and a sense of inclusive patriotism. These values, he said, had been given substance through the experience of Australian soldiers at Flanders and Gallipoli, and were now divested of any entanglements of empire and race: 'For whatever claims Britain and its empire had on those who served and died on the Western Front and at Gallipoli, the primary claim remained Australia's.'[73]

Abbott's and Keating's interventions in 2013 pointed to the new, if sometimes uneasy, mix of state commemoration. The war memorial now stood at the centre of a reconfigured story of the Australian nation and its values in the twenty-first century. Anzac, as expressed in the unknown soldier, was the natural arena in which citizens and government were bound together in a shared sentiment that provided legitimacy and direction to the contemporary state.

'The great pain we feel / Is for you who were our future': The unknown New Zealand warrior, 2004

New Zealanders had also long debated the merits of creating a national shrine to the war dead. Within a year of the signing of the 1918 armistice, Waitomo MP William Jennings raised the idea of a national tomb and asked Cabinet to consider bringing home the remains of 'one of our boys'.[74] Cabinet declined the suggestion, perhaps believing – as Gareth Phipps suggests – that the Westminster Abbey tomb served the purpose of a national memorial.[75] As one commentator observed, 'The British Unknown Warrior is a soldier of British Citizenship – he could have been from any part of the empire.'[76] Furthermore, the repatriation and construction of a tomb would have incurred a large expense at a time when the country was still recovering from the war effort. The idea surfaced again when the Auckland Cenotaph was developed in the 1920s, but was again dismissed.

The RSA reintroduced the notion of a tomb following the end of World War II. Christchurch president D.W. Russell called for two unknown warriors, one for each of the world wars, to be brought home and buried in a proposed Hall of Memories at the National War Memorial in Wellington's Pukeahu/Mount Cook. The proposal was part of a wider campaign to secure government support for the completion of the memorial, which until then had been piecemeal. However, the estimated cost of the RSA's proposal, around £250,000, was deemed prohibitive.[77] Despite support from newspaper editors and military leaders, the lack of state enthusiasm caused the project to flounder.[78] Public interest was muted at best, and communities opted to build local memorials.[79]

The original design of the National War Memorial had been for an institution as grand and prominent in the life of the capital as the Australian War Memorial was in Canberra. Architects Gummer & Ford envisaged it at the terminus of a boulevard akin to Anzac Parade in Canberra, which would run through the centre of Wellington city to the steps of Parliament and create a visual connection between the nation's memorial to its valiant citizen-soldiers and parliamentary democracy. The boulevard never eventuated; not only did the project lack the authority of a federal government, it also failed to take into account Wellington's topography, which did not allow for neat boulevards. By the late twentieth century the area around Wellington's war memorial had become an industrial zone; a motorway would eventually cut across the precinct, further separating it from the city's civic centre. There could hardly be a greater contrast with the Australian War Memorial, which is linked to the formation of Canberra itself as a space of federal authority.

There was also an important distinction to be made between the memorial as monument and shrine, and as museum and research centre. Thanks to the vision of Charles Bean, the Australian War Memorial had secured these roles under one roof. But Wellington claimed a network of cultural sites and institutions. Behind the National War Memorial Carillon and Hall of Memories stood the Dominion Museum, completed in 1933, which shared a building with the National Art Gallery. During the 1980s, as the Australian War Memorial was becoming an institution in the Department of Veterans' Affairs, a different sort of convergence was taking place in Wellington. In 1987 an Act of Parliament incorporated the Dominion Museum and National Art Gallery into what would eventually be established in 1992 as the Museum of New Zealand Te Papa Tongarewa.

Te Papa was tasked with representing a national identity that centred on biculturalism and the Treaty partnership between Māori and Pākehā. When the museum opened in 1998, Gallipoli was nowhere to be seen in the exhibition galleries. The flagship exhibition, *Te Tiriti o Waitangi: Ngā tohu kotahitanga – The Treaty of Waitangi: Signs of a nation* focused on Waitangi as the birthplace of the nation.

The exhibition operated, both conceptually and architecturally, according to Conal McCarthy, 'as the hinge of the nation, cleaving the space into tangata whenua and tangata tiriti [Māori and non-Māori] sections, uniting (or dividing) us, depending on your perspective'.[80]

The tangled web of New Zealand's national cultural institutions reflected the political priorities of 1990 and had implications for the growing interest in commemoration over the 90s and early 2000s. In the year of the Australian unknown soldier's repatriation New Zealand marked the centenary of women's suffrage, which arguably meant more to the majority of the population – not least the nation's women and girls – than the return of an unknown soldier, and a range of projects highlighted women's contributions to the founding of the nation.[81] In 1999, the centenary of the Boer War provided an opportunity for an experimental if modest war commemoration, this time coordinated by historian Jock Phillips.[82] The patchwork of commemorative projects reflected the broad focus on public history promoted through the Ministry of Culture and Heritage following the 150th anniversary of Waitangi in 1990.

As was the case in the Hawke–Keating commemorative projects, the personal style of Helen Clark, Prime Minister of New Zealand 1999–2008, contributed significantly to the particular shades of the repatriation. Historian Graham Hucker argues that Clark's interest in promoting war commemoration was underpinned by her family's involvement in the Great War.[83] But as well, it provided an avenue for Clark, who was also the Minister of Culture and Heritage, to invest in the cultural sector. 'Our creative people,' she declared in 2000, 'help to define us as a nation, and through them we express our unique national identity.'[84]

War commemoration would be a key part of her agenda of cultural recovery.[85] Clark oversaw the renovation and establishment of an unprecedented number of international war memorials, as well as national reconciliation projects such as the pardoning of soldiers executed during the Great War and the 2008 Crown apology to Vietnam War veterans and their families for their treatment by the government and public after the war. Clark's agenda was a project of nation-building that brought together historians, the creative industry, artists and museum curators in 'building the spirit of New Zealand and … understanding the forces that shape New Zealanders'.[86] Old stories of a joint sacrifice in wartime, in a joint citizenship, were renovated for a new century; and Clark, one of the generation who in the past had protested on Anzac Day, now acted to correct the divisions of protest and patriotism.

Military historians in particular gained a lot from this new state commitment to cultural narratives of war and advocated for state commemorative projects – above all, for a tomb for an unknown soldier. In 1999 historian Ian McGibbon recommended the Department of Internal Affairs investigate the possibility of repatriating the remains of a New Zealand unknown soldier as a millennium project, arguing that it would be 'a visible and dramatic way of honouring and remembering the nation's war dead'.[87] McGibbon was supported by RSA national president Pat Herbert who, in a letter in the RSA *Review*, called for public discussion about the possibility of a repatriation. The fact that Canada had followed Australia's lead to repatriate an unknown soldier in 2000 added weight to his argument. Where such a project might once have been considered a statement against empire, a national tomb would now 'bring New Zealand into line with its senior Commonwealth partners'. McGibbon raised the idea again in 2001 at the launch of his guide to New Zealand battlefields on the Western Front, this time with Prime Minister Helen Clark in the audience.[88]

McGibbon was one of a growing cadre of military historians in New Zealand. The New Zealand Military History Committee was formed in the mid-1990s to facilitate public engagement with the nation's military heritage, and as a lobby group for military historians' influence in government policy around the repatriation. In 2003 the committee consisted of McGibbon, New Zealand Defence Force historian John Crawford, independent historian Peter Cooke and RSA historian Stephen Clarke. The committee organised four-yearly conferences: the one in 2003 was supported by the New Zealand Defence Force, the Ministry of Defence, the Ministry of Culture and Heritage and other agencies.[89] Even before the decision to go ahead with the repatriation was made, the idea of an official history of the event was proposed, to be coordinated by Chris Pugsley. The RSA provided sponsorship for Pugsley on the basis that he would undertake work on behalf of the RSA, and used this to bolster its flagging public profile. Politicians and historians were quietly confident that the project would be successful and, given the international precedents, few obstacles were anticipated.

In her official announcement of the project on Anzac Day 2002, Clark said the tomb would be 'a tangible monument for those who lost family members overseas' and would 'remind current generations of the sacrifice of New Zealanders in overseas conflicts and peacekeeping operations'.[90] Media reactions were uniformly celebratory. The *Evening Post* declared the project well overdue: 'Canada and Australia, who have moved more rapidly away from the shackles of Britain than New

Zealand, have in the past seven years repatriated unknown First World War soldiers to tombs in their homelands.'[91] Public responses were also positive: in what remains the largest civic service in New Zealand's history, some 100,000 people would eventually line the streets of Wellington to watch the funeral procession of the unknown warrior.

A coordinating committee, responsible for advising the prime minister on the development of the war memorial and ceremonies around the repatriation, met for the first time in September 2002. It comprised representatives from an array of state agencies, including the Ministry of Culture and Heritage, the Defence Force and Te Puni Kōkiri, principal advisor on government–Māori relations and policy affecting Māori wellbeing. The committee agreed to a deadline of Armistice Day 2003 and discussed the sensitivity of the exhumation.[92] Te Puni Kōkiri representative Eru Manuera, who was also a member of the RSA and the 28th Māori Battalion National Association, stressed the need for Māori input at all stages of the project. By the time Cabinet met the following month, a media strategy, a request for publicity funding and an initial brief for designers were being circulated.

The committee's first goal was to secure support for the repatriation from public stakeholders. Project coordinator Brodie Stubbs of the Ministry of Culture and Heritage addressed a meeting of the RSA executive with an outline of dates, events and details of the proposed redevelopment of the National War Memorial to accommodate the tomb. The executive endorsed the project and was happy to be part of the state project. RSA membership was at an all-time low: as a result of changes to drink-driving regulations and the cost of running venues, clubs were experiencing declining patronage and becoming financially unviable. The repatriation offered an opportunity to raise the RSA's profile among New Zealanders.

The project also received strong support from Māori leaders, with some stipulations: iwi representatives asked that the warrior be disinterred from an area where the Native Contingent and Pioneer Battalion was known to have served, and that Māori leaders be kept informed of progress.[93] The commitment to biculturalism that had emerged since 1990 and the constitutional position of hapū and iwi as Treaty partners with the Crown would be apparent throughout the process. The minister of Māori affairs would be part of the ministerial delegation at all ceremonies connected with the Tomb of the Unknown Warrior. Journalist and Vietnam War veteran Miki Apiti expressed interest in covering the project for Māori audiences, and further publicity was provided through the Te Puni Kōkiri magazine, *Kōkiri Paetae*. Kaumātua John Tahuparae coordinated the turning of the first sod and the hiki tapu (blessing) at the National War Memorial, and tangata whenua were present throughout the exhumation and transportation to New Zealand, throughout which tikanga Māori (cultural and philosophical protocols) were adhered to. The presence of kaumātua and kuia at the disinterment was unusual given the Commonwealth War Graves Commission's strict policies regarding the presence of 'non-essential' people at an exhumation.[94]

The repatriation committee's progress was initially swift. Stubbs followed diplomatic precedents set in the repatriation of the unknown Australian and Canadian soldiers, and was in regular contact with the Australian War Memorial.[95] The New Zealand government's application to the Commonwealth War Graves Commission was a word-for-word copy of the Canadian application, and much of the exhumation ceremony was borrowed from the Canadians as well.[96] The Australian and Canadian events were also reflected in the language of nationhood and cultural trauma that imbued the ministerial briefings to Helen Clark.[97]

The project received significant support from the Ministry of Foreign Affairs, and attention was drawn to the prime minister's visits to London and Paris in 2003 as these provided excellent opportunities to leverage political and public support, both at home and abroad. Clark intended to make the official announcement of the repatriation at the Anzac Day service at Westminster Abbey, home to the Tomb of the British Unknown Warrior. A plan to include New Zealand's last surviving World War I veteran, Bright Williams, in the Westminster service and other publicity events such as the installation itself, had to be abandoned as he passed away in February 2003. His death added to the poignancy of the project and its urgency as a national act of reconciliation.

The French government, eager to heal postcolonial wounds in the Pacific and rejuvenate New Zealand–French relations after the disastrous nuclear-free debate, was enthusiastic about the project and called the planned entombment 'strongly symbolic' and 'positive'.[98] When Clark visited in 2003 the French expressed the hope that she might oversee the exhumation of the body immediately, six months before the planned transportation. Clark rejected this as undignified and unacceptable to tikanga Māori. Furthermore, having Clark at the graveside risked being viewed as a publicity stunt to raise the prime minister's profile.[99]

This was evidence of the attention being paid to the public story of the repatriation. Publicity was coordinated from the Prime Minister's Office and the Ministry for Culture and Heritage, and as in the case of the unknown Australian soldier, the ministry team developed key media messages. Publicists promoted the repatriation at all stages, beginning with the handover ceremony in France; in collaboration with the Department of Veterans' Affairs and the New Zealand Defence Force, they oversaw the development of a tomb logo and catch-phrase, educational packs and an essay competition for school students. TVNZ producers were briefed to mention the project in Anzac Day coverage. Throughout, the tomb was presented as a site of national remembrance for those who had sacrificed their lives in the service of the country, a symbol of unity and national identity that would link all generations of New Zealanders, and a place for war veterans to pay tribute to their comrades. The unknown warrior was first and foremost a New Zealander coming home, and his remains represented and honoured all New Zealanders, regardless of ethnicity or religion, who were lost to their families through war.

It was important that the tomb should reflect this inclusivity through motifs and materials that were symbolic of national identity. The Ministry for Arts and Culture commissioned Studio Pacific Architecture to redevelop the National War Memorial to accommodate the tomb, and in December 2002 Clark called for expressions of interest for the tomb's design.[100] The winner would be announced on Anzac Day 2003.

The ministry received 55 expressions of interest and by April had approved the winning design by Robert Jahnke: a pyramid-shaped tomb that incorporated both Māori and classical patterns and emphasised the connection between the lines of the pyramid and the vertical lines of the War Memorial Carillon. Jahnke used stone, he said, 'as a medium to reference Aotearoa New Zealand and territories beyond our country. South Island pounamu acknowledges New Zealand as the homeland of the Unknown Warrior, while imported black granite acknowledges the land from which the Warrior will be returned.'[101] This crafted narrative – edited by the Ministry of Culture and Heritage leadership team – made political and moral claims on the Unknown's body and located his 'home' in New Zealand.[102] The emphasis on the Carillon appealed to the international context of commemoration: the War Memorial Carillon was a sister instrument to the Peace Tower Carillon at Parliament Buildings in Ottawa, Canada.[103] In this way the New Zealand project resembled the Australian programme, shaped by its institutional and performative elements.

Jahnke's design involved a significant remodelling of the National War Memorial's forecourt and steps. The formal entrance – a staircase, pool and walls – would need to be demolished and dozens of 70-year-old pōhutukawa trees removed. Described as a 'living memorial', these pōhutukawa were originally planted to frame the overall site and were part of a historical pattern of planting in the wider

Wellington metropolitan area. For this reason alone, the design attracted immediate criticism from civic groups. As well, the Professional Historians' Association of New Zealand/Aotearoa (PHANZA) noted that removal of the memorial's formal entrance constituted a major alteration to a historic building and would require public consultation.[104] Despite the Wellington City Council's response – that the steps and forecourt fell outside the boundaries of the main edifice and were therefore not part of the heritage site – further public protest followed. Anzac Day returned to its familiar site of protest as posters campaigning against the renovations appeared on the steps of the war memorial in time for the televised services on Anzac Day 2003. The ministry ignored the protest, and in response the newly formed Serious About Heritage Society (SAHS) organised a public campaign and lodged an appeal in the High Court against the council's decision, arguing that the steps and forecourt should be included in the heritage listing.

By this stage, dozens of projects in the state programme around the repatriation – a New Zealand Post commemorative envelope, a poetry competition, a resource kit for schools, an exhibition at the Waiōuru Army Museum and more – were under development. As well, the committee had commissioned poems from prominent writers to be inscribed on the tomb's canopy.[105] Confident that it would secure court approval, the government told contractors to begin preparations for the development, and in May safety barriers and site offices appeared around the war memorial.[106] The PHANZA/SAHS legal action succeeded, however. Resource consent for the alterations was overturned and the ministry scrambled to submit a new application. Work was delayed, and the committee was forced to postpone the repatriation ceremony to Armistice Day 2004. A consultation process began with PHANZA, the New Zealand Institute of Architects and SAHS to seek a replacement design that would not interfere with the existing site.

The acrimonious debate severely undercut the state programme and led to disputes about which state agency would cover the costs of court action. Meanwhile, a quantity surveyor's report revealed a $400,000 shortfall in the project budget. The New Zealand Defence Force, which up to this point had been entirely supportive of the project, now requested that additional costs be covered by the Ministry of Culture and Heritage. As a result, funding earmarked for various supporting projects was redirected to the redesign and the public outreach programme was trimmed.

It seemed the state was struggling to establish and maintain public authority over the repatriation project. No one in Australia had contested the reconfiguration of the Australian War Memorial's Hall of Memory or the removal of its imposing statue. PHANZA's court action suggested that the prioritisation of military experience in national heritage was at least up for debate. Institutional differences between the Australian and New Zealand national war memorials were also apparent in the names. Australia had a Hall of Memory; the New Zealand equivalent was the Hall of Memories, the plural suggesting there might be multiple ways of remembering, a factor that perhaps also affected the government's ability to assert control over the site.

The early design had not explicitly included mana whenua (Māori territorial rights), and the government now leaned increasingly on Te Ātiawa iwi. As original kaitiaki (custodians) of the site in Wellington, they had the greatest interest in preserving its historical significance. The ceremony to break the first sod for the alterations was marked by recognition of Māori claims to the place, and karakia and a Te Mauri blessing were included alongside prayers in English. Stones collected from three rivers in Taranaki were placed at the tomb site as part of the blessing to symbolise Te Ātiawa links to Taranaki and Wellington and confirm the mana of the site. After the blessing the stones were placed in storage until the interment, at which point they were buried with the unknown warrior. Iwi were also consulted in the development of the tomb's inscription.

A colonial prison had formerly been on the site. Following the Crown sacking of Parihaka, a community established by Taranaki prophets Te Whiti-o-Rongomai and Tohu Kākahi, 195 Taranaki Māori were imprisoned there in 1879 before being sentenced to hard labour. As part of a campaign of public reconciliation in early 2000, a stone monument was raised next to the war memorial to commemorate the Parihaka prisoners.[107] The memorial, something of a 'footnote' to the other state monuments, connected the war memorial with Pākehā–Māori conflict in the nineteenth century, which both usurped Gallipoli as the place of national beginnings and undercut the story of national pride and unity at the repatriation.[108] Reflecting on the repatriation project in 2010, Te Ātiawa historian Rachel Buchanan observed, 'Memories of these complicated foundational wars, including war stories associated with the site on which the tomb has been built, nibble away at this elegant new memorial, diminishing its mana and power.'[109]

These histories and the dispute over the design resulted in uncertainty about the National War Memorial as an appropriate location for the tomb. Rather than encouraging unity, the site challenged the state's authority over the repatriation and divided the government's approach. Whatever site was chosen would carry moral and political significance and shape public reception. One suggestion was to build

The Parihaka Memorial at the National War Memorial Park, raised in early 2000 as part of Te Hīkoi ki Te Waipounamu. The stones of the base represent the Parihaka prisoners, from Taranaki, who were held in nearby Mount Cook Prison in the 1880s. The memorial's quiet statement of resistance and survival in the face of colonial violence forms a simple dialogue with the public monuments attached to the National War Memorial.
Photo: Kevin Hawkins

the tomb at one end of the Hall of Memories. The statue of a grieving family sited there would then be overlooking the Tomb of the Unknown Warrior; the symbolism of this might suit the narrative of family and cultural trauma being healed through repatriation. The concerns raised against this, however, were that a tomb would ruin the overall balance of the original design, and would shift the focus from commemoration of all those who served to only those who died. Others suggested the congested space might cause visitors to walk over the grave. Other sites such as Parliament House and the Auckland War Memorial Museum were considered but ultimately dismissed.

State agencies attempted to guide the discussion as best they could. In a letter to the prime minister, Stubbs pointed out that as 'the tomb must be a symbol of unity and national identity', it would be 'inappropriate and self-defeating if it became a symbol of controversy and divisiveness'.[110] The final design needed to reconcile not only the national past but the national present.

Unlike the United States, Australia and Canada, who had each repatriated an 'unknown soldier', New Zealand chose to commemorate an 'unknown warrior'. Some members of the RSA felt the name sounded aggressive and brought to mind historical images of Māori, but with no formal objection from the RSA the recommendation of the New Zealand Defence Force – arguing, as had its Australian counterpart, that the term 'warrior' better represented the three military services – prevailed.[111] The choice was important: the 1993 Australian precedent was powerful, but the New Zealand repatriation was intended as a distinct act of national independence.

Having missed the 2003 deadline the Clark government now approached Pacific Architecture, and a new design, by artist and sculptor Kingsley Baird, was eventually built into the forecourt steps of the war memorial.[112] The words 'An Unknown New Zealand Warrior – He Toa Matangaro no Aotearoa' were engraved in the slab. The base was inlaid with crosses of Tākaka marble representing the comrades of the unknown warrior, and the bronze slab with pieces of pounamu (greenstone) in the shape of the Southern Cross. Baird described it as 'an expression of the nation's memory and a cross-cultural language of remembrance [that] combines Māori and Pākehā ritual, symbolic and visual elements ... to express remembrance specific to New Zealand's contemporary identity'.[113] A karanga or ceremonial call was inscribed around the base of the tomb in English and te reo Māori: 'Te mamae nei a te pōuri nui / Tēnei ra e te tau' ('The great pain we feel / Is for you who were our future'). Cloaked in the language of loss it was as much a claim on the national past, present and future as Keating's 'He is all of them; and he is one of us.'

Baird's tomb, more sculptural than the Australian Tomb of the Unknown Soldier, was situated not in the Hall of Memories of the National War Memorial or as part of some grand redevelopment, but in an open area between the Carillon and the boulevard beyond. It was exposed to the elements, to children clambering on it and skateboarders using it as a launching pad. Australia's Tomb of the Unknown Soldier, in comparison, was placed in the Hall of Memory at the heart of the memorial. New Zealand's decision not to use the Hall of Memories balanced competing interests. Although the coordinating committee followed the Australian precedent closely in many ways, and despite having ostensible ownership of the Hall of Memories, the state was not able to achieve a unified narrative.

The group present at the New Zealand exhumation ceremony in northern France in November 2004 was more diverse than the Australian delegation 10 years earlier and included veterans and family members. Four representatives of Te Ātiawa attended to provide the karanga and karakia, and collected soil from the area.[114] The remains were placed in a casket in the care of a guard of honour led by Defence Chief Air Marshal Sir Bruce Ferguson and accompanied by a Māori cultural party, and transported to Aotearoa on a special Royal New Zealand Air Force flight. In Wellington, following a pōwhiri (welcoming ceremony), the casket was carried up Parliament's steps into the old Legislative Council Chamber where Governor-General Dame Silvia Cartwright, Prime Minister Helen Clark and other dignitaries laid wreaths. A number of civic leaders including the governor-general, the prime minister, representatives of the RSA and Māori rangatira delivered speeches. Veterans played a central role in the ceremony and ascribed both symbolic meaning and moral authority to the ritual.

In contrast to the Australian War Memorial, site of both the funeral and interment in 1993, Wellington's National War Memorial was the site of the burial only. The funeral took place in Wellington's Anglican cathedral. And whereas the Australian ritual abstracted the unknown soldier into a material symbol of the Australian state, laden with national meaning, in New Zealand the ceremony was open to local communities and included commissioned artistic works. Eight RSA districts were represented rather than just the single national body, and each placed an item of significance from their local area in the tomb.

This sense of a less tightly coiled commemorative project in the New Zealand repatriation was reiterated in the prime minister's address at the memorial service. Clark declared that New Zealanders had gathered 'to honour a warrior who has lain for close to ninety years in foreign soil, and who has now been called back to serve his country once more'.[115] Both the context of the speech and its position, as one address among several on Armistice Day, contrasted significantly with Keating's 1993 eulogy, which was ritually and symbolically about the prime minister as the moral voice of the nation. Clark's speech was considerably longer, at times lapsing into a kind of bureaucratic language; unlike Keating's oration, it has not been remembered. Where Keating reinforced the moral lesson of the Anzacs as 'Australia's story', past, present and future, Clark framed the unknown warrior and the war he died in as but one part of New Zealand's varied history, 'one of the foundations of today's society'.

The story of nationhood based on war experience was further diffused by Clark's focus on grief and healing. As well as speaking of the impact war has had on New Zealand families, she referred to the Commonwealth War Graves Commission, saying its 'worldwide task embodies the spirit of co-operation, peace, and healing'.

Clark framed the repatriation of the unknown warrior as an act of reconciliation – not just of national grief, as Keating had referred to in 1993, but also of personal and global fractures.

Clark, like Keating, was seen as a mediator of public grief and the public's desire for closure through family histories of the war. The media, historians, state sources and Clark herself constructed a narrative around the person of the prime minister as an embodiment of New Zealand commemoration, emphasising the tragedy of war and its impact on families.[116] In her dual roles of prime minister and minister for culture and heritage, Clark embarked on an intentional commemorative policy that underlined the Labour government's foreign policy imperatives. Clark and Keating were not radically different; however, the contested spaces of memory in their respective countries shaped their success.

*

In 2013, the 20th anniversary of the unknown Australian soldier's interment, Michael McKernan wrote, 'It's a very unusual thing to take a man who's been buried for at least 75 years and dig up his remains and bring him back to Australia.'[117] New Zealand's warrior, buried for at least 90 years, was even more unusual.

The 1993 and 2004 acts of repatriation were crucial moments in which earlier forms of remembrance, such as those of 1965, were increasingly re-orientated towards the state. They represented the fundamental claims of Australian and New Zealand statehood, presented as apolitical but in truth deeply enmeshed in the politics of culture after empire. Although the projects were achieved through the vital networks of various groups and institutions, without state support the repatriations of the unknown Anzacs would have languished as mere dreams. In both cases the therapeutic language of trauma abjured politics even as it obscured the irreducible political objective of repatriation: the reforging of national unity.

Differences, however, were evident in the spaces of the memorials, the tombs themselves, and the scripts presented by Keating and Clark. Over the 1980s the Australian War Memorial was revamped with considerable federal expenditure as the nation's chief cultural institution – museum, memorial, archive and research centre – all geared towards promoting an Australian memory of war. Moreover, this memory, located in the war memorial, discouraged critiques of a national remembrance.[118] The Australian myth of Gallipoli was consolidated during the 1990s through a close relationship between institutional networks of war memory and political advocates, and in the absence of any formal Indigenous–state relationships;

the Australian War Memorial housed the 'national spirit' – 'the spirit of the Anzacs' and was an apparent scene of unity.[119] In New Zealand the varied histories around the National War Memorial suggested a different idiom of memory. It was a scene of pluralism.

The tombs themselves were symbolic of this difference: the Tonkin Zulaikha Harford design displaced the statue of the citizen-soldier, exorcising the old Anzac traditions; Baird's tomb invoked a bicultural nation with multiple stories. The carefully drawn line from the Australian War Memorial to the body of the unknown soldier was captured by Keating's prime ministerial speech: magisterial, symbolic and Lincolnian in its language, it was ultimately inscribed on the tomb itself. Clark's voice, in contrast, was one of several at the New Zealand ceremony.

And where the Australian War Memorial sealed off national memory from colonial violence through a carefully constructed project, New Zealand's unknown warrior was more discursive and open to interpretation – an optimistic project undercut by public dissent and ruptured by alternative histories. The fragmented nature of the Unknown Warrior's funeral and entombment reflected the debate that took place around the planning of the tomb. Far from being the unitary site of the Australian War Memorial, the result of a collaboration between military historians, war memorial leadership and the federal government, New Zealand's National War Memorial was a space subjected to myriad claims about national heritage and open to re-inscription through public debate. Any sense of authority over the site was further diffused by the state's biculturalism. The unknown warrior was uniquely informed by both the repatriation and the cultural revival of tangata whenua, as seen in the design of the tomb itself.

The unknown Anzacs bookend a period in which New Zealanders and Australians pursued a converging national agenda of war commemoration, one that would be a key interface for understanding the relationship between the two nations, past, present and future. This meeting of sentiment and security defined a new era of Anzac commemoration.

NEW ZEALAND
WW100

New Zealand's centenary logo is a stylised Anzac poppy, a symbol originally linked to the battlefields of the Western Front but adopted for use with Anzac commemorations in the 1920s. Ministry of Culture and Heritage

100 YEARS OF ANZAC
THE SPIRIT LIVES
2014 - 2018

The Australian centenary logo suggests that the Anzac spirit – courage and mateship – is alive and well a century after the Gallipoli landing. Department of Veterans' Affairs

One of many Anzac murals that appeared during the Anzac Centenary in New Zealand. This one recreates the legend of John Simpson Kirkpatrick, who used donkeys to provide first aid and carry wounded soldiers at Gallipoli. Simpson and his donkey have been depicted and described in statues, books and other resources throughout Australia and New Zealand. Artist: Bruce McLachlan. Photo: Matthew Anderson

Anzac pilgrims disembark at Anzac Cove, 25 April 1965, having travelled from Greece on the MV *Karadeniz*. In the centre of the first group, with brown hair, is the young 'unofficial correspondent' Ken Inglis, who would go on to write the seminal account of the pilgrimage, ensuring its enduring importance in the history of Anzac commemoration.
Photo: World War I veteran Hugh Clifton Belliss. Wairarapa Museum

The Anzac commemorative medallion struck in 1967 by the Australian government in consultation with the New Zealand government. The medal depicts Simpson and his donkey framed by eucalyptus and fern leaves, with St Edward's Crown, the centrepiece of the United Kingdom's Crown Jewels, at the top. The belated creation of the medal and its mix of imperial and national symbolism reflect the fraying networks of commemoration at the time of the 50th anniversary of Gallipoli. Australian War Memorial, Canberra

The promotional poster for the international release of *Gallipoli* depicts the film's protagonist, Archy, being struck down by machine-gun fire at the Battle of the Nek. The image reinforced the myth of the inevitable sacrifice of Anzacs at Gallipoli. National Sound and Film Archive Australia

A poster for *Gallipoli: The New Zealand story* – the exhibition, the book and the documentary, 1985. The design is suggestive of the artwork used in the promotion of Weir's *Gallipoli* and the transformation of the Anzacs from real people into cultural archetypes. Auckland War Memorial Museum

The Tomb of the Unknown Soldier at the Australian War Memorial. The inscription reads 'An Unknown Australian Soldier killed in the war of 1914–1918'. The gap between the floor of the Hall of Memory and the tomb's slab suggests the space between the sacred and profane. Photo: Andrew Taylor. Australian Broadcasting Corporation

Opposite: Guards flank the Tomb of the Unknown Australian Soldier in the Hall of Memory at the Australian War Memorial, Canberra. The columns in the apse behind, representing the 'four freedoms', lead the visitor's eyes from the tomb to the domed ceiling above. Australian War Memorial, Canberra

An architect's vision of the National War Memorial, Dominion Museum and Art Gallery, Wellington, 1930. Note the generous avenue leading from the steps of the memorial into the heart of Wellington city. In fact, there was no city planning for this sort of avenue. Gummer & Ford (GF12), Special Collections. Architecture Archive, University of Auckland Libraries and Learning Services, Auckland

The National War Memorial precinct prior to its 2015 renovations. The pōhutukawa trees, which formed the heart of the PHANZA legal action against the initial MCH redevelopment in 2003, are evident. Photo: Andy Palmer. Ministry of Culture and Heritage

Opposite, top: The Tomb of the Unknown Warrior on the steps of Pukeahu National War Memorial Park, Wellington.
Photo: Kevin Hawkins

A wreath stands before the statue *Mother and Children* in the Hall of Memories at Pukeahu National War Memorial Park. Following legal action by the Professional Historians' Association of New Zealand/Aotearoa against the early design for the Tomb of the Unknown Warrior, Ministry of Culture and Heritage officials considered placing the tomb at the foot of the statue. Office of the Clerk, Parliament of New Zealand

The inscriptions on the Tomb of the Unknown New Zealand Warrior. The words of the lower engraving are cut to varying depths to suggest a person's breath. Photo: Kevin Hawkins

The Australian War Memorial in Hyde Park, London. The memorial was designed by Tonkin Zulaikha Greer in collaboration with artist Janet Laurence, and is intended to give the appearance of growing unevenly out of the earth. Photo: Tanya Arya

The Southern Stand, New Zealand War Memorial, Hyde Park Corner, London. The pillars of wrought iron, topped with slanting crosses, may be interpreted in a number of ways, including as soldiers standing at attention. Each is inscribed with national symbols such as the silver fern and koru. According to sculptor Paul Dibble, 'through the words and images, any New Zealander visiting the memorial will recognise home, and British people may learn something of the relationship between our two countries'. Photo: Tanya Arya

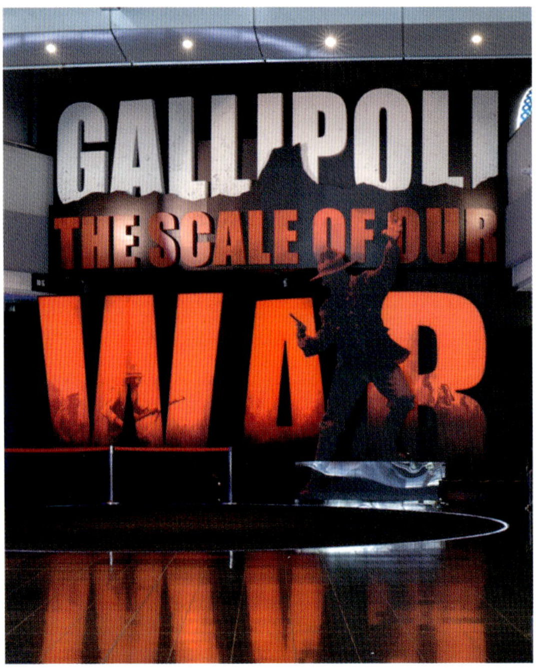

Above: One of the larger-than-life models in the exhibition *Gallipoli: The scale of our war*. Lieutenant Colonel Percival Fenwick was among the first to land on Gallipoli. Depicted here contemplating the body of a fallen comrade, Fenwick represents despair at the loss of life during the early stages of the battle.

Left: The entrance to the exhibition. Photos: Michael Hall. Museum of New Zealand Te Papa Tongarewa

TE TIRITI | THE TREATY
WAITANGI 175

The logo for the 175th commemoration of the signing of Te Tiriti o Waitangi/The Treaty of Waitangi, 2015, which basically reproduced the one used for the 150th commemoration in 1990. The white heron/kōtuku evokes the whakatauki or proverb: 'He kōtuku rerenga tahi' – 'A white heron's flight is seen but once'.
Te Puni Kōkiri

The Australian Memorial at the Pukeahu National War Memorial Park. The red stone pillars, sourced from India, are designed to evoke the ochre landscape of the Australian desert.
Photo: Kevin Hawkins

The Sir John Monash Centre, an extension of the Australian War Memorial at Villers-Bretonneux in France. Unveiled on Anzac Day 2018, the centre is Australia's largest offshore commemorative site and tells the story of the nation's Anzacs on the Western Front. The project cost over $100m. The centre was designed by Cox Architecture with Williams, Abrahams and Lampros. Photo: John Gollings

Coloured Diggers, a painting by Tony Albert. Recognition of the service of Black Diggers grew in the lead-up to the Anzac Centenary, thanks to the work of artists and media like NITV. The cartoon explores some of the motives these 'forgotten heroes' had for serving in the Australian armed forces, and indigenises one of the iconic moments in the history of twentieth-century warfare – the raising of the United States flag on Iwo Jima, Japan, in World War II. The soldiers are raising the Australian Aboriginal Flag. Acrylic on canvas, 2013. Australian War Memorial, Canberra

Chapter 6

'A destiny forever linked'

Trans-Tasman friendship and the triumph of Anzac, 2001–07

The turn of the twenty-first century was marked by a convergence of trans-Tasman remembrance. The disputed meaning around Anzac Day that had arisen over the 1960s and 1970s was now defined by a consensus: Anzac Day was truly 'when the nation salutes itself'.[1] The concept of 'mateship', expressing both something 'distinctly Australian', as Prime Minister John Howard asserted when he attempted to enshrine the word in the preface of the Australian Constitution in 1999, and the bond between the Anzac nations gained new importance in the political language of Anzac remembrance.[2]

All history prior to 1915 was 'before the Anzac dawn', according to historian Karl James.[3] When New Zealanders and Australians commemorated the centenary of the Boer War, it was to celebrate 'the fathers of the Anzacs'.[4] Others traced an 'Anzac genesis' to the nineteenth-century New Zealand Wars, when regiments of Australian settlers, dubbed 'blood brothers' by historian Jeff Hopkins-Weise, took arms against Māori.[5] This notion of 'blood-lines' as a kind of proto-Anzac experience where Australians and New Zealanders fought together translated easily to the joint Australian and New Zealand military actions in Asia and the Pacific.

A political symmetry – the 'Anzac bond' – emerged between the John Howard and Helen Clark governments and became a means of defining, arguing and adapting a range of political problems. As Rosemary Baird points out, the 'Anzac spirit' was integral to the emotional appeal of cooperation between Australians and New Zealanders.[6] Both Howard and Clark leaned on a mutual Anzac policy to explain their national security interests, especially in response to the Iraq War, in which Howard wanted to re-establish a strong Anglo–American alliance while Clark was more interested in carving out a small peacekeeping role with minimal defence commitments. Both leaders mixed the personal and the political in the use of remembrance to rationalise their actions as prime ministers, but whereas Howard used war commemoration to legitimise otherwise controversial commitments to wars in Afghanistan and Iraq, Clark claimed a more centrist stance stressing, in Graham Hucker's turn of phrase, New Zealand's 'historic right of attendance'.[7]

The experience of the sesquicentennial commemoration in New Zealand in 1990 had cast a long shadow. Clark's engagement with Anzac commemoration was the result of a different thread of debate in New Zealand society around Waitangi Day. Māori perspectives on the Treaty and history of protest on Waitangi Day itself had resulted in a more diverse commemoration than took place in Australia. Clark herself struggled to understand the antagonism of some Māori towards official Waitangi Day celebrations and, in her time as prime minister, sought to avoid what she called the annual 'silly season' every 6 February.[8] Anzac Day provided a more useful story of unity. The shared memory of Gallipoli was a celebration of democracy, existing outside of ideology and above partisan politics. Public commemoration in Australia and New Zealand, however, continued to highlight the deeper structural differences in the work of memory, which Clark and Howard's 'Anzac bond' could only paper over at best.

The Anzac bond

On the eve of Anzac Day 2001 in Canberra, Prime Ministers John Howard and Helen Clark unveiled a sculpture that celebrated the bond between Australia and New Zealand. The New Zealand Memorial consisted of two bronze arches framing the entrance to Anzac Parade, the capital's commemorative avenue. Anzac Day was the epicentre of two centuries of trans-Tasman contact, and the monument expressed this affinity between the two nations. The arches represented the handles of a Māori kete or basket, a visual rendition of the whakatauki (proverb), 'Mau tena kiwai o te kete, maku tenei' –'Each of us at a handle of the basket.'[9] Now in her third year of office, Clark spoke of the memorial as a symbol of 'our shared history, values and memories, and our common endeavours and sacrifices, in peace and war'.[10]

Howard quoted from soldier-poet Leon Gellert's poem 'Anzac Cove': 'There's a sound of gentle sobbing in the South.' Gellert, he said, 'was speaking of the sense of shared grief held by so many people in our two nations during that terrible costly campaign'.[11] The sense of a vast trauma uniting Australians and New Zealanders in the twenty-first century magnified the theme of Anzac commemoration as it

Prime Ministers John Howard of Australia and Helen Clark of New Zealand and one of the arches of the New Zealand Memorial, Canberra. The memorial was designed by Kingsley Baird in collaboration with Māori painter and weaver Toi Te Rito Maihi. Photo: David Grey. Reuters had developed since the 1980s, from Weir's *Gallipoli* to Hawke's 1990 pilgrimage and Keating's eulogy for the unknown soldier. Howard was enthusiastic about the new state configuration of Anzac commemoration and declared Anzac Day 'more evocative of the Australian spirit than any other day in our calendar'.[12]

Howard had been developing an official script of trans-Tasman Anzac policy since 1997 when he made his first trip to New Zealand as Australia's prime minister. At an official lunch at Parliament House in Wellington with then-Prime Minister Jim Bolger, Howard spoke of the 'easy naturalness' of the relationship between Australia and New Zealand – 'our two peoples and our two societies' – which was based, he said, on the 'deep and intricate bonds of history and tradition and culture and shared experience and common values which bring our two countries together'.[13] The relationship was not 'embedded entirely in nostalgia and in the past', however:

> [I]t is a modern, contemporary relationship built upon the shared interests of the two countries in the Asia-Pacific region, a recognition that we have to work together in that region if we are to realise our full potential. And also our common experiences over the past decade with economic reform.[14]

In the wake of a period of economic disruption that had seen high numbers of New Zealanders move to Australia, fragmentation of the Anzus alliance and divergent nuclear policies, Howard presented a story of Australia and New Zealand drawing closer on issues of defence, shared markets, immigration and social security. Anzac remembrance formed a bridge between the two countries that could provide an axis for relationships across the Asia-Pacific region, perhaps even globally. As political scientist Matt McDonald observed, Howard's 'Anzac policy' was based on the emergence of state-centred Anzac commemoration rather than directly referring to 'Anzac memories'.[15]

The countries' shared interests in the Asia-Pacific region came to the fore with the United Nations-mandated intervention in East Timor following the Timorese independence vote in late 1999. Known as the International Force East Timor (or Interfet), the mission involved around 20 countries led by the Australian government and some 5000 Australian troops. Howard framed the intervention as a way of protecting 'the birth of small nation'; it was also a chance for Australia to play an active role in its regional interests and align more closely with the United States.[16] American involvement in Timor failed to materialise, however – a blow to Howard, who in an interview suggested 'the Australian public would not understand America not being involved given the depth of the relationship and the contributions we've made in the past' – a reference, presumably, to the world wars, Vietnam and Korea.[17] Australians, he said, could not avoid 'the moral responsibility' of the mission and needed to 'stand up for the right of these people to determine their own future'.[18] Although Interfet was a UN force with contributions from other Commonwealth nations, including Canada and Britain, a common perception in this Australia-led mission was that 'only the Kiwis are really solid and sticking by us', as one commentator said.[19] These moral and political demands of 'sticking by' national values and interests were filtered through war memory.

Helen Clark was elected prime minister in 1999, and Howard found in her a willing and enthusiastic partner in this Anzac statecraft. In March 2000 Clark made her first trip to Australia in her new role.[20] At their first joint press conference the two prime ministers unveiled the design for the New Zealand Memorial, intended as a gift to the people of Australia to mark the 2001 centenary of Australian federation and symbolise, as Howard said, 'the close and enduring relationship which our two countries have had'. It was an 'important symbol of our friendship, a reminder of our shared history and the determination in relation to those matters that the association continue in a very open and very well-developed way'. He linked the project to the ongoing collaboration in East Timor, 'the most reassuring element' of which was 'the ready and very strong support from New Zealand'.[21]

In this initial meeting of the 'Anzac prime ministers', peacekeeping operations provoked discussion around defence spending and collaboration. Both countries were reviewing defence plans for the new decade. The Howard government had released a white paper outlining expansion across all three branches of the Australian Defence Force, and Clark had committed to modernising the New Zealand Army.[22] Media commentators suggested, however, that Clark was in fact stepping away from her government's military commitments by reneging on the purchase of new fighter squadrons and naval frigates. According to one, Clark was 'bludging or free-loading' on Australia's defence effort.[23] 'New Zealand turns back on tradition of Anzac' read one Australian headline.[24] In response, Clark cited the Interfet mission as indication that the two nations were 'committed to the highest level of cooperation'. If there was any doubt about New Zealand's commitment to the Anzac bond, 'there will be other opportunities for us to show in a practical way just how important that is to us'. The shift away from the conventional fighting forces of the Cold War, as Clark put it, only made sense in a trans-Tasman arrangement; she valued 'the ongoing very close relationship the two countries have enjoyed for a century' on matters of national defence.[25]

This trans-Tasman diplomacy mixed easily with memorial projects. On Anzac Day 2000 Howard undertook the first of two visits that he would make to Gallipoli as prime minister. At the dawn service he talked of the 'remarkable legacy' the Anzacs had left to all Australians and New Zealanders, as 'a heritage that requires of each of us a conscious decision to do what is right regardless of the resistance we meet or the fears we hold'.[26] At the Turkish international service that followed at Mehmetcik Abide, Howard spoke of how the sacrifice of the Anzacs in the Gallipoli campaign had 'forged a bond between our two countries that will never be broken'.[27] Clark also attended the international service but did not speak. Nestled in Minister of Foreign Affairs Phil Goff's speech at the dawn service a year later, however, were themes of a trans-Tasman Anzac policy. Every 25 April, Goff claimed, 'we commemorate comradeship'; Gallipoli was the place where 'the special bond between New Zealanders and Australians was first forged in the heat of battle', a bond now expressed in the 'cause of peace' in Timor and Bougainville.[28] Gallipoli was where 'the Anzac spirit was born' and forged a 'friendship [that] remains as important today'.[29]

The accusations of New Zealand 'bludging' around defence shifted to negotiation of a new social security agreement for New Zealanders living in Australia. Some of this work had been done in previous meetings in which the Clark government had agreed to tighten up 'sloppy borders' and crack down on overstayers.[30] In a Wellington meeting in early 2001 Howard and Clark declared 'a win-win for both countries': New Zealanders living in Australia would retain their status as de facto permanent residents but would have reduced access to Australian welfare and health care.[31] Clark expressed a desire to put to rest the image of the 'Bondi bludger' – Australian media slang for New Zealanders living in Australia – an 'irritant' that she said had undermined cooperation between the two countries.[32] Both Clark and Howard lauded the new arrangement as an expression of the Anzac bond. When journalists queried whether the federal government's 'cutting back on payments' in fact compromised this bond, Howard swatted away concerns with a bold rhetorical flourish: 'Nothing will ever undermine the Anzac spirit.'[33]

The Clark and Howard governments pursued widely different security arrangements; as analyst Hugh White observed, Australia and New Zealand were 'not on the same bus'.[34] Yet there was an important transaction here: in exchange for Clark's reduction in security expenditure, Howard would reduce federal spending on New Zealanders' welfare in Australia as part of his platform of 'cracking down' on the porous Tasman border without threatening the flow of economic migrants.[35] In turn, the Clark government would support Australian-led initiatives to shore up democracy in Asia and the Pacific. The Anzac bond provided a way to imagine, understand and massage ongoing relations, and to gloss over differences in defence and social security policy to the mutual benefit of both governments.[36]

Howard and Clark managed this relationship through direct references to the Anzac experience. At the final official lunch of his New Zealand trip Howard toasted 'the friendship between the people of Australia and the people of New Zealand'.[37] He and Clark had attended the Anzac Day commemorations at Gallipoli a few months earlier and had encountered a crowd of young Australian and New Zealand pilgrims. 'The most astonishing thing ... to me,' Howard said, 'was to move amongst some 12,000–15,000 young Australians and New Zealanders who were making what was visibly a pilgrimage to that very special place in the world that means more to us, our two peoples, than any other place on Earth':

> The history of a relationship is very important, the sentiment and the emotions of a relationship are very important, but so is the modern-day flesh and blood of it. You need both. You need the history and the emotions but you also need the common-sense, coincidence of interests.[38]

This shared framework of remembrance could also be applied to contemporary practical concerns between the governments. Howard suggested both nations should concentrate 'on the modern-day reality': the Anzac bond was a 'sophisticated relationship built on common needs, common values and common interests', including the 'practical and sensible, rational working out of common issues'. Democracy, decency, tolerance and openness were the hallmarks of contemporary Australia and New Zealand.[39]

This Anzac policy was cemented with the installation of the New Zealand Memorial in Canberra. As Clark noted in her address, the edifice of the Australian War Memorial loomed over the ceremony, framing the whole commemorative project. This institution, the heart of Australian nationhood, would now provide a cornerstone for an emerging revivification of a trans-Tasman commemoration of Anzac. That morning, with Australian War Memorial director Steve Gower, she had opened a new version of the exhibition *Gallipoli: The New Zealand story*. Renamed *New Zealand: The other Anzac*, it offered 'moving stories of trans-Tasman mateship in times of war' and aimed to promote New Zealand's military heritage to an Australian audience and 'put the "NZ" back in Australian perceptions of Anzac'.[40] The exhibition would travel to the Museum of New Zealand Te Papa Tongarewa at the end of the year, where it was hoped it would help 'a new generation of New

Zealanders learn about the grim forging of their nation'. Clark emphasised the 'story of courage and partnership in adversity' in her dedication speech: 'Our cooperation endures today as New Zealand and Australian servicemen and women continue to serve together in East Timor, Bougainville, the Solomon Islands, and other endeavours.'[41]

A host of Australian commemorative projects followed in which Howard conveyed his moral and political values through the Anzac policy. When opening the RSL National Congress four months later, he spoke of 'the opportunity last year on Anzac Day on Gallipoli Peninsula ... to be involved with the Prime Minister of New Zealand in dedicating the new memorial and taking part in the services' as 'the most emotional experience I've had as Prime Minister of Australia'. It had been 'a powerful message to me of the growing relevance of our history and the growing interest of the young in the sacrifices of earlier generations'. He touched on contemporary concerns, stating that Australians 'live in a region which is probably more turbulent, more unsettled and therefore potentially more threatening than it might have been 25 years ago'.[42]

The Anzac bond was deployed to shore up national security: through defence, social cohesion and border protection. In August 2001 a Norwegian container ship, MV *Tampa*, picked up 440 asylum seekers after their ship sank in the Indian Ocean. The *Tampa* planned to bring these people to Australia; however, in the face of growing unauthorised migration over the past decade and electoral calls for the government to stay tough on border protection, the Howard government refused to allow the ship access to Australian ports.[43] After an intense international stand-off between Australia and Norway, Clark contacted Howard and offered to relocate 151 of the refugees to New Zealand; the rest would be sent to Nauru and processed as asylum seekers. Both Howard and Clark framed their cooperation around the crisis as proof of an enduring Anzac bond. 'Can I say to Helen Clark,' Howard announced in an interview with the ABC's Barrie Cassidy, 'I appreciate very much the stance that she has taken.'[44] New Zealand had demonstrated, once again, that it was 'Australia's best friend'. Reflecting in 2005 on this early period of cooperation and consensus as a 'turning of the page', Howard spoke of the 'feeling of a new optimism and a new era'.[45]

Anzac and the 'war on terror'

The 1999 East Timor intervention had helped to develop a perception of how Australia might act as a leading regional partner in the Anzus alliance. Initial gestures asserting an Anzac bond became the premise for more extensive cooperation in the wake of the Al Qaeda terrorist attacks in the United States on 11 September 2001. The attacks had personal significance for Howard, who was in Washington at the time hoping to negotiate a new Australian–New Zealand–US alliance, and the experience gave him some authority in the ensuing 'war on terror'.[46] Howard invoked the Anzus treaty, offering a blank cheque to the US government for its response to the attack. When the Bush administration rolled out a retaliatory invasion of Afghanistan, the base of the Al Qaeda attacks, Howard committed Australian support. This activation of Anzus highlighted differences in the respective security priorities of Australia and New Zealand – a divergence that would become more apparent in subsequent years. In a media release on Anzac Day 2002, the first following the 11 September attacks, Howard wrote of the forces serving in Afghanistan: 'Our young soldiers, sailors and airmen stand today as their Anzac forebears did more than three quarters of a century ago – willing to serve their nation and eager to defend its freedoms.'[47] Clark also committed New Zealand forces to the war in Afghanistan, but these were confined to Special Air Service (SAS), intelligence and naval contingents.[48]

Clark travelled to Sydney in February 2002 as part of the preparatory work on the next stage of trans-Tasman cooperation: the pursuit of international trade. The year 2003 would mark the 20th anniversary of the Closer Economic Relations agreement, which Clark celebrated as 'making solid progress towards realising our longer-term ambition of a single economic market' – something which, incidentally, she had opposed as a junior parliamentarian in 1983.[49]

The two prime ministers were soon sharing a stage again, this time at the funeral of the Queen Mother. Howard announced his intentions to attend the funeral, a role traditionally reserved for the governor-general. Clark followed suit, promoting the trip as a chance to collaborate with other Commonwealth leaders. An informal summit followed between Clark and Howard, Canadian Prime Minister Jean Chrétien and British Prime Minister Tony Blair.[50]

A month later Howard presided over the funeral of Gallipoli veteran Alec Campbell, who died at the age of 103. In the final few years of his life Campbell had become the reluctant face of Howard's Anzac policy: in 1999 he was awarded

The last Australian Gallipoli veteran, Alec Campbell, nicknamed 'The Kid', during his service in the AIF. The photo first appeared in in the *Weekly Courier* on 19 August 1915 in an article about Tasmanian men who had responded to 'the empire's call', and became popular at the time of Campbell's death. He was the archetypal image of the Anzac boy-soldier caught up in an imperial conflict of which he had little understanding. Tasmanian State Library and Archives, Hobart

the 80th Anniversary Armistice Remembrance Medal, in 2002 the Centenary Medal, and he had featured with two others on a set of stamps issued to mark Australia Day 2000.[51] Campbell's family sought a private burial but bowed to a request by the Howard government for a full-blown state funeral, at which the prime minister himself would give the eulogy. Campbell aligned perfectly with the image of the Anzacs under the state configuration of Anzac Day. Since veteran Ted Hughes had been buried as the 'last Anzac' at a state funeral in 1997, Campbell was deemed the last 'participant': he had not been a soldier but went to the war as a boy and carried water to the troops.[52] He was a fresh-faced Archy, an innocent, literal child-soldier. His oft-quoted ambivalence towards Anzac Day – 'I joined for adventure … There was not a great feeling of defending the Empire. I lived through it, somehow. I enjoyed some of it. I am not a philosopher. Gallipoli was Gallipoli' – was the perfect, muted anti-imperial foil to the emotional cachet of public commemoration.[53] The Australian War Memorial quickly elevated Campbell to a pantheon of national heroes, memorialised as a national treasure who 'embodied the spirit of Anzac', the 'last human link to Gallipoli and all that place symbolises'.[54]

At the funeral Howard presented a tour de force of Anzac policy. Having portrayed Campbell as the personification of the Anzac spirit, he asserted that 'new wars' would now be incorporated in Australia's military heritage. On behalf of the Australian people, Howard committed to a 'silent promise':

> We signal our understanding that the freedom under which we shelter needs to be nurtured and, at times, defended anew. We think of the men and women of the Australian Defence Force now serving in Afghanistan, East Timor, Bougainville, and elsewhere.[55]

A silent promise is one for which consent is assumed, not requested. Howard comfortably fitted the war on terror into a heritage of military service, framing the response in traditional terms and military retaliation as both natural and laudatory. Once again he fused this remembrance with the national trait of mateship, expressed in the need to fight for beleaguered democracy. Campbell's funeral provided an occasion to mark the end of an era; remembrance now became the focal point for action and responsibility into the future. Howard presented a claim on national memory that was above partisan critique, even as his speech pointed to an irresistible emotional course of action in the present.[56]

The Bali bombings in August 2002 were the third incident in an emotional trifecta. Eighty-two Australians and three New Zealanders were killed in terror attacks on nightclubs in Bali, and Howard's response was immediate and resolute. To suggestions the attacks were motivated by Australia's leadership in the East Timor mission, he responded, 'It is the practice of democracy, and the ideals of freedom, and the character of our societies that [the terrorists] despise.'[57] Ten days later Howard and Clark met in Mexico for the annual APEC ministerial summit, during which they talked at length about forging a shared counter-terrorism strategy. 'The tragedy in Bali has touched both of our countries,' Howard announced in a Los Cabos interview:

> It drives home to both of us the common threat of terrorism in our region and the need for countries such as Australia and New Zealand to continue to work very closely together ... We have in the past, and we'll continue to do so with a redoubled sense of urgency in the future.[58]

The Bali bombings gave further impetus to an escalation of the war on terror, a shift already under way over the course of 2002. In January of that year President Bush delivered an address to the US Congress in which he warned of an 'axis of evil', which included authoritarian regimes in Iraq and Iran, and broadened the definition of the war on terror to encompass proactive military interventions. Howard expressed support for Bush's agenda in his own congressional speech in June 2002.[59] It was the address he had intended to deliver during his Washington trip in September 2001, and in it he presented a narrative of Australian and American military cooperation that dated back to the Battle of Hamel in France in 1918. Howard's father Lyall had participated as a signalman for an Australian reserve unit in the battle. The reference to Hamel was a transliteration of the Anzac bond to an American audience, weaving geopolitics with remembrance both personal and national. 'From that moment to this, we've been able to count on each other when it has mattered most,' Howard said. Without American intervention in World War II, '[Australia's] history and society would have been totally different'; America was now 'under attack' and Australia was 'immediately there to help'.[60]

After the Bali bombings, the need to act decisively aquired an irresistible logic for the Howard government. Returning to Australia for what would be the prelude to the invasion of Iraq, Howard gave an interview on the *Today Show* with Steve Liebmann in which he spoke of 'a strong possibility of American action after 9/11'. Despite growing political opposition, and with the threat of an Australian Senate inquiry and motions condemning a 'first strike' policy, Howard stated: 'If that occurs, then Australia could well be asked to participate.'[61] The day before, Howard had opened a new memorial in Papua New Guinea to mark the 60th anniversary of the Battle of Kokoda. With this commemoration of Australian military deaths in mind, Liebmann questioned 'the wisdom of sending Australian soldiers into another war on the other side of the world'. Howard responded: 'To start comparing what happened in World War II with any possible hypothetical Australian military involvement in relation to Iraq is a little disproportionate.' In his mind, the conflict in Iraq was motivated by 'very legitimate concern about the failure of a country to comply with Security Council resolutions'.[62] War remembrance became a field on which to play out debates about foreign policy, but one that Howard used selectively.

Howard travelled to New Zealand in 2003 amid growing protests against an Australian commitment to the Iraq invasion, and this visit also highlighted some tensions in the Anzac bond. He opened a new consulate office in Auckland and laid a wreath at the Auckland War Memorial, but eschewed a public walk lest he be harangued by protesters. At the joint press conference announcing the objectives of the annual trans-Tasman talks, Helen Clark focused on economic negotiation. A 'good exchange on the position of the two economies' was followed by an agreement to cooperate closely on counter-terrorism. The backdrop to the press conference was, however, the protests against the war: some activists were condemning Howard as a 'warmonger'. Clark said she was 'determined that New Zealand isn't going to lose good friends or damage friendships over this'. Media representatives queried whether Australia's military commitment was linked to the Howard government's pursuit of a Free Trade Agreement (FTA) with the United States – something Howard strenuously denied – and whether the failure of the Clark government to support the war underpinned the decision to pursue a separate FTA rather than a shared trans-Tasman agreement. Parallels were drawn between any invasion of Iraq and past opposition to the Vietnam War, in which Helen Clark had herself taken part: 'If you weren't prime minister today,' journalist Mark Sainsbury asked Clark, 'could you envisage yourself across the road with that protest?' Clark declined to answer the question.[63]

Howard used the New Zealand visit to mobilise public support for the war in Iraq through recourse to remembrance. Historical allusions abounded. In a TV One interview Howard solemnly declared that he would ask Australians to 'remember the victims of Bali if soldiers go in to fight against Iraq', provoking the satirical headline, 'Who do you think you are kidding, Mr Howard?', a parody of the theme song of the 1960s television series *Dad's Army*, 'Who do you think you are kidding, Mr Hitler?'[64] By the end of his visit Howard had reframed his vision of the Anzac bond – a 'very close and very treasured friendship' – as a reason to act together decisively against terrorism. In a speech at the official dinner he reiterated the legacy 'of history, of language, of culture and very importantly, of shared values' between Australia and New Zealand. In the face of the threat of international terrorism, 'we are … reminded of the things that matter to us most, and that is the way of life we have and the things that we believe in, and the things that we stand for'. Australia and New Zealand, Howard said, 'will tread paths together': 'Nations that share democratic values in the end will share common goals and common aspirations.'[65] It was as much a message for Australian audiences at home as a statement to his dinner guests.

This filtering of Australian politics through trans-Tasman Anzac remembrance was coupled by the Howard government's commitment to celebrating heritage at home. In 2002 Howard announced the allocation of $50m for a national heritage project. Australians were invited to nominate sites of national significance across three themes: 'a wide and ancient land', 'building a nation' and 'the Australian spirit'. At the launch of the project the prime minister celebrated the theme of nation-building and the core value of mateship, and spoke of Australians' 'fellowship, selflessness and cooperative self-reliance evident in all times of adversity', essential for coping with the country's vast and rugged environment and crucial also 'in times of war and conflict'.[66]

The first of these heritage sites was, of course, Gallipoli, the nomination of which completed the national claim on the site made by Hawke in 1990:

> Although it's not on Australian territory, anyone who has visited the place will know that once you go there you feel it is as Australian as the piece of land on

> which your home is built. And it has a powerful and ongoing influence on the psyche, not only of older Australians, but as we so frequently now remark and rejoice in the fact that it also has a powerful and growing impact on the psyche of younger Australians who see visiting that place as being increasingly some kind of rite of passage for them as young Australians.[67]

In 2003 Howard announced the nomination of Anzac Cove as an Australian heritage site, noting that it had the 'enthusiastic support' of Prime Minister Helen Clark, which lent legitimacy to the project as well as impetus for negotiations with the Turkish government on improving infrastructure at the cove. The nomination was part of a suite of Anzac initiatives that included the digitising of Bean's war correspondence alongside some 200 newspaper articles, images and interpretive pieces through the C.E.W. Bean Foundation.[68] According to some, Howard's pursuit of Anzac policy was verging on overkill, and his frequent invocation of mateship was regularly satirised by the Australian media.

By this time Howard had signalled that Australia would be committed to American intervention in Iraq irrespective of UN approval.[69] Debate raged about the country's involvement in the war. Clark, on the other hand, contrived a difficult

'An Amazing Thing', by Michael Leunig. Leunig satirised Prime Minister John Howard's overuse of the terms 'Anzac spirit' and 'mateship' in his political speeches, and his tendency to make speeches on matters of importance for the edification of the nation. Michael Leunig

balance between supporting allies and not being drawn into significant military commitments. Asked whether the 'Anzus alliance still had any vestige of authority', she explained her reluctance in terms of the lack of UN support and the breakdown of the diplomatic process.[70] Her goal was a rapprochement with the United States in the hope of opening up American domestic markets to New Zealand produce while avoiding military entanglements.[71] Ultimately, a compromise was struck: New Zealand would not send troops but would contribute to postwar building projects in Iraq and the removal of mines under a UN mandate.

This delicate navigation on New Zealand's part was illustrative of a pattern towards the midpoint of the decade: the use of Anzac remembrance, with occasional reference to the 'Anzac bond', to navigate public legitimacy for military intervention. In 2004, the second year of the war, Howard made a surprise 29-hour round trip to Iraq for Anzac Day to support the Australian troops in Baghdad 'in a just cause' and 'to personally thank them'.[72] In a breakfast speech at Camp Victory he likened the assembled military personnel to modern-day Anzacs: 'You are seeking to bring to the people of Iraq, who have suffered so much for so long, the hope of liberty and the hope of freedom, and your example, your behaviour, your values, belong to the great and long tradition that was forged on the beaches of Gallipoli in 1915.'[73] Despite public ambivalence towards Australia's involvement in the war, his trip was hailed a success; according to the Australian Defence Association it was a 'morale booster' for the Australian troops.[74]

By linking his trip to Anzac Day Howard avoided any criticism of partisan politics. Leader of the Opposition Mark Latham had no choice but to support it, agreeing that 'Anzac Day should be above politics', although Democrat leader Andrew Bartlett commented that the prime minister was 'very good at trying to bask in the reflected glory or the bravery of our troops'.[75] There was little space for Howard's political opponents and critics to manoeuvre in this fusion of personal–political memory: it was difficult to separate the sacrifice of the troops, so lauded in the rubric of Anzac commemoration, from the prime minister, who had become its chief purveyor.

Howard's visit to Iraq took place at the height of Australian public criticism of the government's commitment to the war, and fuelled increasing accusations that Howard, in his blend of remembrance and defence policy as 'military heritage', was militarising Anzac commemoration. *Why the War Was Wrong* (2003), edited by Raimond Gaita, contained a number of essays by prominent Australians criticising the government's commitment to Iraq and a pattern of leadership that was increasingly 'presidential', as Mark McKenna put it.[76] The broadside was an amplification of the largest anti-war protest movement since the Vietnam War. Some quarter of a million marched in Sydney, and in March 2003 protesters climbed onto the roof of the Sydney Opera House and painted 'NO WAR' in red letters on the white tiles.[77] The latter doubled as an affront to the new Anzac heritage regime, in which 'heritage' was a vital evocation of national values.[78] The decision by the Clark government not to join the 'coalition of the willing' – the United States-led multinational force – meant there was no equivalent anti-war movement in New Zealand, which in turn limited the public's critique of Anzac policy.

Clark modelled her use of commemoration on that of her Australian counterpart. Speaking on the parliamentary motion to recognise the repatriation of the Unknown Warrior on Armistice Day 2004, she staked a personal claim on the official commemoration. Like Howard, she referred to her ancestors who had participated in the war, recalling family graves in battlefields in France and Belgium, 'portraits of great-uncles in military uniform', and how 'as children we all knew their story':

> Understanding more about how, where, and why those ordinary New Zealanders died, and about the impact on my family, has helped me understand the forces and events that shaped our people, our country, and its values. And it has reinforced for me a determination that we must never forget, and that their memory should be honoured for all time. That is the spirit in which we have worked to return the remains of this one soldier, as a permanent memorial to the fallen, and as a place where succeeding generations might reflect on the sacrifices made in our name.[79]

Clark had been cultivating this 'determination to remember', centred on her family's history, since the beginning of her time in office. As early as 1999 she suggested to her parliamentary colleagues that World War I had 'cast a very long shadow over the family'; and while visiting Flanders in 2003 she remarked that the war had 'caused great distress and heartbreak in the family'.[80]

It was clear that by 2004 Clark was more confident in positioning her commitment to national identity through personal remembrance of the trauma of war. Clark's Anzac policy evolved to focus heavily on her relationship with the RSA as she developed an image of herself as the advocate for veterans. In the inevitable mixing of personal and political she frequently posed for photographs with ageing veterans, and declared 2006 the Year of the Veteran to coincide with the 90th birthday of the RSA. The commemorative year would be a 'lasting expression of appreciation to those who have served New Zealand in times of war or emergency'.[81] In 2009 Clark would apologise to veterans of the Vietnam War: an 'honour march' to Parliament, a ceremony at the citizens' memorial and a $30m compensation package accompanied the official apology.[82]

Political experience was another part of the rationale for Clark's apparent affinity with Anzac commemoration. As an MP in the dying days of the Lange Labour government she had witnessed the difficulties in establishing consensus for a national celebration on Waitangi Day. Michael Bassett's leadership in cultural policy in the 1990 Commission had shown the possibilities offered through a dedicated Ministry of Culture and Heritage; on the other hand, the growing importance of state commemorative projects justified direct steering by the Prime Minister's Office.[83] Clark married these precedents in her role as the first New Zealand prime minister to also hold the arts portfolio.[84] Anzac commemoration was a way to combine the political and sacred acts of state leadership.

Furthermore, the overshadowing of official celebrations at Waitangi Day by a show of protest and dissent had affected Clark directly. In 1998 she was publicly humiliated at Waitangi when, as deputy leader, she was refused speaking rights on the marae grounds because she was a woman. She swore never to return to the site of the Treaty signing if elected as prime minister.[85] This stance was not without political risk. A section of the Pākehā public was, however, increasingly disaffected by Waitangi Day protests. Head of the Fisheries Commission Shane Jones supported Clark's Waitangi policy and suggested Māori ran the risk 'of destroying Waitangi Day in terms of the rest of the country being prepared to take it seriously as a national holiday'.[86] When asked about the 1998 incident in 2004, Clark replied, 'Everyone has decided they are sick of the fiasco ... they want to move on.'[87] The controversy continued to be a source of irritation, however; mobbing protesters soured the conciliatory 'return' to Waitangi Day. By the end of the year the Clark government had passed the Foreshore and Seabed Act, in an attempt to extinguish customary claims on coastal access and resources.[88] In 2009 she again refused to participate in the ceremony and organised an alternative programme, hosting a commemorative breakfast down the road from Waitangi before visiting an alternative marae and walking onto the Treaty Grounds without an official welcome.[89]

Clark's disaffection with iwi politics, and the political dichotomy between Waitangi/dissent and Anzac/unity, were possibly behind the government's decision to give the green light to the police 'anti-terror' dawn raids on Tūhoe iwi in 2007. The arrest of several Tūhoe activists on charges of terrorism – later reduced to illegal firearm charges – was indicative of the moral panic around terrorism playing out in the Tasman. Although Clark faced a different context of protest from her Australian counterpart, she employed a similar strategy of memory that leaned heavily on the celebration of the Anzac spirit. The disruption of Waitangi Day celebrations provided the necessary foil for a new political enthusiasm for Anzac Day.

Hyde Park memorials and the 90th anniversary of Gallipoli

From 2003 to the end of their terms as prime minister – in 2007 and 2008 respectively – both Howard and Clark retreated further into the safety of commemoration. Their early collaboration settled into a series of significant international commemorative projects.

The first of these was the installation of the Australian War Memorial in London. The 'AWM London', as it came to be dubbed, commemorated Australian service personnel who served in the world wars, and was dedicated by Queen Elizabeth II on Armistice Day 2003 in the presence of Tony Blair and John Howard.[90]

The concept of a London memorial was first proposed by Blair and Howard in July 2000 as part of the suite of projects to mark the centenary of Australian federation, and was approved on 11 January 2003.[91] Over an 11-month period, the Australian and United Kingdom governments worked with the Australian War Memorial and Commonwealth War Graves Commission to plan the memorial, which would be sited at Hyde Park Corner, a place with enormous public cachet.[92] The Australian government provided £3m for a monument that would 'weave personal and official memory together in a poignant claim for tolerance and inclusion'.[93]

The chosen design was by the Australian firm that designed the tomb of the unknown soldier, Tonkin Zulaikha Greer (earlier Tonkin Zulaikha Harford) in collaboration with artist Janet Laurence.[94] Its 'broad-sweeping and open Australianness' would contrast with the 'ceremonious conventionality of old-world edifices' – the Wellington Arch and the Royal Artillery that stood nearby.[95] Tonkin Zulaikha Greer proposed the use of Australian granite as 'a literal fragment of Australian earth given presence at the very heart of the old Empire'.[96] The project of Anzac commemoration that had been unfolding since the 1990s would now return to the imperial heartland.

Howard led a delegation to participate in the dedication ceremony.[97] Following a rendition of 'Waltzing Matilda' and before an audience that included thousands of Australians, he delivered an august speech on what had become the great theme of his time in office: the spectre of the war on terror underpinning the demands of contemporary Anzac remembrance. In dedicating the new memorial, he suggested Australians should 'reaffirm the enduring hope of a world set free from hate', and acknowledged 'the terrible power of those forces that would conspire against such a dream'. 'These young Australians we honour here comprehended those truths,' he said – truths that had always 'bound together the peoples of Great Britain and Australia in deep and unique friendship' tied by 'history, by shared language and law, but most important of all, by an enduring belief in human dignity and the democratic freedoms that should be the birth-right of all'.[98]

The London memorial dedication was followed by the 90th anniversary of the Gallipoli landing in 2005. Howard met with the New Zealand Cabinet in February 2005 to discuss details of the occasion. The dawn service and subsequent services at Lone Pine and Chunuk Bair would follow the formats of the past, and there was some discussion around pre-commemoration activities and how to ensure these were 'appropriate and dignified', as Howard put it, adding that he was 'very happy with the co-operation that Australia has with New Zealand on this issue'.[99] Clark shared this language of reassurance, saying the commemorative services 'will be dignified, they will be appropriate, and I'm very confident we'll have a good outcome on that'. This echoing of 'dignity', 'appropriateness' and 'confidence' belied some tensions, however. For one, Howard's decision to declare Anzac Cove the first listing in Australia's federal heritage project had reinforced the assumption that Australians had some prerogative to the site, which had raised eyebrows in both New Zealand and Turkey. Now Clark scuttled the idea to have Australian singer John Farnham perform as part of the pre-dawn service entertainment. Howard for his part was reluctant to restrict pilgrim numbers, aware that this would limit the presence of Australians at Anzac Cove.[100]

As the 90th anniversary approached, Clark and Howard were keen to emphasise joint Tasman interests in peacekeeping and relief work. The two defence forces had worked together closely to provide relief in the wake of the 2004 Boxing Day tsunami in Thailand a few months earlier. It was 'a truly Anzac effort', Clark declared.[101] Howard agreed: the Anzac bond was 'an old relationship' and 'a very close one'; not only 'steeped in history' but 'bound ever more tightly' over the course of the Clark–Howard partnership, through economic integration, the fight against terrorism and the ongoing deployment in Afghanistan. The 90th anniversary, he claimed, would be 'a wonderful opportunity to demonstrate again the real friendship that the people of Australia have towards the people of New Zealand, and the high regard in which I hold the people of New Zealand, and the commitment I have to ever closer relations between our two peoples whose destiny is forever linked together.'[102]

This notion of a linked destiny captured the paradox of Anzac in the Howard–Clark partnership: Anzac was part of a distinctive Australian culture, but managed through trans-Tasman linkages. It was a shared national mythology, which repudiated historian Keith Sinclair's 1986 suggestion that New Zealand actually pursued 'a destiny apart'.[103] Clark would repeat this language of destiny in her dawn service speech at Gallipoli: 'Out of catastrophe, each of our nations emerged with a new sense of certainty about our own destiny and our place in the world.'[104]

The ceremony was marked by a series of controversies that reflected the relationship between myth and counter-myth in making Anzac policy. The playing of the Bee Gees' song 'Stayin' Alive' to entertain the crowd before the dawn service, drunken behaviour from some Australian pilgrims, reports of Turkish complaints about Howard's claim to Anzac Cove as a site of Australian heritage, and Howard's decision to attend a barbecue at the Beach Cemetery with personnel from the HMAS *Anzac* instead of the New Zealand-led Chunuk Bair service – all expressed the new moral geography of Gallipoli that now enmeshed the actions of the Australian prime minister. Howard was expected to account for these anomalies. He was quick to emphasise the importance of the commemoration, and the suggestion that he had snubbed the New Zealand service caused him to respond somewhat indignantly that no other prime minister 'has tried harder than I have to keep the New Zealand relationship in good repair'.[105]

Clark avoided any blame for the questionable proceedings, and Howard defended the goings-on. He suggested the dawn service was 'a rite of passage' for young people, and any disorderly behaviour was the action of a minority and to be expected at such a large gathering. If anything, it indicated young Australians' need for better education about their Anzac values and history.[106] In the same year, in what he hoped would be the prelude to an extensive revamp of the national school curriculum, Howard rolled out the Values for Australian Schooling campaign, which aimed to 'instil Australian values among students'. The resource featured a watermark of the classic Anzac image of Simpson and his donkey.[107]

Clark had a tendency to leverage commemoration as an electoral strategy. In an address at the opening of the RSA national annual meeting in the anniversary year she highlighted the success of the unknown warrior repatriation, proudly reminding the audience that her government had 'seen the project through' and

Cartoonist Murray Webb depicted Helen Clark and John Howard standing with Turkish Prime Minister Tayyip Erdoğan on the beach of Anzac Cove. In Webb's lampooning of the 90th anniversary, the national leaders are implicated in various controversies: Howard barbecues sausages as if at a festival; Clark is dressed in traditional Māori costume and wields a mere (club), despite the Turkish ban on the performance of haka; and Erdoğan digs up human bones, the ultimate sacrilege, in pursuit of Anzac diplomatic support.
ATL DX-101-068, Alexander Turnbull Library, Wellington

expressing the hope that, in light of this commitment, 'New Zealanders will not vote for a return to past failures.'[108]

There was an element of this strategy also in the establishment of New Zealand's own memorial in London. Named *Southern Stand*, the memorial, by sculptor Paul Dibble and architect John Hardwick-Smith, consisted of 16 cross-shaped bronze standards decorated with text, patterns and small sculptures representing aspects of New Zealand life. The standards brought to mind 'soldiers in procession … pou-whenua markers around Māori ancestral sites, or Celtic … standing stones' and were reminiscent of 'warriors during haka, the defensive bat in cricket, the barrel of a shouldered gun'.[109] The memorial commemorated 'the enduring bonds between New Zealand and the United Kingdom and the shared sacrifice during times of war.

It is a symbol of both our common heritage and of New Zealand's distinct national identity.'[110]

In a smaller ceremony than the Australian memorial dedication, Clark joined Queen Elizabeth II, Tony Blair and 1500 official guests and members of the public to unveil the New Zealand Memorial in Hyde Park on 11 November 2006.[111] Like its Australian counterpart, the monument was the first 'devoted to the special bond between New Zealand and the United Kingdom'. In the words of New Zealand High Commissioner Jonathan Hunt, it would 'serve as a focal point for future generations to celebrate the likes of Anzac and Waitangi Day'.[112] Speaking alongside RSA president John Campbell, a key collaborator, Clark spoke of the genesis of the memorial as 'the desire to commemorate the shared sacrifice of New Zealanders in times of war, alongside the people of Britain':

> Our country owes much to the generations of British migrants who have brought their values and aspirations to our land. They came to islands where indigenous people were well settled, and the story of the adjustment of Māori, British and other settlers to each other is a large part of the story of our South Pacific nation.[113]

The deeper text of the memorial – of war service encompassed within a longer Pacific story – is an example of Clark's use of commemoration to foster New Zealand's international relations; the memorial was soon referred to in diplomatic memos as 'an outstanding piece of public diplomacy'. New Zealand's history and contemporary identity had been 'paraded in the centre of London … before an audience from the very top of British society', and 'the special relationship' between New Zealand and the United Kingdom dominated media coverage.[114] Commentators hoped the memorial would 'cement in a highly visible way' the New Zealand–UK relationship 'in the heart of London'.[115]

This memorial was the first project of a 2006–10 strategic plan to develop 'new symbols of nationhood' in New Zealand, akin to Howard's heritage regime. The second was the 2007 commemoration of the centenary of Dominion Day – a short-lived public holiday established in 1907 to mark the colony's symbolic promotion to 'dominion' status. According to Clark, Dominion Day was 'one of many steps on New Zealand's long journey of nation building'. There was, she said, 'a real sense that many are exploring with renewed pride what it means to be a New Zealander', a factor visible in the annual pilgrimages to Gallipoli and growing attendance at Anzac Day ceremonies. 'I hope the day will come when people feel as compelled to come out to the many community events on Waitangi Day.'[116]

The commemoration of Dominion Day was one of a dizzying array of such projects.[117] These were also occasions to explore constitutional questions: the 2007 proceedings, for example, looked toward a review of the nation's unwritten constitution and proposed the idea of a Treaty-led Upper House.[118]

On both sides of the Tasman, the Anzac bond set a pattern for international commemoration over the course of the decade that culminated in the Australian government's announcement of its intention to erect a monument in Wellington as a counterpart to the bronze arches on Canberra's Anzac Parade. Inspired by the shared memorial projects in London's Hyde Park Corner, the Australian monument would be the first component in the expansion of the National War Memorial precinct into a New Zealand memorial peace park.[119] The commemoration of the Anzac bond had come full circle.

The monument was Howard's final commemorative project. By November his government had been defeated and Howard had lost his electoral seat.

*

On Anzac Day 2008 Clark met with newly elected Australian Prime Minister Kevin Rudd to discuss what would, in the end, be her own final commemorative project: the dedication of a statue of a New Zealand soldier on Sydney's Anzac Bridge. Clark was the senior political partner in this relationship and she stepped up to deliver a speech in which she embraced the language of trans-Tasman friendship now familiar to audiences of the Anzac prime ministers: 'Since this bridge was renamed a decade ago, the flags of both our nations have proudly flown here,' she began. The bronze statue of an Australian World War I soldier that had graced the bridge for the past eight years would now be 'joined by his mate, symbolising the extraordinary and close friendship between New Zealand and Australia in times of war and peace ... Our soldier stands there now, facing his mate the Australian digger [as] an enduring testimony to the unique bonds between us.'[120] The Anzac Bridge flanked by the two 'mates' was the perfect rendition of the Anzac bond that had developed over the first decade of the new millenium.[121]

In many respects the commemorative projects of the Anzac prime ministers merely accentuated the major theme of official commemoration laid down since 1990 and the repatriations of the Unknown Anzacs: the site of Gallipoli as a place in which Australians and New Zealanders encountered their past and, through the Anzacs, their relationship to one another. Anzac Cove was 'ground zero' of national identities that shunned any trace of racial or imperial loyalties.

The rhetoric and ritual of 'Anzac policy' was transnational, and both governments used the imagined shared memory of Gallipoli strategically. At dawn services, press conferences and especially in New Zealand territory, Howard frequently referred to the Anzac bond to advance his domestically contentious foreign policy; Clark similarly wrapped fraught defence and economic decisions around the concept of past unity. Both presented Anzac memory as a military heritage above ideological critique. When we place the two cultures of Anzac nationalism side by side, the political effect of this public remembrance becomes apparent.

The Howard–Clark partnership reflected the political and cultural context of the early twenty-first century and the personalities of those in office. Both took the cultural memory of Anzac to its logical conclusion. The new state-centred commemoration of Anzac bolstered the basis for the war on terror as well as other contemporary military commitments, and the Anzac bond exemplified the way contemporary political crises could shape commemoration. The Anzac nations had found a surer footing, defined by this modern relationship rather than a legacy of colonisation. The issue of whether Indigenous communities would accept or contest this new public narrative would define the lead-up to the Anzac Centenary.

Chapter 7

'The price of citizenship'

Indigenous media and the Anzac revival, 2005–15

Between the 90th anniversary of Gallipoli in 2005 and the centenary in 2015, increasing prominence was given to Indigenous stories of war and histories of colonial violence.

The growing political and cultural assertiveness of Indigenous Australian and Māori communities had resulted in two notable developments in Indigenous–state relations, both in 1984. *Out of the Silent Land*, a federal government report on the media needs of Aboriginal communities in Australia, drew attention to negative depictions of Indigenous people in the media that were affecting their self-perception, public opinion and public policy. Across the Tasman, the Waitangi Tribunal published a report on the rights of tangata whenua to have te reo Māori preserved under the terms of the Treaty of Waitangi, and recommended that te reo be enshrined as one of New Zealand's official languages.[1] Both reports identified the ways non-Indigenous cultural production had worked to disrupt and obscure Indigenous cultures and languages; any cultural and social recovery for Indigenous communities would need to be supported by dedicated Indigenous media.

In New Zealand the Māori Television Service was launched in 2004. As part of its competing demands – to be an avenue for Māori language revival while appealing to a general audience in a competitive global media environment – Māori Television became one of the major proponents of the Anzac revival. Between 2004 and 2005 it developed an unprecedented live, all-day broadcast on Anzac Day, streaming services from Gallipoli and around New Zealand and providing a programme of documentaries, film, live music, theatrical performances and panel discussions with veterans, historians, military personnel and politicians. Australia's National Indigenous Television (NITV) was launched in 2007 as a subsidiary of the Special Broadcasting Service (SBS), and promoted recognition of Indigenous Australian war service as part of its wider content for Indigenous communities. Both NITV and Māori Television reflected what Tim Rowse calls the 'renovation of the national'– the use of Indigenous communities in altering postcolonial configurations of statehood.[2]

According to historian James Bennett, visual media such as film, documentary and television accommodate the 'narrative strategies and forms' of Indigenous oral histories more readily than traditional historical scholarship.[3] Changes to the cultural memory of war in Australia and New Zealand cannot be understood without reference to NITV and Māori Television, both of which contributed to increased Indigenous engagement with Anzac commemorations. John Hartley and Alan McKee argue that a mediated Indigenous public space offers possibilities for new notions of citizenship arising from an emphasis on culture and identity belonging to place rather than being based on rights and obligations to the state.[4]

Māori Television explored the involvement of Māori soldiers in the Māori Pioneer contingent Te Hokowhitu a Tū (The Sons of the War God Tū) during World War I, and the 28th (Māori) Battalion (also known as the Māori Battalion) during World War II. In Australia, NITV programming relied on earlier media productions about 'forgotten warriors' – the term for Aboriginal and Torres Strait Islander soldiers who served in the Australian military.

Commemoration is shaped by stories and institutions, as well as the deeper constitutional patterns of public life. Over the course of Māori Television's Anzac Day coverage from 2005 to 2015, the Pioneer contingent and the Māori Battalion – and by extension, the Māori Battalion Association – gradually replaced the RSA as the primary image and voice of veterans and paved the way for later emphasis on alternative voices, such as those of women and Pasifika soldiers, and discussions of colonial violence. There was no such transformation in Australia, where Indigenous soldiers continued to be submerged in the general ranks of the Anzacs. NITV's focus on 'forgotten warriors' did, however, help to make public the historical wrongs against Indigenous Australians, within the site of Anzac Day. This translation of Indigenous Australian pasts into public history is an ongoing process.

Remembering together: Early Anzac Day coverage by NITV and Māori Television

The idea of an Anzac Day broadcast was an early part of the pitch for a dedicated Māori broadcaster. Initial discussions proposed a live broadcast of Waitangi Day, but this was deemed potentially divisive. Part of the rationale for promoting Anzac Day instead was that coverage of this commemoration might make Māori Television more palatable to non-Māori audiences.

The proposal to run a live, all-day Anzac broadcast was ambitious: until now, public and commercial broadcasters had provided only limited content on the day. In the 1990s television coverage of Anzac Day consisted of evening news bulletins and current affairs programmes; radio programming was dedicated to dawn and morning ceremonies.[5] In 2001 a campaign by broadcaster Sue Scott for a minute of silence at 10am on Anzac Day, across all radio stations and television channels, was the closest anyone had come to a unified media approach.

Māori Television was launched on 28 March 2004 and rapidly positioned itself as the voice of the nation on Anzac Day. The 25 April broadcast that year was funded by the government agencies Te Puni Kōkiri and Te Māngai Pāho. The following year, 2005, the broadcast centred on the 90th Anzac celebrations led by the Howard and Clark governments. Anzac Day became the service's flagship broadcast, its success reflected in a 37 percent growth in the average number of general viewers in 2007. By 2009, Māori Television was reaching more than 1.5 million New Zealanders each month.[6]

The 2004 and 2005 Anzac Day broadcasts were easily the most significant Indigenous stories of commemoration on television in Australian and New Zealand history. A number of production elements presented this as a bicultural project: viewers were welcomed by well-known Māori broadcasters who established the programme as a professional production of interest to both Pākehā and Māori; and presenters and guests spoke in both te reo Māori and English. In 2006 the broadcast was branded as *Nā Rātou, Mō Tātou* (Let's honour them together). The theme spoke to both Māori and Pākehā and used the personal form tātou – together – to suggest unity.

The broadcasts presented a selection of films and documentaries that had emerged from a burgeoning Māori creative sector in the 1980s and 1990s. Films like Wiremu Grace's *Turangawaewae* (2003) and Taika Waititi's *Tama Tū* (2005) portrayed a Māori history of war beyond the typical official commemoration, and focused on autobiographical and biographical accounts. The films asserted Māori autonomy: *Tama Tū* depicted members of the Māori Battalion as 'soldiers who owed no allegiance to a flag but fought and died in their thousands because they were warriors at heart'.[7] Audiences were also entertained with dramatic films in which trauma was overcome through turangawaewae (belonging) – an appropriate metaphor for Māori Television's emerging position as an interlocutor of national identity.

NITV was set up in 2006 and was initially carried by cable and satellite providers only, along with limited over-the-air transmissions in certain remote areas.[8] Anzac commemoration was not among its 2007 priorities. In the news bulletin producers adhered to familiar content featuring Indigenous art, music, sport and traditional ceremonies, and productions such as the serial *Culture Warriors*.

In 2007 NITV included a series of news reports on the Redfern Black Diggers march, which was first held that year. Black Diggers are the Aboriginal and Torres Strait Islander service personnel who fought in the wars as part of the Australian military.[9] Then in 2008, for the first time, NITV produced a live broadcast from Redfern of the Welcome to Country, a traditional ceremony bringing visitors onto ancestral land, followed by highlights of the march to St Saviour's Church for the closing ecumenical service. The broadcast included six short stories about Indigenous veterans, and featured interviews by reporter Paula Maling and panellist David Huggonson, curator of the 2000 exhibition *Too Dark for the Light Horse*, which told the story of Aboriginal and Torres Strait Islander people who were members of the Australian armed forces. Until this exhibition, the fact that Indigenous Australians had fought in the AIF was virtually unknown, and the depiction of their martial prowess was itself an important and powerful narrative, in stark contrast with the stereotypical images of passive childlike victims of colonialism. Huggonson said of the Redfern march, 'It is very important the younger members of the Aboriginal community and the general Australian public recognise the contribution that the Indigenous population of this country has made to the defence of this nation in every war since the Boer War.'[10]

NITV's focus recalled Glen Stasiuk's *The Forgotten*, which first screened on ABC in 2001. Stasiuk's documentary examined 'the prejudice faced by Indigenous soldiers in the armed forces and the honour they felt representing their nation'.[11] It emphasised the place of Indigenous soldiers in the arena of commemoration in Australia and recounted stories of Indigenous Australians who fought in battles that predated Gallipoli and were linked to resistance against early colonialists.

The Kalkadoon resistance featured prominently as the foundation of this Indigenous military tradition. Located in Queensland, the Kalkadoon Nation fought against colonial forces in the 1880s. The affray culminated in a pitched battle between some 600 warriors surrounded by a heavily armed colonial force in 1884 at Battle Mountain in northern Queensland.[12] In its Anzac Day coverage in the 1990s and 2000s, the *Koori Mail* described 'the spirit of the Kalkadoon' – the writer purposely appropriating the theme of the Anzac spirit – and equated the Kalkadoons at Battle Mountain standing 'in the face of withering fire' to the 'foolhardy but no less heroic attack on the Turks at Anzac Day'.[13] The warriors' heroic action at Battle Mountain 'was in the best Anzac tradition', the author wrote, adding: 'It may be fairer to say that our troops in Gallipoli performed in the best Kalkadoon tradition.'[14]

The celebration of colonial resistance was crucial to the language of *The Forgotten*. According to Stasiuk, Indigenous people had 'displayed … rare courage and fighting qualities' throughout colonial history while 'retaining their culture, identity, and sense of self-worth', and were the foundation of the Indigenous contribution to Australian military expeditions.[15] Given the social conditions and racial discrimination that Aboriginal people experience, this story of a military tradition predating Gallipoli was significant.[16]

The 2005 and 2006 Māori Television broadcasts also referred to earlier documentary work. Key here was *Māori Battalion – March to Victory*, produced by Tainui Stephens and released in 1990 through TVNZ. Interviews and footage from this were used throughout Māori Television's Anzac Day broadcasts and were instrumental in shaping the image and language of Māori remembrance. Stephens had longstanding ties to the Māori media sector and was a co-executive producer of Māori Television when the Anzac Day broadcast won the 2007 Air New Zealand Screen Award for Best Event Broadcast. Reflecting on the making of *March to Victory* in 2013 he noted: 'The Māori Battalion presents us with one of the great stories of our country':

> When we made the documentary we knew we were dealing with a tragic and noble but vital part of our Nation's story. We treated it seriously and aimed beyond recording the mere facts of the war of these men – to trying to capture how they felt about it.[17]

The documentary told the stories of five men who served with the unit and emphasised the role of Sir Āpirana Ngata, the government minister who advocated for the battalion's formation and was thus its koro, or father figure. Ngata argued that Māori involvement in the war effort was 'the ultimate price' for the privilege of imperial citizenship. The price was certainly high: over two-thirds of the 3500-strong battalion were injured or killed, and the impact on postwar Māori communities was enormous. This 'price of citizenship' narrative was reiterated in a number of ways in the all-day broadcasts with their emphasis on family duty, tribal honour and return, but was balanced by the concept of the army as an institution in which Pākehā and Māori worked and fought side by side. *March to Victory* portrayed the battalion volunteers as having originated in a warrior tradition, 'in harmony with the land' and 'trained in the art of war'. Stephens hoped the documentary would help give young Māori a sense of pride in their culture.[18]

Māori Television's programming placed the role of the Māori Battalion Association alongside that of the RSA in the nation's commemorative landscape. RSA president John Campbell was invited to appear at the end of the inaugural 2005 programme and delivered a brief statement congratulating Māori Television on the success of its first full broadcast. Subsequent programming was dedicated to coverage of the association's annual reunion. The president of the Māori Battalion Association also gave an extensive interview, and viewers were offered an explanation of the battalion's structure along tribal allegiances. Images of elderly battalion veterans were overlaid with historical footage of their departure and return to local marae as 'sons of the god of war'. Scenes of veterans weeping at grave sites – 'remembering those who had failed to return' – presented a sympathetic narrative of ageing veterans.[19]

The success of the Māori Battalion Association was twofold: first, it asserted the mana or prestige of battalion members; and second, it included whānau (family members) and iwi at a time when the state was reorganising national cultures of remembrance. By the 2000s, many of the association members marching in parades were in fact family of the original Māori Battalion members. Women seemed to hold a special role in this new remembrance; in 2007 a group of Māori women in Sydney successfully argued to be included in the George Street parade despite strict rules about the participation of non-military personnel, a fact that suggests the Māori Battalion exerted some authority in trans-Tasman Anzac commemoration also. Many women were interviewed as part of the Māori Television coverage, which further enabled viewers to imagine the battalion through the lens of whānau and iwi as much as warriors in a national war effort. The RSA would eventually welcome a broader membership also: it launched its own national association for 'all New Zealanders' in 2014.[20]

Structures of memory: Citizenship and reconciliation in NITV and Māori Television

Māori Television's 2005 and 2006 Anzac Day coverage established the broadcaster globally as a leading Indigenous television media producer. In 2008 the service hosted an international summit of Indigenous media, which members of NITV attended. The Australian network was facing numerous internal changes that would culminate in its relaunch under the SBS in 2012 as a free-to-air channel.[21] Emulating the immense success of the Māori Television broadcast, NITV's commemorative coverage was increasingly framed by the language of reconciliation and citizenship. The reconciliation movement in Australia promoted dialogue and collaboration between Indigenous and non-Indigenous Australians, the recognition of historical wrongs and a commitment to equality and respect.

NITV built on its 2007–08 stories of Indigenous soldiers. 'Anzac Harry Allie', a 2011 episode of the series *Living Black* – a flagship NITV programme – showcased the breadth of Indigenous war experience in Australia.[22] It presented Anzac commemoration as 'a chance to reflect on the Indigenous contribution to Australia's wartime effort', and borrowed the language of Australian remembrance by celebrating those who 'made the ultimate sacrifice for our freedom'.[23] The programme was based on an interview with Allie, an air force warrant officer until his discharge in 1989, in which he described his enlistment as a positive experience linked to family tradition, and his time in the armed forces as an opportunity for self-improvement and friendship. The interview was interspersed with scenes from Indigenous commemorations such as the Redfern Black Diggers march. A mentor of Indigenous youth in later life and one of the organisers of the march, Allie spoke of the importance of Anzac Day as 'a day of equality, especially for our young people, especially for women'.

By 2011 the Indigenous content of NITV's Anzac Day coverage had increased significantly. According to one of the channel's first commissioning editors, Tanya Denning Orman, a Birri and Guugu Yimithirr woman, the intention was 'to ensure the stories of our First Nations were not forgotten in … Australian recognition and commemoration'.[24] Content was providing an Indigenous lens on the day, creating space in the commemorative landscape for Indigenous Australian audiences.

NITV widened its Anzac programming further in 2012, screening documentaries and interviews and general programmes. *Living Black* dedicated a major episode, 'A Spirit Returns', to the theme of Indigenous recognition, and this was accompanied by an episode of *Awaken*, 'The Anzac Legend and Legacy'.[25] Both included interviews with Indigenous people about family members who had served in the world wars. The subject of 'A Spirit Returns' was Frank Archibald, a Gumbaynggirr man who died fighting on the Kokoda Trail in Papua New Guinea during World War II; it recounted his family's efforts to raise funds in order to visit his grave, to bring soil from his tribal lands and perform a traditional smoking ceremony. Frank was the only family member not buried in Australia, and the ceremony would guide his spirit home. The story featured a rehearsal of the ceremony, with Indigenous elder Michael Jarrett reading the ritual words in the Gumbaynggirr language overlaid with an explanation of its significance by NITV reporter Dan Conifer. Indigenous culture and cosmology were foregrounded in the implicit evocation of the Anzac spirit, and wove the language of the dislocation and losses of war with reconciliation through Indigenous ways of being and knowing. The episodes would be replayed in subsequent years and were syndicated online for other news sites.

Programming continued to be framed by themes of reconciliation. *Grow*, in April 2012, for example, framed war remembrance within the aims of the Australian Reconciliation Barometer project, a biennial study of public attitudes towards reconciliation.[26] In 2013, amid calls for the New South Wales state government to build a dedicated memorial to Indigenous Australian soldiers, NITV affirmed Anzac Day as a site of recognition and celebration of a positive self-image for Indigenous peoples.[27] The coverage of their war experiences was one way of acknowledging Indigenous Australians' part in the life of the nation, to 'show that we did actually represent our people and the whole of Australia', as the programme's byline stated. In the NITV rationale, the Anzacs who had founded the nation and its promises of political citizenship through the landings at Gallipoli were not only white; Black Diggers were also founding pioneers, and had paved the way for the recognition and equality of Indigenous peoples. This version of the Anzac story was particularly evident in the 2013 programming, which memorialised Indigenous soldiers fighting for land, culture and country – a reimagining of the mantra 'for God, for King, and for country'.

The 2013 coverage included a replay of *The Forgotten*. The programme guide described how Glen Stasiuk's documentary questioned 'the motives of these Aboriginal soldiers and their experience in the Australian Armed Forces – further exploring that indeed, Aborigines and Islanders showed that the "digger legend" – one of the most profound and positive of Australia's self-images – encompasses black Australians as well'.[28] The approach resonated with NITV viewers. One stated how *The Forgotten* gave Anzac Day 'a whole new meaning': '[As] a proud Aboriginal woman in the twenty-first century, problems are easier to tackle knowing that many brave Indigenous men gave their lives and served to secure a better future for past, future generations and me.' Another, a non-Indigenous viewer, found it 'an exceptional programme at a very appropriate time'.[29]

The use of Anzac to express Indigenous relationships and identity was a central part of later NITV coverage. Family accounts of Indigenous men who returned from wartime physically and mentally broken identified contemporary and historical identity and solidarity as part of a wider struggle for dignity and legal rights by Indigenous peoples in Australia.[30] Despite their role in Australia's security, and the lack of racial discrimination 'in the trenches', these men returned home to disenfranchisement and systemic racism. They were 'the forgotten'. NITV made this language of 'the forgotten' and reconciliation central to its Anzac Day coverage in the lead-up to the Anzac Centenary, and aired *Anzacs: Remembering our heroes*, a documentary about the military efforts of Aboriginal and Torres Strait Islander people who defended the Thursday, Goods and Horn islands, along Australia's northern coastline, the front lines of Australia's defence in World War II.[31]

Speaking at the 2005 dawn service at the unofficial monument to Indigenous military personnel in Canberra, just outside the Australian War Memorial, Indigenous elder Kelton Pell spoke of how, 'even in times of darkness and injustice – even when they could not vote or hold citizenship of their own land – Aborigines fought alongside their comrades of all races and earned a fighting reputation as fine as any Australian'.[32] Newspaper coverage of Black Diggers marches also included this language of equality: 'Anzac Day means a great deal, not only for those people who gave their lives for our freedom,' one veteran stated, 'but hopefully in the future it will also have a unifying effect by bringing more of our veterans and their families forward to take their rightful place.' Another said that going to war 'gave me equality with my non-Indigenous colleagues and I was recognised as a citizen of Australia'.[33]

Reflecting in 2016 on the development of coverage over the decade, NITV presenter Luke Briscoe stated, 'It is widely understood that Anzac Day signifies what it is to be an Australian … but if Australia is to achieve reconciliation, the nation needs to recognise the roles played by Indigenous Anzacs in those events.' NITV's commemorative programming and online content was 'paying tribute to the military efforts of the Indigenous peoples of Australia', bringing to light forgotten stories of 'Black Anzacs' and, through programmes such as *Awaken*, examining the sacrifices of Aboriginal and Torres Strait Islander servicemen and women. Briscoe concluded that the coverage was 'a burning reminder that Australia still needs to pays its formal respects to the Indigenous Anzacs'.[34]

Stories of the Māori Battalion connected Māori Television to narratives of state-building around Anzac. Both Māori Television – an outcome of the Treaty partnership and recognition of te reo as a taonga or prized treasure – and the Māori Battalion – a unique institution of Indigenous recruitment in both world wars – were the result of the place of Māori in the constitutional life of the nation. Different threads of memory and identity were being woven into the Anzac revival.

The centrality of the Māori Battalion Association in Māori Television's inaugural broadcasts did not pass without criticism: some viewers considered the emphasis to be an overstatement of Māori involvement. As one online commentator put it, 'The only problem with the Māori Television coverage is that they think the Māori Battalion won the war on their own.'[35] Others noted omissions and limitations of the coverage, saying the celebration of the Māori Battalion Association obscured the fact that returning Māori soldiers were denied land under soldier settlement schemes and were subject to assimilationist government policies, and the ways in which many iwi had faced persecution and imprisonment for refusing to join the war effort.[36] These difficult narratives were submerged beneath the construct of a unified nation. Historian Danny Keenan was disappointed by Māori Television's enthusiasm for its Anzac Day broadcast in 2006, arguing, 'New Zealand did not come of age on the beaches of Gallipoli; it came of age on our own battlefields, like Rangiriri. The war that mattered – that forged the nation we are today – was fought on our own soil.'[37]

Subsequent documentaries focused on the battalion's four companies. Produced in consecutive years, each programme gave a brief history of one company along with interviews from surviving members, and drew on the voices of whānau and communities to explore the impact of having so many of their menfolk go off to war. Stories of each soldier's tūrangawaewae or place of belonging articulated Māori as tangata whenua. Historical continuity was established with *Te Hokowhitu a Tū* in 2008. The 2009 and 2012 programming focused on D Company, known as Ngāti Walkabout; in 2010 *Ngā Morehu Hoia o Te Rua Tekau mā Waru* depicted the reunion of A Company, 'the Gumdiggers', at Ōrākei; and *Hitler and the Gumdiggers* (2010), directed and produced by Tainui Stephens, explored Ngāpuhi stories.[38] In 2014 *Ngā Uri o Ruku te Kapa* focused on B Company, 'the Penny Divers'.[39] In the same year *Te Marutuna o te Tangata: The Commanders* connected the battalion to the approaching centenary through the fact that its leaders began their military careers during World War I.[40]

At the centre of the 2013 broadcast was *The Final Hui: 28th Battalion Association*, a Māori Television report on the association's hui (meeting) in December 2012.[41] With the number of surviving veterans dwindling, the decision was made to wind up the association, and its symbol of leadership, a greenstone mere or club, was ceremonially entrusted to the Waiōuru Army Museum. In an assertive claim of spiritual ownership of a sacred site of Anzac commemoration, the formal closure of the association took place at the National War Memorial in front of the Tomb of the Unknown Warrior.

Warriors still: Alternative histories

As well as exploring European theatres of war, Māori Television ran stories about the war in the Pacific. The 2009 broadcast examined the NZEF expedition to capture German Sāmoa in the Great War, and through this the Māori Pioneer Battalion, which had around 50 Samoan members, became a framework for understanding relations between Māori and Pasifika people.[42] Segments of the programme also looked at the 600 or so volunteers from Tonga, Niue and Rarotonga who joined the war effort. The broadcast bypassed traditional scholarship that struggled to incorporate diverse experiences of war and home fronts. In Māori Television's coverage, these men were New Zealanders with Pasifika, Māori and Pākehā identity.

In 2011 Māori Television screened the documentary *Ngā Toa o Te Moana-Nui-A-Kiwa: Warriors of the Pacific*, which focused on the battle between Allied troops and the Japanese in the Solomon Islands.[43] Paramount chief of Mono Island John Goldie spoke at length on the impact of the occupation of the Solomon Islands, and suggested the arrival of New Zealand troops helped to forge a close relationship between the people of New Zealand and Mono Island, a 'sharing of blood' in a common Pasifika history. Contemporary NZDF troops stationed in the Solomon Islands as part of the 2003–17 Regional Assistance Mission to the Solomon Islands, Operation Helpem Fren, were described as 'a new generation of New Zealand soldiers' sharing in this Pacific lineage.[44]

Unlike Pākehā representations of the RSA, which tended to privilege soldiers' stories over those of family, the Māori Battalion Association provided a space in which to situate the stories of women and families. In *Amoiha Te Mauri*, literally

‘Uphold the legacy’, veterans’ interviews were followed by discussions with whānau, including daughters and granddaughters.[45] *Morēna Whānau* in 2014 emphasised soldiers’ familial and social ties, and in 2015 showcased an interview with Hinemoa Awatere, editor of *Awatere: A soldier’s story*, her grandfather’s biography about family and the legacies of war and trauma.[46] *The Black Legacy* (2014) depicted Māori singer Whirimako Black’s journey to Monte Cassino to understand the battle in which her father fought, and which affected him profoundly, both physically and mentally. The documentary, which the family called ‘a journey of discovery of our father’, explored the way his experience with the battalion shaped his character as a father and grandfather.[47]

This focus on whānau was a feature also of *Ngarimu VC* (1993), about the life of battalion member Te-Moananui-a-Kiwa Ngārimu, a Ngāti Porou and Te Whānau-ā-Apanui soldier and the first Māori to be awarded the Victoria Cross. The documentary screened as part of the 2013 broadcast, and told of his childhood on the East Coast, his enlistment and leadership.[48] A second segment followed, ‘The Whānau Remembers’, which contained footage from 1993 interviews with Ngārimu’s sisters recalling the brother ‘who never came home’.[49]

The broadening of war memory also extended to narratives of violence preceding World War I. At the 150th anniversary of the Battle of Gate Pā, one of the last conflicts of the Waikato-Tauranga war, Governor-General Jerry Mateparae acknowledged the New Zealand Wars ‘as an integral part of this nation’s story’, saying the qualities of ‘the Anzac spirit’ – courage, commitment, comradeship and compassion – were equally applicable to the battle at Gate Pā: ‘In years to come, as we give greater acknowledgement to the conflicts which occurred within New Zealand … sites like Pukehinahina … will also come to embody the quality of our national esteem – our collective mana – and have a greater meaning for all New Zealanders.’[50] Mateparae’s connection between Anzac and the colonial wars was indicative of the shared public languages of remembrance that had been crafted through Māori Television’s Anzac Day coverage.

The 2015 centenary broadcast was anchored in two documentaries. The first, *Ngā Rā o Hune: The Days of June*, told the story of Waikato-Maniapoto men arrested for resisting conscription during World War I. The second, *Shovels and Guns*, was the culmination of 10 years of Māori Television’s Anzac Day broadcasts.[51] Narrated by historian Monty Soutar, it depicted the experience of the Māori contingent at Gallipoli. These documentaries represented the progression of Māori Television’s Anzac Day coverage, from tentative support for the Anzac project to the assertion of an Indigenous space within the narrative of 'the price of citizenship', and took a particularly Māori form of remembrance: the spiral of past, present and future was connected, backwards, to wars of settlement and World War I, and forwards, to shaping the national future.

This coverage shows the potential for Indigenous media coverage to ascribe new meanings to Anzac Day, and indicates one of the central paradoxes of increased Indigenous participation in Anzac commemoration, what Brendan Hokowhitu calls 'the condition of being postcolonial' – the problems for Indigenous media entities of producing an Indigenous world-view with state funding.[52] Tensions unfolded in the NITV coverage between stories of colonial violence and state structures of commemoration. In its role as national broadcaster, NITV's coverage of these themes was both important – enhanced precisely by its status as 'national' – and fraught, situated as it was in the political economy of SBS and federal government funding. Programmers handled this carefully. In the 2011 and 2012 broadcasts, for example, documentaries about the Frontier Wars were purposely screened once the official Anzac Day programming was finished, as a way of placing colonial violence outside of the space of Anzac coverage and therefore outside of the structures of state commemoration and memory. NITV and its cultural stories operated in 'silences' of Australian Anzac commemoration and historical configurations of the country as terra nullius. To the Indigenous way of thinking, the Australian nation was enclosed within country. As librarian and essayist Nathan Sentance observes, Aboriginal notions of country extend beyond territoriality to encompass sky, land, sea, seasons, creation spirits and stories encompassing past, present and future.[53]

One programme in 2014 examined dissent and disruption among Indigenous communities during wartime, such as the story of Guugu Yimithirr people of North Queensland, who were forcibly removed from their land during World War II. However, NITV's publicity for its Anzac Centenary programming did not refer to the Frontier Wars as part of its coverage; instead, it focused on 'Australia's military efforts in every war Australia has fought in [from] 1901 to 2015'. NITV had never before defined such a specific boundary to its commemoration broadcast.

This challenge was apparent in NITV's coverage of the annual Frontier Wars march along Anzac Parade in Canberra. After filming confrontations between police and march participants, NITV journalist Myles Morgan was harassed by ACT police.[54] Upon discovering Morgan's affiliation, officers on duty accused Morgan of failing to provide the 'fair and equitable coverage' required by Australian taxpayers. In their eyes, remembering the Frontier Wars on Anzac Day apparently fell short of what was fair and equitable.

*

The collision of Indigenous and state-centred stories of war in NITV programming is at the heart of the trade-off in state-funded Indigenous media participation in Anzac commemoration. The political culture of Anzac commemoration comes with constraints that are both narrative and – as police actions at the Canberra march suggest – physical. This coercion demarcates what is considered official and what is heterodoxical; what is 'fair and equitable coverage' when it comes to Anzac Day; what, in effect, supports the narrative of pride and celebration and what does not. As a site of recognition and reconciliation, Anzac Day is an incomplete re-founding of a nation. As historian Geoffrey White notes, representing war history as a national memory is likely to be an unstable and unfinished process, as 'unfinished histories' of militarism, empire and sacrifice jostle alongside one another.[55] This instability is a constitutive element of a national cultural memory: an instability and open-endedness evident in Indigenous media coverage of the Anzac revival.

Māori Television and NITV's Anzac Day programming in the years 2005–15 accommodated shared memories that were not simply limited to nationhood. They expressed the Anzac spirit in local, family, tribal and imperial contexts, redrawing geographies of memory through connections to Asia and the Pacific; giving space to families and women's voices; and suggesting deeper histories of colonial violence and traditions of remembrance that were distinctly Indigenous. Both asserted an Indigenous presence and, in doing so, reshaped the public space of Anzac commemoration.

Chapter 8

'The maintenance of memory'

National myth and the Anzac Centenary, 2015

In marking the Anzac Centenary, the Australian federal government outspent any other country; and although on a smaller scale, New Zealand's centenary programme – WW100 – was still the largest commemoration in the country's history.[1] On both sides of the Tasman the public assent given to these projects evinced the seismic transformation of Anzac Day since 1965. But what was remarkable about the centenary programmes was not so much the two governments' orchestration of a diplomatic commemorative event but the way the remembrance made claims on history, memory and culture through an array of heritage projects, while rendering these actions as apolitical.

It is useful to consider the centenary as part of a continuum rather than a stand-alone event. The 75th, 90th and 100th anniversaries of Gallipoli can be understood as stages in the reconfiguration of the Anzac nation, each one reinforcing the role of the Prime Minister's Office in orchestrating commemoration. The proposition in 1990 that the 75th anniversary was a 'once-in-a-lifetime opportunity', as stated in the Australian commemorative programme, now seems quaint in light of the extraordinary financial and political commitment made for the centenary on both sides of the Tasman.[2]

According to Australia's Anzac Centenary Advisory Board, the role of the federal government was to 'ensure that the Anzac Centenary is commemorated in a very special way' that reflected 'the values and qualities that [Australians] link inextricably to the name, "Anzac"'.[3] The government orchestrated educational and cultural programmes totalling some $325m of state and federal tax funding, and a dedicated federal Anzac Centenary minister oversaw all expenditure.[4] The centenary was 'not simply about what happened a hundred years ago, as if it were past and gone': rather, '[Australians] fought then on a global scale to defend the values we shared with many other nations and this commitment continues today.'[5] The Anzac Centenary was as much about Australia in 2015 as a memorial to the dead.

In New Zealand close to $15m was distributed through Creative New Zealand and New Zealand on Air for hundreds of centenary-themed cultural productions, including plays, exhibitions and television programmes.[6] Local government provided hundreds of thousands of dollars' for commemorative projects, and the Lottery Grants Board allocated another $17m. The $120m expansion of the National War Memorial precinct within Pukeahu National War Memorial Park was the government's largest project, and the Auckland Cenotaph database was digitised at a cost of $330,000.

Although the official centenary spanned four years from 2014 to 2018, most of the projects reached the public in 2014 and 2015 – 'a very condensed time frame to see hundreds of war-related cultural works', as journalist Michelle Duff observed.[7] Carolyn Holbrook argues that despite some evidence of 'Gallipoli fatigue', the popular engagement with the day continued to suggest the public had a profound attachment to Anzac mythology.[8] Above all, the centenary commemorations pointed to the narrow script that had emerged around Anzac, and the place of Gallipoli as the foundation of this national myth. When the two countries' commemorative programmes are placed side by side, however, the deeper patterns, convergences and disparities in the politics of commemoration in 2015 become apparent.

The spirit of Anzac: Pundits, critics and revisionists in the Anzac Centenary

The dawn service at Anzac Cove in 2015 was the emotional epicentre of the centenary commemorations. Prime Ministers Tony Abbott and John Key, British royalty and 10,000 pilgrims of all ages attended the service in person, while hundreds of thousands of Australians and New Zealanders watched and listened at home.

The Anzac Cove event was shared somewhat unevenly between the two countries. The audience was entertained with a programme framed by references to Charles Bean's letters, despatches and diary entries, interspersed with government-funded documentaries celebrating the Royal Australian Navy and other Australian contributions. It had all the hallmarks of the influence of the Australian War Memorial and the project, begun by Inglis in 1965, of recovering Bean as 'the Australian historian'.[9]

The New Zealand government's contribution was decidedly different. The haka, banned by Turkish authorities in 2005, was reintroduced into the proceedings. The 1984 documentary *Gallipoli: The New Zealand story* was taken off a dusty shelf at New Zealand Sound Archives Ngā Taonga Sound and Vision and segments played before the dawn service. The dated footage of Leonard Thornton in his tweed jacket paled in comparison to the slickness of the Australian production: a quiet voice attempting to claim a small space against an avalanche of colourful new Australian cultural productions.

The Australian hype was not without its critics and revisionists, however. A 2013 editorial in the *Australian*, directed at the federal centenary commission as it prepared to draw up plans for the commemorative period, exhorted them to 'ignore the tortured arguments of the intellectuals and listen to the people, the true custodians of this occasion'. The committee should acknowledge that 'the current intellectual zeitgeist is at odds with the spirit of Anzac' and recognised neither the significance of the war nor the patriotism it inspired. The national values of 'honour, duty and mateship are foreign to their thinking': 'They may be experts on many things, but on the subject of Anzac, they have little useful to say.'[10]

There was a cadre of historians ready to critique the commemoration after the event. Rather than threatening the anniversary, however, any polemic by academic historians only reinforced its significance. The annual conference of the Australian Historical Association in 2015 interrogated foundational histories such as the one offered at Anzac Cove, and swathes of the proceedings were dedicated to revising the Anzac myth.[11] Plenary speaker British historian Peter Mandler confessed he was perplexed by the sheer scale of academic commentary offered on the Anzac revival; he knew of no other national body of historians who spent so much time talking about one topic.[12] Across the Tasman, where no editorials shrilled with tortured intellectual arguments, the New Zealand Historical Association conference in November was a smaller affair. Historians appeared to be more interested in the 800th anniversary of the Magna Carta than the WW100 programme.[13]

In the end there was little public dissent about the centenary commemoration plans – with a few exceptions. In 2015, in a last-ditch attempt to control the commemoration and contend with the vast tidal flow of public ownership of 25 April, the Melbourne RSL decided to limit the number of descendants of World War I veterans marching in the Anzac Day parade, out of fear that the tiny contingent of veterans themselves might be swamped.[14] The following year, in protest, an alternative march was organised for excluded families; organisers voiced the hope that this would eventually replace the RSL march.[15]

Later in the commemorative period, a small silent vigil was held at the Wellington citizens' memorial on Anzac Day 2017 to highlight the killing of civilians by New Zealand special forces operating in Afghanistan in 2003, which had recently come to the public's attention. The protesters were confronted by a 12-year-old boy, who shouted that Anzac Day was not the day for such action.[16] Footage of this went viral, and a subsequent online poll on the *AM Show* suggested two-thirds of listeners agreed with the boy and believed protesting on Anzac Day was 'inappropriate'.[17] It seemed the formative history of protest on Anzac Day was long forgotten.

A massive exhibition titled *Gallipoli: The scale of our war* was unveiled at the Museum of New Zealand Te Papa Tongarewa in 2015. With an $8m price tag, *Gallipoli* was the centrepiece of the WW100 programme, designed to create a 'heightened awareness' of New Zealand's experience during the war and 'leave a lasting and impactful memory of this most important of events in New Zealand's history'.[18] A joint venture between Te Papa and renowned special-effects company Weta Workshop, the exhibition told the story of the NZEF during the Gallipoli campaign through eight historical figures, chosen for the letters, diaries and photographs they left behind.[19] Visitors walking through the exhibition encountered giant realistic models, 2.4 times life-size, in cameo scenes in dimly lit spaces. Each scene offered a snapshot of the Gallipoli experience and was accompanied by an array of visual, textual and spatial narratives, including a specially composed soundtrack and interactive multimedia platforms.[20]

As the title of Te Papa's *Gallipoli* suggested, the exhibition collapsed the wider 1914–18 war into the 1915 campaign while also reflecting the new national language – Gallipoli was 'our war'. In concept and practice, the exhibition was a twenty-first-century 'New Zealand story'; it assembled multi-textual, theatrical and cinematic elements in New Zealand's leading cultural institution to achieve what Australian creative and institutional networks had in the 1980s at the Australian War Memorial. Drawing on Peter Weir's 1981 film, Weta Workshop artists used the tragic slaughter of young men to form the exhibition's emotional narrative, and the digital artwork offered a pastiche of 1980s imagery.[21] The publicity image of a New Zealand officer in a classic 'lemon squeezer' hat emphasised national iconography and echoed Shadbolt's *Once on Chunuk Bair*. Indeed, Chunuk Bair formed the dramatic climax of the exhibition: this was 'our place', as invoked by the men in Shadbolt's play. William Malone VC was, once again, a crucial component in this myth-making: his Quinn's Post bunker was recreated in the exhibition and his diaries were narrated by a voice actor. This was Malone as Shadbolt's Connolly, selectively trimmed of his religious and imperial loyalties. Like the writers and researchers of the earlier exhibition, *Gallipoli: The New Zealand story*, in the absence of a centralised national war collection the exhibition designers literally manufactured their own.[22]

The exhibition's historical director, Chris Pugsley, adapted his book *Gallipoli*, with its interpretations of a war experience that forged New Zealand's nationhood after empire, as part of the exhibition's narrative, and reproduced his work in digital models of the peninsula and Chunuk Bair. Gallipoli was a foundational place of nationhood and the basis of Pugsley's argument, advanced in 1984, that although 'we did not even consciously go to war as New Zealanders', the experience of Gallipoli 'established a reputation and a sense of identity that is important to … who we are'.[23] This was a repudiation of Inglis' assertion (itself an echo of Bean) that New Zealanders were 'colourless' and without nationalism. Rather than being one among many contested historical interpretations, 'our war' was an absolute claim on national memory. 'This exhibition,' Pugsley proclaimed, 'will determine how New Zealanders remember the Gallipoli campaign for the twenty-first century.'[24]

The Te Papa exhibition became a focal point for other creative projects.[25] One, the animated film *25 April* (2015) directed by Leanne Pooley and produced by Matthew Metcalfe, was in essence a cinematic adaptation of the exhibition. In a *Metro* interview Metcalfe noted that he needed 'at least a couple of … characters to be at Chunuk Bair': 'In terms of New Zealand, it was the most important battle: we actually mark 8 August [when the troops arrived at Chunuk Bair] as a really important date here, rather than the day of the landing.'[26] Metcalfe's claim echoed the creative trend started by Shadbolt in which Chunuk Bair was represented as a moment of national birth. The handful of New Zealand veterans at the 1965 pilgrimage who escaped the Australian-dominated itinerary to visit the Chunuk Bair memorial would no doubt have approved.

Gallipoli, with its giant models like synthetic versions of the repatriated Unknown Warrior, transformed Te Papa into a figurative war memorial. Almost a million visitors passed through the exhibition in the first 12 months, making it the most successful in the museum's history – so successful that it was extended until at least 2022.[27] Te Papa became a kind of 'Anzac Mecca' for New Zealanders in the way the Australian War Memorial had for Australians in the 1990s. There were tensions between different myths: Pugsley reduced the number of Māori figures in the exhibition to reflect the statistical presence of Māori soldiers in the 1915 campaign, while curators argued that Te Papa's commitment to biculturalism required an equal balance of Māori and non-Māori.[28]

In Canberra the Australian War Memorial chose a 'centenary experience' as the flagship community event of the federal centenary programme. *Spirit of Anzac Centenary Experience* was a touring exhibition that took the work of national remembrance to communities across Australia through a mix of visual displays, artefacts, audio, film and curated local histories.[29] Any sense that the Australian War Memorial might have missed out on the spotlight during the commemorative period was dispelled when, in 2018, the federal government committed an eye-watering $498m for a nine-year revitalisation of the precinct. The institution had been named the seventeenth most-visited tourist site in the world, ahead of icons such as the Sydney Opera House and Uluru/Ayers Rock.[30]

Frontiers of memory: New monuments, memorials and museums

In New Zealand a reversal of priorities took place. The designation of Waitangi Day as a major commemoration theoretically gave it equal importance with Anzac Day. The year 2015 was also the 175th anniversary of the signing of the Treaty, the 150th anniversary of which, organised by the 1990 Waitangi Commission, had been marked by fervent and sometimes volatile debate. In 1990 the governor-general and RSA had taken care of the civic duties of the 75th anniversary of Gallipoli. Now, in 2015, public attention was trained on Gallipoli and the WW100 programme instead, and Governor-General Jerry Mateparae was left to oversee the official Waitangi commemoration.

'Waitangi 175' rehashed the 150th logo and offered a calendar of events that centred on Mateparae's visit – the first by a governor-general since 1840 – to Māngungu, site of the largest Treaty signing event.[31] In his Waitangi Day speech, in a clear echo of the language of 'the price of citizenship' mediated through Māori Television over the previous decade, Mateparae acknowledged the irresistible pull of the Gallipoli centenary and reflected on 'the responsibilities and obligations of citizenship – in addition to the rights and privileges that we all enjoy'.[32] In a twenty-first-century amendment to the celebrations, for the first time ever the ceremonies at Waitangi were live-streamed in the way of Māori Television's Anzac Day broadcasts.[33] But even the emphasis on debate about the Treaty claims process through the 'Talk

Treaty' project, in which prominent Māori and non-Māori New Zealanders spoke candidly about what Te Tiriti meant for them, could not elevate the anniversary to the levels reached by the Anzac Centenary.[34] On this occasion, commemoration of the signing of the Treaty of Waitangi was relegated to the back seat.

This shift in state priorities was also expressed in the expansion of the National War Memorial into Pukeahu National War Memorial Park. The alterations would make room for a commemorative site to accommodate monuments to New Zealanders' wartime allies, similar to the cluster of memorials in Canberra's Anzac Parade and those at Hyde Park, London. The first monument to be established, the federally financed Australian memorial, was intended as a twin to the New Zealand Memorial in Canberra and represented 'the deeds of the Anzacs and our most important relationship in war and in peace', as Prime Minister John Key stated in his dedication address.[35] Designed by Tonkin Zulaikha Greer, the architectural firm that installed the unknown Australian soldier in 1993 and the Australian War Memorial in London in 2004, it comprised a number of carved red sandstone pillars invoking the Australian landscape. In dedicating the memorial in the week before the centenary, Key delivered a speech replete with tropes of the trans-Tasman friendship: 'The Anzac spirit has been defined in many ways – mateship, courage, integrity – but what it means in practice is that we can knuckle down and work together anywhere from a solid foundation of mutual trust.'[36] The memorial's construction had not been without controversy. The sandstone representing 'the red heart of Australia' was in fact sourced from Agra, India, as a cheaper alternative to Australian rock. The Anzac bond came at a price that, according to some visitors, was 'wrecking the narrative' of the memorial.[37]

The redevelopment at Pukeahu was telling in other ways. In 2014, in an effort to avoid a re-hash of the 2003 debate about the heritage value of the site, the government passed emergency legislation to 'expedite the building of the National War Memorial Park'.[38] The National War Memorial Park (Pukeahu) Empowering Bill bulldozed the planning safeguards that had been a source of contention 12 years earlier, and removed the right to object and appeal under the Resource Management Act, the Historic Places Trust Act and the Public Works Act. Among others, historian Rachel Buchanan queried the government's unseemly haste, noting that New Zealanders might have expected to have 'plenty of time to prepare, very carefully, for the planning, design and construction of a beautiful, sophisticated, challenging war memorial that showed sensitivity to the military history of the significant piece of Māori land' on which it would be built.[39] Instead, the emergency powers obviated public discussion; there was barely enough time even for the RSA to express moral support.[40] The intervention was a flexing of political muscle by a state firmly in control of Anzac commemoration, and the fact that there was little public outcry indicates the changing custodianship of Anzac Day.

Although focused mainly on Gallipoli, the Anzac Centenary also included commemoration of the Western Front and other theatres of war. The Australian federal government announced its next commemorative project the day after the centenary dawn service. The Sir John Monash Centre would be a massive expansion of the Australian National Memorial at Villers-Bretonneux, a French war cemetery containing the graves of some 40,000 Australian World War I soldiers. The centre would form the hub of the Australian Remembrance Trail that ran through France and Belgium, and would, as Prime Minister Abbott announced, tell 'the whole story of Australia's part in the Allied victory here on the Western Front'.[41] Abbott was completing the work of his Liberal predecessor John Howard, whose government originally proposed the new centre in 2005.[42]

Questions were immediately asked about the AUD$100m budgeted for the centre, the lion's share of which would come from the federal defence budget rather than the Department of Veterans' Affairs. As historian David Stephens pointed out, the expenditure set a new precedent: nowhere in the world had a commemorative project of this magnitude been budgeted for by a defence ministry.[43] One French journalist politely commented that the centre 'proposes a very Australian version of the war'.[44] The new director of the Australian War Memorial, former politician Brendan Nelson, defended the focus and the expense; the centre was 'a great engineering feat', he said, adding: 'Anyone who thinks that World War I, and what the diggers did, doesn't have anything to do with us today really needs to re-examine what it means to them to be an Australian … Young people in particular will be energised by the creative use of technology to bring the story to life.'[45] Like Te Papa's *Gallipoli* exhibition, the Monash Centre offered an immersive 'enhanced interpretation' of the war, in this case through 'a cinematic barrage of light, gunfire, grenades and re-enactments of bloody conflict'.[46] It was, in the view of one writer, 'an exemplar for other nations to follow and from which other museums might learn something about the maintenance of memory'.[47]

Perhaps not to be outdone as the Sir John Monash Centre was opened by Australian Prime Minister Malcolm Turnbull to enormous media attention, in 2018 the New Zealand government purchased a former mayoral residence in Le Quesnoy, France, to be renovated as an interpretive centre for its own commemorative trail,

Ngā Tapuwae.[48] Former Prime Minister Helen Clark was invited to become the new museum's patron and, in terms similar to Nelson's appeal to youth, expressed the desire to 'make sure those stories of young New Zealanders who travelled to the other side of the world a century ago are passed on to future generations'.[49] With a smaller budget, this time from the Ministry of Culture and Heritage, New Zealand's museum was considerably less showy than the Monash Centre but nonetheless spoke to a perennial theme in the history of Anzac commemoration: where Australian remembrance leads, New Zealand follows.

The international arena of the commemoration was apparent when, in the lead-up to the centenary dawn service, the Australian and New Zealand governments announced that the two nations would engage in a joint military training mission in Iraq to help the Iraqi army fight Islamic State (ISIS).[50] Once again the Anzacs at Gallipoli were linked with the contemporary defence forces as Prime Ministers Abbott and Key affirmed their wish 'to ensure Australia and New Zealand's unique shared heritage and Anzac legacy is used as a catalyst for further cooperation, peace-building and the promotion of democracy, human rights and the rule of law into the future'.[51] Previous trans-Tasman military cooperation in Afghanistan, East Timor and the Solomon Islands was said to have 'kept faith with the original Anzacs'.[52] John Blaxland of the Strategic and Defence Studies Centre at the Australian National University noted the irresistible pathos in the idea that the centenary would see 'the great-grandsons of Anzac involved as bit-players in a fight against a Middle-Eastern supposed caliphate'.[53] Although no substantial intervention against Islamic State eventuated, the emotional and rhetorical power of a modern Anzac military expedition to the Middle East, set against the backdrop of the centenary programmes, was descriptive of the Anzac revival. The political sanction and acceptance of war experience was linked to the very foundations of nationhood. The 'sons [and daughters] of the Anzacs' in the modern defence forces were intertwined with Australian and New Zealand identity, the relationship between the two nations, and the projection of their roles on the international stage.

Indigenous commemoration was also woven into the fabric of the centenary. In Australia various productions and ceremonies promoted the legacy of Black Diggers, and NSW Governor David Hurley attended the official Redfern march.[54] In 2014 the Queensland Theatre Company performed *Black Diggers* by Tom Wright, directed by Wesley Enoch.[55] In an interview with Nancy Haxton on the ABC Radio programme *PM*, Enoch stated:

> There's sometimes a forgetting, a very convenient forgetting of what Indigenous Australians have done, and I think World War I is one of those things when we have this commemoration to say, in fact this nation has been a very diverse nation for a very long time ... I know we look back and we think of our mythology as a very white Anglo-Saxon mythology, but in fact it's always diverse and we've been conveniently forgetting that.[56]

Like forgotten warriors, Black Diggers operated as a shibboleth for the reconciliation of Australian nationhood through the recovery of Indigenous war experiences and relationships. In March 2015 the first memorial dedicated to Aboriginal and Torres Strait Islander men and women in the Australian Defence Force was unveiled in Sydney's Hyde Park. The sculpture, *Yininmadyemi – Thou Didst Let Fall* was designed by Aboriginal artist Tony Albert and depicted seven bullet cases, four standing and three on their sides. Although some criticised the design's militancy, it was nonetheless an important statement of recognition in Australia's Anzac nationhood.

This public acknowledgement of Indigenous involvement was supported with investment by the academy: 'Serving Our Country: A history of Aboriginal and Torres Strait Islander people in the defence of Australia', a four-year Australia Research Council project, documented the historical contributions of Aboriginal and Torres Strait Islander people in the Australian defence and auxiliary services from the Boer War to 2000.[57]

The exhibition *For Country, For Nation*, which explored stories of Indigenous war experience from pre-colonial times to the present, opened at the Australian War Memorial.[58] Given the institution's long and complex history in relation to Indigenous representation, the exhibition was significant and suggested 'a willingness to tell a deeper story about Australia's frontier past'.[59] A number of artworks, stories and artefacts offered the possibility of national reconciliation between Indigenous and non-Indigenous Australians. Army reservist Gareth O'Connell stated that there was continuity between the Frontier Wars and the role of Indigenous soldiers in Australia's overseas wars; Anzac was 'a modern incarnation of that spirit in defending our country'.[60]

These cultural productions around Indigenous war experience, especially the exhibition, offered new iterations of the Anzac story – but within the confines of the state. As Federica Caso observed in her political analysis of the exhibition, although 'the inclusion of Indigenous soldiers in official war commemorations is a sign of Indigenous resurgence and recognition, as long as the Memorial refuses to include the Frontier Wars, this recognition legitimises colonial authority'.[61]

Foundational myths and the quicksand of public memory

The annual Redfern Anzac Day Aboriginal and Torres Strait Islander Black Diggers March in 2015 was the largest in the event's seven-year history. Thousands of Indigenous and non-Indigenous Australians lined the streets of the Sydney suburb, and NITV journalists interviewed military personnel, veterans and their relatives and streamed stories around the nation. Many spoke of their pride at having Indigenous diggers, 'those who were often forgotten when they returned home from war', recognised by the public.[62] Lance Corporal Natalie Whyte, serving with the Royal Australian Army Ordnance Corps, was pleased to see Anzac remembrance galvanising the local community, saying, 'The march ... gets everyone of all types together ... the day has grown from the Indigenous perspective.'[63] Redfern resident Ebony Allen said the event offered her a way to better connect with her Indigenous heritage: 'The march is really important for the community because there are not many things out there that specifically look at the contributions of Aboriginal and Torres Strait Islander servicemen and women during the war.'[64]

Black Diggers and forgotten warriors pointed to the impasse of Anzac memory: the names provided symbolic recognition of Indigenous involvement, but because they were claimed within the broader Anzac story, these symbols could hardly undermine the national remembrance of Gallipoli. In fact, the inclusion of Indigenous stories lent the legacy of 1915 greater credibility as a moment of national unity.

The following year Māori Television launched its latest programming theme, *Nō Tātou te Toto/The Blood We Share*, stating, 'It's been 101 years since blood was spilled at Gallipoli, but for Māori Television that blood has provided the foundation for a new campaign to show the war is a history all of Aotearoa shares, despite our own personal histories.'[65] *Nō Tātou te Toto* was emblematic of the way Māori media had become established as a purveyor of Anzac memory and collective belonging.

*

The festive atmosphere of the centenary period belied a deeper constitutional turmoil in the Australian state. In December 2015 a parliamentary committee was appointed to oversee bipartisan collaboration for a referendum on the recognition, in the preface of the federal constitution, of Indigenous Australians. The council, comprising both Indigenous and non-Indigenous community leaders, struggled to achieve consensus.

The Frontier Wars remembrance march in Canberra, 25 April 2015, organised by the Indigenous Australian group Lest We Forget the Frontier Wars. Aboriginal and Torres Strait Island activists have established a tradition of commemorating the Frontier Wars on Anzac Day despite the lack of support from authorities. Photo: Michael Anderson

Several months later a convention of Indigenous elders met at Uluru and released the *Uluru Statement from the Heart* (2017), which made a plea for a different national collective memory to that offered at the Anzac Centenary.[66] Belonging, for Indigenous peoples, was 'a spiritual notion' linked to ancestral claims of sovereignty over an ancient land rather than to the fruit of military violence in 1915. *The Uluru Statement* asserted the need for a constitutional voice for Indigenous Australians within the structures of federal law-making, and for a process of 'makarrata'.[67] From the Yolngu word meaning 'conflict resolution, peacemaking and justice' and 'a coming together after a struggle', makarrata was intended to capture the aspiration for 'a fair and truthful relationship with the people of Australia'. With the establishment of a 'Makarrata Commission' to 'supervise a process of agreement-making between governments and First Nations', the beginning of a new foundational story might be possible.

The federal committee established to respond to the statement recommended, as part of this process of makarrata or treaty-making, that the Australian government undertake to repatriate from overseas and domestic institutions all ancestral remains of Aboriginal people and Torres Strait Islanders taken by Europeans during colonisation; and that the government consider the establishment, in Canberra, of a national resting place of commemoration, healing and reflection for any that could not be linked to a particular community.[68] This spiritual return to the nation's capital, akin to the repatriation of the unknown Australian soldier, suggested a willingness to rework the foundations of the federal state to include Indigenous sovereign claims.[69] Indigenous Australians, it was hoped, would be counted in the ranks of the Anzacs as Black Diggers and also heard as the constitutional heart of the Australian state.

In New Zealand, where the Treaty of Waitangi had been largely sidelined in 2015, stories of military conflicts on New Zealand's own territory during the nineteenth century featured in Māori Television's programme of documentaries. A decade after historian Danny Keenan's attack on Māori Television's ostensible capitulation to the myth of Gallipoli as the birthplace of the nation, Vincent O'Malley published his seminal history of the Waikato War, *The Great War for New Zealand*. The title, a paraphrase of the words of Māori rangatira Wiremu Tāmihana in 1865, invoked the spectre of World War I and proposed a new layer to New Zealand's national memory of war. 'My point is not that we shouldn't be marking the First World War,' O'Malley wrote:

> Of course we should. Remembering the Great War does not, in itself, make us forget the New Zealand Wars. Neither is it a question of creating some kind of equivalence between the two wars. The Waikato conflict was important for its own reasons and in its own ways. It was different from the 'total war' that came to characterise the major conflicts of the twentieth century. But the relative neglect of the Waikato War seems telling.[70]

Unlike Keenan, whose 2006 comments suggested a dichotomy between Gallipoli and New Zealand's own wars of settlement, O'Malley offered a conciliatory strategy that drew on the language, practices and emotional resonance of Anzac commemoration in the second decade of the twenty-first century. The frontiers of Anzac memory were gradually developing space to encompass stories of colonial violence.

O'Malley's was not the only voice calling for change. In December 2015 a group of students had delivered a petition of 13,000 signatures to Parliament requesting the establishment of a new national day to commemorate 'those who lost their lives here in New Zealand, both Māori and colonial', whose 'blood was shed on New Zealand soil; their lives were given in service to New Zealand'.[71] And as Crown and iwi leaders considered ways to commemorate the 150th anniversary in 2014 of the Battle of Ōrākau, the final battle of the Waikato Wars, Governor-General Jerry Mateparae added his own pitch for a new cultural infrastructure of commemoration: 'Many nations have battles that take on mythic proportions for their peoples. For New Zealanders, Ōrākau is one of those battles, one of those places.' At the commemoration ceremony at the battle site, just outside Te Awamutu, Mateparae spoke of the 'mutual respect, honour, and the basis of reconciliation' provided by remembrance, saying, 'It is my hope that this place and its story becomes firmly etched in our nation's collective memory. I hope the children who are here today and all New Zealanders will encourage their children and their mokopuna [grandchildren] to come here for the 200th anniversary commemorations in 2064.'[72]

The first Rā Maumahara or national day of commemoration of the sacking of Kororāreka, the first battle in the northern war, was held on 11 March 2018 in Kororāreka/Russell, hosted by Te Tai Tokerau iwi.[73] The Rā Maumahara drew on some of the practices of Anzac commemoration while focusing on the worlds of hapū and iwi. The following year, 28 October was selected as the permanent day of commemoration, to coincide with the Declaration of Independence by the United Tribes in 1835. The day augured a fresh era of commemoration and a new wave of remembrance in New Zealand.

*

The centenary of Anzac in 2015 was something of a 'memory orgy', according to historian Joan Beaumont, and received enormous political and financial commitment from the governments of both Australia and New Zealand.[74] Yet in the following three years Anzac Day attendance at Gallipoli declined markedly, and by 2018 registrations for the dawn service had virtually collapsed.[75] 'Have we lost our desire to commemorate this most important moment in our military history?' asked radio broadcaster Chris Smith: 'Have we forgotten Gallipoli?'[76]

Did the commemoration generate greater understanding of the experience of war and violence in the twentieth century? The federal Department of Veterans' Affairs suggested it had given Australians 'a broader understanding of Australia's military experience and its impacts', along with lessons that would 'enhance future commemoration programs to carry forward the Anzac spirit and the values of service and sacrifice'. No qualitative or quantitative evidence was offered for these claims.[77] In New Zealand, the reflection was more deliberate. In April 2019 the WW100 steering committee published a report on the outcome of the New Zealand centenary programme.[78] Survey results indicated the near complete exposure of the New Zealand public to the remembrance; 93 percent of New Zealanders over the age of 15 were touched by the centenary, and 82 percent of respondents agreed World War I was relevant in shaping the national identity. Respondents were asked what came to mind when they heard the words 'First World War'. The most common responses were 'death', 'Gallipoli' and 'Anzac'. These clichés – conflating Anzac, Gallipoli and World War I – were redolent of the 'the New Zealand story' and the new nationalist historiographies of the war that appeared in the 1980s. In shared trans-Tasman war memory, the Anzac experience at Gallipoli was interpreted as the end of a national innocence. The implications for the trajectory of the Anzac myth and its web of political and cultural relations are less certain, and more analysis is yet needed.

Despite the enormous investment in the Anzac Centenary, the focus of public attention was surprisingly narrow and returned to key themes and sites that had emerged over the course of the Anzac revival.[79] National myth is always an unfinished story, and its creation is a process that needs constant maintenance; narratives that are intended to stabilise state institutions and secure political order are themselves profoundly unstable. Cultural remembrance by the state results in an uneven, episodic attention to its own foundations; beyond official commemoration, Anzac seems to revert to quieter and more local networks of remembrance. The connections to the past will continue to be recreated in the future.

Jay Winter writes that historians of commemoration find themselves part of a 'stream of memory' they did not create.[80] There is clearly a latticework of networks and institutions that give substance to public remembrance. There is also a dissonance as the national myth of Anzac continues to occlude other threads of Australia and New Zealand's past by demanding the reassertion of national memory. Cultural remembrance is both fragile and incomplete. The ostensibly firm foundation of myth at Gallipoli relies on an official maintenance of remembrance, and although extensive political investment was brought to bear on the architecture of cultural memory in the Anzac Centenary, the results were mixed.

*

The Anzac revival has given new direction to the practices, places and language of memory in Australia and New Zealand, and has resulted in forms of commemoration that also acknowledge the violence of the colonial past. The constitutional movements for makaratta and commemoration of the New Zealand Wars are evidence that the evolution of Anzac Day in Australia and New Zealand must always be considered in light of the political and cultural needs of society.

Since 1965, stories of Gallipoli and World War I have been rewritten to express a new national spirit in Australia and New Zealand that asserts a cultural belonging that is independent of empire. The Anzacs, once seen as imperial citizen-soldiers, are now understood as heroic victims of violence who gave their lives in sacrifice for democracy, freedom and friendship – language that saturated the Anzac Centenary in 2015. Where once the commemoration of Anzac Day flowed from the personal experiences of these men and their social networks, in the twenty-first century this national remembrance is focused on public audiences, especially young people.

The connection between Gallipoli as a national place and Anzac Day as a national practice is a relatively recent development. How we experience Gallipoli is important: informed by the imagery of films, plays, exhibitions and narratives, Australians and New Zealanders gather at dawn services and imagine the bond they share as citizens and descendants of the Anzacs. The new myth of Gallipoli also comes with a moral geography: remembrance of the battle gives Australians and New Zealanders a prism through which to examine public values and measure the extent to which public actions and narratives match up to the legacy of the Anzacs.

Why and how Gallipoli is remembered depends on the forces that shape public culture. The 'work of memory' is carried out by individuals and groups such as networks of historians and artists, and institutions such as museums, memorials and governments. It is captured in written and visual media, and is structured by constitutional conditions of the state. These 'agents of memory' bring the violence of the past into the foreground to work against or alongside conflicting and contradictory cultural stories, movements and places of protest, revision and dissent. And while remembrance gives the state a sense of permanence and stability, it also makes the story of Anzac more iterative and subject to change and co-option. Moreover, Anzac commemoration is shaped across cultures of nationalism and the interactions between Australia and New Zealand.

Anzac Nations shows, above all, how national history-writing has been a powerful factor in imagining the past. Analysis of the centenary peels back the sense of permanence and inevitability and shows the tradition of remembering the Anzacs to be the result of the work of groups and institutions and the stories they share, contingent on and shaped by circumstances. Alternative claims of collective belonging and foundation – the ancient sovereignty of Indigenous cultures and the active partnership of the Treaty of Waitangi – continue to present challenges to the Anzac nations. While the geographic distance of Anzac Cove allows Gallipoli to be easily repurposed every 25 April, 'home' sites like Waitangi or Sydney Cove are disrupted by these alternative claims and the ongoing concerns of Indigenous communities.

This is part of the contradiction of national cultures in which competing public stories are told and heard. The hero-victim absolving the nation of the sins of imperial war; 'the broken years' and 'the New Zealand story' translating the personal trauma of the Anzacs to the nation itself; 'the Anzac bond' that expresses the maintenance of a trans-Tasman commemoration; and public translations of Indigenous concepts of 'forgotten warriors' and 'the price of citizenship' – all were evident in the 2015 centenary, and all give a particular inflection to the Anzac revival. Cultural memory provides a common language, practice and imagination that draws on the past and can be co-opted and contested – shaped by stories and institutions, as well as the deeper constitutional patterns of public life.

Abbreviations

ABC Australian Broadcasting Corporation
ACT Australian Capital Territory
ADF Australian Defence Force
AIF Australian Imperial Force
Anzus Australia, New Zealand, United States Security Treaty
APEC Asia-Pacific Economic Cooperation
AWM Australian War Memorial
CND Campaign for Nuclear Disarmament
FTA Free Trade Agreement
Interfet International Force East Timor
NITV Australian National Indigenous Television
NZEF New Zealand Expeditionary Forces
NZUSA New Zealand University Students' Association
PHANZA Professional Historians' Association of New Zealand/Aotearoa
POWs prisoners of war
PYM Progressive Youth Movement
RNZ Radio New Zealand
RSA Royal New Zealand Returned and Services Association
RSL Returned and Services League of Australia
SAHS Serious About Heritage Society
SAS New Zealand Special Air Service
SBS Special Broadcasting Service
SOS Save Our Sons
TRT Turkish Television
UN United Nations
WAR Women Against Rape
WW100 NZ First World War Centenary Programme

Glossary of te reo Māori

haka vigorous dance with actions and rhythmic chanting
hapū kinship group, tribe
hiki tapu blessing
hui meeting
iwi extended tribe
kaitiaki custodians
karanga ceremonial call
karakia prayer, blessing
kaumātua elder
kete basket
koro male elder, grandfather
kuia female elder, grandmother
mana whenua territorial rights
Māoritanga the Māori world-view
marae village, courtyard in front of the wharenui
mere club
mokopuna grandchild, descendant
pounamu greenstone
pouwhenua boundary marker
pōwhiri welcoming ceremony
rangatira chief, person of high rank
tangata tiriti non-Māori citizens
tangata whenua the Māori people
taonga treasure
Te Moananui a Kiwa the Pacific Ocean
te reo Māori the Māori language
tikanga Māori Māori cultural and philosophical protocols
turangawaewae place of belonging
waka canoe
waka taua war canoe
whaikōrero speech
whakairo carvings
whakapapa genealogy
whakatuaki proverb
whānau family
whare house
wharenui meeting house

Notes

INTRODUCTION

1. Tony Abbott, '2015 Gallipoli dawn service', 25 April 2015: www.aph.gov.au/About_Parliament/Parliamentary_Departments/Parliamentary_Library/pubs/AnzacDay2016/Speeches
2. John Key, 'Speech at dawn service in Anzac Cove in Gallipoli', *Scoop*, 26 April 2015: www.scoop.co.nz/stories/PA1504/S00333/john-keys-speech-at-dawn-service-in-anzac-cove-in-gallipoli.htm
3. Avishai Margalit, *The Ethics of Memory* (Cambridge, Mass.; London: Harvard University Press, 2004), 95.
4. Stuart Hall, 'Thinking the diaspora: Home-thoughts from abroad', *Small Axe: A Caribbean Journal of Criticism*, 6, 1 (1999): 1–24, 4. See also Stuart Hall, 'The West and the rest: Discourse and power', in Stuart Hall and Bram Gieben (eds), *Formations of Modernity* (Cambridge: Cambridge University Press, 1994), 222–37.
5. Ben Wellings, *English Nationalism and Euroscepticism: Losing the peace* (London: Peter Lang, 2012). See also Ben Wellings, 'Lest You Forget: Memory and Australian nationalism in a global era', in S. Sumartojo and B. Welling (eds), *Nation, Memory and Great War Commemoration: Mobilizing the past in Europe, Australia and New Zealand* (Bern: Peter Lang, 2014), 45–59.
6. Steven Loveridge, 'Sentimental equipment': New Zealand, the Great War and cultural mobilisation' (PhD thesis, Victoria University of Wellington, 2013), 5. See John Fousek, *To Lead the Free World: American nationalism and the cultural roots of the Cold War* (Chapel Hill, NC: University of North Carolina Press, 2000), 9; Margaret Wilson, *The Struggle for Sovereignty: New Zealand and twenty-first century statehood* (Wellington: Bridget Williams Books, 2015), 16.
7. *Sydney Morning Herald*, 26 April 1921; L. Napper, *The Great War in Popular British Cinema of the 1920s* (London: Palgrave Macmillan, 2015). See for example, *Katoomba Daily*, 10 May 1932.
8. Eric Bogle, 'And the Band Played Waltzing Matilda', Australia, Franklyn B. Paverty, 1979.
9. Philippa Mein Smith, 'The "NZ" in Anzac: Different remembrance and meaning', *First World War Studies*, 7, 2 (2016), 193–211.
10. Both Indigenous Australians and Māori soldiers returned from their service to find themselves locked out of soldier land settlement and other welfare schemes. See for example Michael Roche, 'Failure deconstructed: Histories and geographies of soldier settlement in New Zealand circa 1917–39', *New Zealand Geographer*, 64, 1 (2008), 46–56; Noah Riseman, 'Evolving commemorations of Aboriginal and Torres Strait Islander military service', *Wicazo Sa Review*, 32, 1 (2017), 80–101.
11. A difference supposedly rooted in the fact that Australians rejected conscription. K.S. Inglis and Jock Phillips, 'War memorials in Australia and New Zealand: A comparative survey,' *Australian Historical Studies*, 24, 96 (1991), 179–91.

12. Jo Hawkins, *Consuming Anzac: The history of Australia's most powerful brand* (Perth: UWA Publishing, 2018).
13. Carolyn Holbrook, *Anzac: The unauthorised biography* (Sydney: New South Books, 2014), 1–10.
14. See the 2013 edition of Paul Fussell's *The Great War and Modern Memory* (New York: Oxford University Press), with an introduction by Jay Winter, for an entrance to this historiography.
15. K.S. Inglis, 'The ANZAC tradition', *Meanjin*, March 1965.
16. K.S. Inglis, *Sacred Places: War memorials in the Australian landscape* (Melbourne: Melbourne University Press, 1998).
17. Paul Morris, 'Who are we? New Zealand identity and spirituality', in James H. Liu et al. (eds), *New Zealand Identities: Departures and destinations* (Wellington: Victoria University Press, 2005), 242–54
18. See John Anthony Moses and George F. Davis, *Anzac Day Origins: Canon DJ Garland and trans-Tasman commemoration* (Sydney: Barton Books, 2013).
19. Ibid. As Canon Garland had famously declared, 'There is no room for anything but a solemn observance of Anzac Day.'
20. Joan Beaumont, *Broken Nation: Australians in the Great War* (Sydney: Allen & Unwin, 2014).
21. Christina Twomey, 'Trauma and the reinvigoration of Anzac: An argument', *History Australia*, 10, 3 (2013), 85–108. Other works clustered around these psychological themes of remembrance are Beaumont, *Broken Nation* and Alistair Thomson, *Anzac Memories* (rev. edn), (Melbourne: Monash University Publishing, 2013).
22. Alan Moorehead, *Gallipoli* (Ware, Hertfordshire: Wordsworth Editions, 1997) (first published 1956), 309.
23. Stanton Hope's 1934 account of Gallipoli was widely read by New Zealand and Australian audiences. Hope distinguished between 'tourists' who, for example, complained about the weather and poor roads and 'the men on pilgrimage', who would not complain because 'they will recall too vividly the agony of the long dragging marches'. Stanton Hope, *Gallipoli Revisited: An account of the* Duchess of Richmond *pilgrimage-cruise* (London: W.W. Stanton Hope, 1934), 19. For an example of New Zealand reports, see *Evening Post*, 27 July 1934.
24. See Hawkins, *Consuming Anzac.*
25. Bruce Scates, *Return to Gallipoli: Walking the battlefields of the Great War* (Cambridge: Cambridge University Press, 2009), 103.
26. Ian McGibbon, 'In the footsteps of the New Zealanders: Gallipoli', in Kynan Gentry and Gavin McLean (eds), *Heartlands: New Zealand historians write about where history happened* (Auckland: Penguin, 2006), 90–106. See also the centenary project, 'Ngā Tupuwae/New Zealand First World War Trails': https://ngatapuwae.govt.nz/
27. Brad West, 'Dialogical memorialization, international travel and the public sphere: A cultural sociology of commemoration and tourism at the First World War Gallipoli battlefields', *Tourist Studies*, 10, 3 (2010), 209–25. For a recent discussion on the posterity of the Ataturk quote see Peter Stanley, 'Talking Turkey': http://honesthistory.net.au/wp/talking-turkey/
28. Mark McKenna, 'Anzac Day: How did it become Australia's national day?', in Henry Reynolds and Marilyn Lake (eds), *What's Wrong with Anzac?* (Sydney: New South Books, 2010), 110–34; Holbrook, *Anzac*, 166–206; Frank Bongiorno, 'Anzac and the politics of inclusion', in S. Sumartojo and B. Wellings (eds), *Nation, Memory and Great War Commemoration* (Bern: Peter Lang, 2014), 81–97, 82.

29. Jenny Macleod, 'The fall and rise of Anzac Day: 1965 and 1990 compared', *War & Society*, 20, 1 (2002), 149–68.
30. Commemorative diplomacy invokes the foundational work of Matthew Graves, most recently focusing on 'memorial diplomacy' and the uses of the past in international relations. See Matthew Graves, *Memorial Diplomacy: The international politics of the past* (London: Palgrave Macmillan, 2018).
31. Graeme Hucker, 'A determination to remember: Helen Clark and New Zealand's military heritage', *Journal of Arts Management, Law, and Society*, 40, 2 (2010), 105–18; Mark McKenna, 'Keeping in step: The Anzac "resurgence" and "military heritage" in Australia and New Zealand', in Sumartojo and Welling (eds), *Nation, Memory and Great War Commemoration*, 151–67.
32. See for example Finlay Macdonald, 'Remembering Gallipoli', *New Zealand Geographic*: www.nzgeo.com/stories/remembering-gallipoli
33. Matthew Haultain-Gall, *The Battlefield of Imperishable Memory: Passchendaele and the Australian legend* (Melbourne: Monash University Press, 2021).
34. Holbrook, *Anzac.*
35. Mark McKenna, 'The history anxiety', in Alison Bashford and Stuart Macintyre (eds), *The Cambridge History of Australia: Volume 2: The Commonwealth of Australia* (Cambridge–New York: Cambridge University Press, 2013), 561–80; Miranda Johnson, 'Burdens of belonging: Indigeneity and the re-founding of Aotearoa New Zealand', *New Zealand Journal of History*, 45, 1 (2011), 102–12, 111.
36. Paul Ashton and Paula Hamilton, 'Unfinished business': Public history in a postcolonial nation', in Daniel Walkowitz and Lisa Maya Knauer (eds), *Contested Histories in Public Places* (Durham: Duke University Press, 2009), 71–98, 74. See also Peter Cleave, *Making Sense of a Small State: The body of memory and the ritual of acknowledgement in Aotearoa-New Zealand* (Palmerston North: Campus Press, 2015).
37. Jenny Hocking, *The Dismissal Dossier. The Palace Connection: Everything you were never meant to know about November 1975* (Melbourne: Melbourne University Press, 2017).
38. Marcia Russell, *Revolution: New Zealand from fortress to free market* (Auckland: Hodder Moa Beckett, 1996).
39. Philippa Mein Smith, *A Concise History of New Zealand* (Melbourne: Cambridge University Press, 2011), especially chapter 9.
40. Jock Phillips describes New Zealand anti-nuclearism, for example, as an expression of 'a postcolonial yearning for a new nationalism', in 'New Zealand and the Anzus alliance: Changing national self-perceptions, 1945–88', in Richard Baker (ed.), *Australia, New Zealand, and the United States* (New York: Praegar, 1991), 194; James Curran and Stuart Ward, *The Unknown Nation: Australia after Empire* (Melbourne: Melbourne University Press, 2006).
41. Chris Laidlaw, *Rites of Passage: Beyond the New Zealand identity crisis* (Auckland: Hodder Moa Beckett, 1999).
42. See Michael Belgrave, *Historical Frictions: Māori claims and reinvented histories* (Auckland: Auckland University Press, 2005). Tony Ballantyne has outlined the emergence of an ideology of biculturalism in history writing: *Webs of Empire: Locating New Zealand's colonial past* (Wellington: Bridget Williams Books, 2012), 50–64.
43. Helen Robinson, 'Making a New Zealand Day: The creation and context of a national holiday', *New Zealand Journal of History*, 46, 1 (2012), 37–51.

44. Indigenous Australians were only recognised as federal citizens in 1967. Bob Hawke, 'Speech by the prime minister at the handover ceremony of the Young Endeavour Sydney', 26 January 1988: https://pmtranscripts.pmc.gov.au/release/transcript-7279
45. *New Zealand Herald*, 7 January 1990.
46. *Canberra Times*, 27 January 1987.
47. Manning Clark, *A History of Australia: The old dead tree and the young tree green, 1916–1935* (vol. 6) (Melbourne: Melbourne University Press, 1987).
48. Ann Curthoys, 'Losing our way after the imperial turn: Charting academic uses of the postcolonial', in Antoinette Burton, *After the Imperial Turn: Thinking with and through the nation* (Durham, NC: Duke University Press, 2003).
49. Richard White, 'Inventing Australia revisited', in Geoffrey Curgenven Bolton and Wayne Hudson (eds), *Creating Australia: Changing Australian history* (St Leonards: Allen & Unwin, 1997), 21. For a more recent overview of these debates, see Freya Willis 'A reconciled nation? Mabo and the reimagining of Australia's national history', *Journal of Australian Studies*, (2021) DOI: 10.1080/14443058.2021.1974922
50. Henry Reynolds, *Aborigines and Settlers : The Australian experience, 1788–1939* (Melbourne: Cassell Australia, 1972).
51. Giselle Byrnes, *The Waitangi Tribunal and New Zealand History* (Oxford: Oxford University Press, 2004), v–vi.
52. Bill Schwarz, *The White Man's World* (Oxford; New York: Oxford University Press, 2011).
53. Alistair Thomson, *Anzac Memories: Living with the legend* (Oxford: Oxford University Press, 1994), 5.
54. Scott Worthy, 'Communities of remembrance: The memory of the Great War in New Zealand, 1915–1939' (MA thesis, University of Auckland, 2001), 8–9.
55. Deborah Montgomerie, 'Anzac anthems: New Zealand history and the two world wars', Winter Lecture, University of Auckland, Auckland, 2009.
56. Ian McGibbon, *The Oxford Companion to New Zealand Military History* (Melbourne: Oxford University Press, 2000).
57. Chris Maclean and Jock Phillips, *The Sorrow & the Pride: New Zealand war memorials* (Wellington: Historical Publications Branch, 1990); Mein Smith, 'The "NZ" in Anzac'.
58. Bruce Lincoln, *Between History and Myth: Stories of Harald Fairhair and the founding of the State* (Chicago: Chicago University Press, 2014), 114.

CHAPTER ONE

1. Helen Robinson, 'Lest we forget?: The fading of New Zealand war commemorations, 1946–1966', *New Zealand Journal of History*, 44, 1 (2010).
2. *New Zealand Herald*, 26 April 1946; Robinson, 'Lest we forget?', 76–91.
3. N.P. Webber, *The First Fifty Years of the New Zealand Returned Services Association 1916 to 1966* (Wellington: New Zealand Returned and Services Association (NZRSA), 1966), 6; *New Zealand Listener*, 15 April 1965, 3.
4. Robinson, 'Lest we forget?'.
5. See John Anthony Moses and George F. Davis, *Anzac Day Origins: Canon DJ Garland and trans-Tasman commemoration* (Sydney: Barton Books, 2013), 242.
6. The fact that the pilgrimage only included a one-day visit to Gallipoli led to complaints that

it had been hijacked by the interests of World War II veterans: *Australian*, 25 November 1964. Matthew A. Crotty, 'Gallipoli 1965: The unhappy pilgrimage', Australian Historical Association Conference, Australian National University, Canberra, 2018.

7. Inglis' reflections in 2015 can be seen at: https://insidestory.org.au/letters-from-a-pilgrimage/
8. Ken Inglis, 'Letters from a pilgrimage: Ken Inglis' despatches from the Anzac tour to Gallipoli, April–May 1965': http://apo.org.au/node/54313. Also see Bruce Scates' recent reflections on the pilgrimage: Bruce Scates, 'Letters from a pilgrimage: Reflection on the 1965 return to Gallipoli', *History Australia*, 14, 4 (2017), 530–44.
9. Alan Cocker, 'Malcolm Ross, journalist and photographer: The perfect war correspondent?', *Pacific Journalism Review*, 22, 1 (2016), 152–66.
10. *Evening Post*, 26 April 1965.
11. 'Meeting of the organising committee minutes,' 5 February 1965, Ceremonials and Celebrations, 1964–1973, ABFK 7494 W4948/71 35/1/2 1, Archives New Zealand (ANZ), Wellington.
12. Mitchell to Holyoake, 15 March 1965, Ceremonials and Celebrations, 1964–1973, ABFK 7494 W4948/71 35/1/2 1, ANZ, Wellington.
13. *Press*, 26 April 1965; *New Zealand Herald*, 26 April 1965.
14. *New Zealand Herald*, 24 April 1965.
15. Rotorua was also central to the North Island and avoided the politics of having the reunion in Auckland or Wellington.
16. *Evening Post*, 26 April 1965. The army, navy and air force were present at the major metropolitan services – Auckland, Wellington and Christchurch, whereas regional centres had solely the army. See 'Minutes of the principal personnel officers' committee,' PPO 65 M3, 9 February 1965, Ceremonials and Celebrations, 1964–1973, ABFK 7494 W4948/71 35/1/2 1, ANZ, Wellington.
17. *Canberra Times*, 15 March 1965.
18. Ibid.
19. *Canberra Times*, 27 April 1965.
20. *Age* (Melbourne), 21 April 1965.
21. Ibid.
22. *Age*, 26 April 1965.
23. Ibid.
24. *Advertiser* (Adelaide), 26 April 1965.
25. *Western Herald*, 30 April 1965; *Fairfield Broadcaster*, 27 April 1965.
26. *Age*, 22 April 1965.
27. Ibid.
28. Ibid.
29. Ibid.
30. *Western Herald*, 26 March 1965; *Valley Hill Times*, 30 April 1965; *Sunday Telegraph*, 25 April 1965. See also *Sunraysia* (Mildura), 22 April 1965, and *Bendigo Advertiser*, 24 April 1965.
31. *Biz*, 21 April 1965.
32. *Age*, 28 April 1954.
33. *Evening Post*, 24 April 1965.
34. *Anzac Plus Fifty: People at war*, 25 April 1965, NZBC.
35. Ibid.
36. *Te Reo o te Māori*, 25 April 1965, NZBC.

37. *Age*, 23 April 1965.
38. *Canberra Times*, 9 January 1965.
39. *New Zealand Herald*, 26 April 1965.
40. *Canberra Times*, 26 April 1965.
41. *Western Herald*, 26 April 1965.
42. Such news stories – aired on the national broadcasting service – also suggested a changing technological context of memory. *ABC News*, Australia: ABC, 1965. The clip was recently published online under the title 'Should Anzac Day marches continue?': www.youtube.com/watch?v=YZXekvN-dws
43. *Canberra Times*, 17 March 1965. The New Zealand archives show no indication as to whether this was an official New Zealand government policy or simply a convenient excuse given by Menzies.
44. The medal was designed by veteran and sculptor Raymond Ewers. Harold Holt, 'Statement by the Prime Minister, the Rt. Hon. Harold Holt, in the House of Representatives: Commemorative medallion and badge', 16 March 1967: https://pmtranscripts.pmc.gov.au/sites/default/files/original/00001524.pdf
45. Graham Seal, '... and in the morning ...': Adapting and adopting the dawn service', *Journal of Australian Studies* 35, 1 (2011), 49–63.
46. 'Anzac Day', *Journal of External Affairs*, April (1965), 12–15.
47. *Age*, 22 April 1965.
48. *Canberra Times*, 11 May 1965.
49. *Age*, 26 April 1965.
50. *New Zealand Herald*, 26 April 1965; 24 April 1965.
51. *Radio Listener*, April 1965.
52. *Age*, 23 April 1965.
53. *Age*, 26 April 1965.
54. *Zealandia*, 22 April 1965.
55. *Age*, 26 April 1965.
56. *Mirror*, 25 April 1965.
57. *Canberra Times*, 9 April 1965.
58. *Sydney Morning Herald*, 27 April 1965.
59. *Evening Post*, 26 April 1964.
60. *Canberra Times*, 24 April 1965.
61. *Canberra Times*, 10 November 1963.
62. *Walkabout*, 1 April 1965.
63. Stephen Clarke, *After the War: The RSA in New Zealand* (Auckland: Penguin, 2016) 92–94; Holyoake to Mitchell, 8 June 1964, Ceremonials and Celebrations, 1964–1973, ABFK 7494 W4948/71 35/1/2 1, ANZ, Wellington. The idea of the trust would ultimately be rejected as unwieldy as a result of its administration and the inconvenience and frustration that would inevitably arise because of differing public and business attitudes to this form of licensing. Instead, the law would allow businesses to operate after 1pm as if it were a standard Saturday afternoon. See W. Hutchings, 'Anzac Day – Afternoon Activities', Secretary of Defence, 4 March 1967, 35/1/2, Ceremonials and Celebrations, 1964–1973, ABFK 7494 W4948/71 35/1/2 1, ANZ, Wellington.
64. *Press*, 13 November 1933.
65. *New Zealand Herald*, 26 April 1965.

66. Office of the Prime Minister, CM (64) 21, 4 June 1964, Ceremonials and Celebrations, 1964–1973, ABFK 7494 W4948/71 35/1/2 1, ANZ, Wellington.
67. Holyoake to Mitchell, 8 June 1964, Ceremonials and Celebrations, 1964–1973, ABFK 7494 W4948/71 35/1/2 1, ANZ, Wellington.
68. *Dominion*, 17 July 1964.
69. The lack of RSA action was viewed as reflecting an executive council largely made up of World War II veterans, without an appreciation for the World War I focus.
70. 'MN 314/3/1', Ceremonials and Celebrations, 1964–1973, ABFK 7494 W4948/71 35/1/2 1, ANZ, Wellington.
71. Letters requesting government help include: Dobbie to Minister of Lands, 20 July 1964; Minister of Defence to Connelly, 17 July 1964, Ceremonials and Celebrations, 1964–1973, ABFK 7494 W4948/71 35/1/2 1, ANZ, Wellington; 'CM (64) 21', Ceremonials and Celebrations, 1964–1973, ABFK 7494 W4948/71 35/1/2 1, 6, ANZ, Wellington.
72. Ministry of Defence to A. Connelly MP, 17 July 1964, Ceremonials and Celebrations, 1964–1973, ABFK 7494 W4948/71 35/1/2 1, ANZ, Wellington.
73. Draft letter of 17 July 1964, Ceremonials and Celebrations, 1964–1973, ABFK 7494 W4948/71 35/1/2 1, ANZ, Wellington.
74. Cabinet memo RJ EOP, 20/7/64, 1/5/8, Ceremonials and Celebrations, 1964–1973, ABFK 7494 W4948/71 35/1/2 1, ANZ, Wellington.
75. Minutes of the meeting of principal personnel officers committee, 20/6/2, 20 October 1964, Ceremonials and Celebrations, 1964–1973, ABFK 7494 W4948/71 35/1/2 1, ANZ, Wellington.
76. *Australian*, 11 May 1965.
77. Ian Maddocks and Seumas Spark, '"Taim bilong uni": Ken Inglis at the University of Papua New Guinea', *History Australia*, 14, 4 (2017), 545–60. In 1967, two years after his participation in the pilgrimage to Gallipoli, Inglis would become inaugural professor of history and then vice-chancellor at the University of Papua New Guinea as the small island moved towards independence from Australian colonial administration. A 'missionary' of Australian history amid a fragmenting imperial world, he would go on to have a distinguished career as one of Australia's leading historians.
78. Inglis, 27 April 1964, Ken Inglis Papers, 1951–circa 2004, NLA, Canberra.
79. Inglis to Klaus, 13 July 1964, Ken Inglis Papers, 1951–circa 2004, NLA, Canberra.
80. *Canberra Times*, 27 April 1965; 27 April 1965; 15 April 1965.
81. Ken Inglis, 'The Anzac tradition', *Meanjin*, 24, 1 (1965), 25–44; Ken Inglis, 'Return to Gallipoli', *Australian National University Historical Journal*, 3 (1966), 43–62.
82. Geoffrey Hutton, 'Gallipoli: As seen by Turks', *Age*, 21 April 1965.
83. Jenny Macleod, 'The fall and rise of Anzac Day: 1965 and 1990 compared', *War & Society*, 20, 1 (2002), 149–68.
84. Ken Inglis, 'C.E.W. Bean, Australian historian', the John Murtagh Macrossan lecture, University of Queensland, Brisbane, 1969.
85. Ibid.
86. As quoted in John Lack, K.S. Inglis and Jay Winter, *Anzac Remembered: Selected writings by K.S. Inglis* (Melbourne: Melbourne University Press, 1998).
87. Ibid.
88. Inglis, 'C.E.W. Bean, Australian historian', 50.
89. Inglis, 'Letters from a pilgrimage'.

CHAPTER TWO

1. Brian Easton, *The Whimpering of the State: Policy after MMP* (Auckland: Auckland University Press, 1999), 28; Peggy Koopman-Boyden and Claudia D. Scott, *The Family and Government Policy in New Zealand* (Sydney: Allen & Unwin, 1984), 139.
2. James T. Sparrow, *Warfare State* (Oxford: Oxford University Press, 2011). Stephen Loveridge has written substantive commentaries on the relationship between interwar commemoration and military mobilisation: see 'Another great war?: New Zealand interpretations of the First World War towards and into the Second World War', *First World War Studies* 7, 3 (2016), 303–25.
3. For a recent summary see Nick Irving, 'Global thought, local action: Australian activism during the Vietnam War 1961–1972' (PhD thesis, University of Sydney, 2017).
4. Jeff Doyle, 'Dismembering the Anzac legend: Australian popular culture and the Vietnam War', *Vietnam Generation*, 3, 2 (1992), 109–25.
5. See for example Nick Scott, 'Black-bans and black eyes: Implications of the 1971 Springbok rugby tour', *Labour History*, 108 (2015), 145–63. *New Zealand Herald*, 26 April 1979.
6. K.S. Inglis, 'Remembering Anzac', in *Remembering Anzac*, 228–47; Ken Inglis, 'Kapferer on Anzac and Australia', *Social Analysis*, 29 (1990), 67–73.
7. *Sydney Morning Herald*, 25 March 2015.
8. For early instances of anti-Anzac Day rhetoric, see the *Honi Soit* University of Sydney student newspapers, editions 7 and 9, 1958.
9. Susanne Davies, 'Women, war, and the violence of history: An Australian perspective', *Violence Against Women*, 2, 4 (1996), 359–77, 375.
10. Graham Seal, '… and in the morning …': Adapting and adopting the dawn service', *Journal of Australian Studies* 35, 1 (2011), 49–63, 49.
11. *Canberra Times*, 26 April 1966.
12. Ibid.
13. Some helpful general works include Ian McGibbon, *New Zealand's Vietnam War: A history of combat, commitment, and controversy* (Auckland: Exisle Publishing, 2010); Brent Coutts and Nicholas Fitness, *Protest in New Zealand* (Auckland: Pearson Press, 2013); Roberto Rabel, *New Zealand and the Vietnam War: Politics and diplomacy* (Auckland: Auckland University Press, 2005); Jeff Doyle, Jeffrey Grey and Peter Pierce, *Australia's Vietnam War* (Austin: University of Texas Press, 2002); John Murphy, *A Harvest of Fear: A history of Australia's Vietnam War* (Sydney: Allen & Unwin, 1993).
14. As quoted in Kevin Clements, *Back from the Brink: The creation of a nuclear-free New Zealand* (Wellington: Allen & Unwin, 1988), 23.
15. Stuart Macintyre, *A Concise History of Australia* (Cambridge: Cambridge University Press, 2004), 209.
16. *Canberra Times*, 18 September 1965.
17. *Australian*, 26 April 1971.
18. 'Bias looks at a phoney protest', *Woroni*, 5 June 1968; see also Jonathan Gaul, 'Holt and the emotive conscription issue', *Canberra Times*, 29 March 1966.
19. 'SOS statement' (brochure), NAA A6122 1668, 59, National Archives of Australia (NAA), Canberra.
20. Joy Damousi, *The Labour of Loss: Mourning, memory, and wartime bereavement in Australia* (Cambridge: Cambridge University Press, 1999), 336.

21. '[Posters promoting peace, and denouncing war]', 1970-1979, Eph-C-PEACE-1970s, National Library of New Zealand (NLNZ), Wellington.
22. *New Zealand Herald*, 26 April 1971.
23. *Press*, 26 April 1968.
24. K.S. Inglis, *Sacred Places: War memorials in the Australian landscape* (Melbourne: Melbourne University Press, 1998), 379.
25. *West Australian*, 26 April 1969.
26. *Age*, 26 April 1971, *Sydney Morning Herald*, 26 April 1972.
27. Barry Lee offers rich insights into various rationales and relationships that shaped young people's memberships of PYM in the 1960s: 'Struggling to make the world a better place: Exploring some experiences of activists in the Auckland Progressive Youth Movement (1965–1977)', (PhD thesis, Auckland University of Technology, 2019), 208–10.
28. 'Youth Manifesto', Auckland PYM, 1969, was a toned-down version of a leaflet that was originally written by Auckland anarchists: Barry Lee collection on the Progressive Youth Movement, Auckland Branch, 1969–c. 1972, University of Auckland Library (UAL), Auckland.
29. 'Wanted: A new militancy', Christchurch PYM (brochure), 1969, Barry Lee collection, UAL, Auckland.
30. *Canta*, end-of-year supplement, 1972, Barry Lee collection, UAL, Auckland.
31. 'PYM attacks newspaper', *Salient*, 24 October 1969.
32. *Salient*, 24 September 1969.
33. Ibid.
34. Murray Horton, private papers, Christchurch.
35. *Christchurch Star*, 27 April 1971.
36. *Press*, 26 April 1972.
37. Elsie Locke, *Peace People: A history of peace activities in New Zealand* (Christchurch: Hazard Press, 1992).
38. See Judith Bright's contribution in Anne Else (ed.), *Women Together: A history of women's organisations in New Zealand – Ngā Rōpū Wāhine o te Motu* (Wellington: Daphne Brasell Associates Press and Historical Branch, Department of Internal Affairs, 1993).
39. *New Zealand Herald*, 26 April 1966.
40. *Otago Daily Times*, 26 April 1967; *Press*, 26 April 1967.
41. Rabel, *New Zealand and the Vietnam War*, 161, 360.
42. *New Zealand Herald*, 22 April 1970.
43. Jenny Carylon and Diana Morrow, *Changing Times: New Zealand since 1945* (Auckland: Auckland University Press, 2014); Rabel, *New Zealand and the Vietnam War*, 296.
44. Speech by Right Hon. Norman Kirk, Prime Minister of New Zealand, 'New Zealand and South-East Asia: A policy for the Seventies', Dominion Executive Council Records, 12 June 1973, NZRSA, Wellington.
45. *Evening Post*, 27 April 1970.
46. Notably, these student activists wore suits to the parade, in contrast to the 'bohemian' style of more radical groups such as the PYM.
47. *Evening Post*, 24 April 1971.
48. For example, see Patrick Hagopian, *The Vietnam War in American memory: Veterans, memorials, and the politics of healing* (Amherst: University of Massachusetts Press, 2009).

49. Gnanasunderam to Nathan, 9 August 1971, Barry Lee collection on the PYM, Auckland Branch, 1969-ca 1972, UAL, Auckland.
50. Kay Goodger, 'Proceedings of the Women's Liberation Conference', *Socialist Action*, 4, 6 (1972), 1
51. *Salient*, 24 April 1978.
52. *Canberra Times*, 8 October 1975; *Tharunka*, 26 May 1976; *Canberra Times*, 14 September 1976.
53. See for example, *Tharunka*, 1 May 1978; and 28 May 1979.
54. Mary Daly's *Radical Feminism*, a central text in 1978 that explored the issue of rape in modern society, was influential in the emergence of WAR and similar collectives. See Meredith Burgmann, 'The Women Against Rape in War collective's protests against Anzac Day in Sydney, 1983 and 1984': https://epress.lib.uts.edu.au/journals/index.php/mcs/article/view/4222
55. *Tharunka*, 1 May 1978.
56. Ibid.
57. Peter Stanley, 'Anzac Day as it was reported', in Michael McKernan and Peter Stanley (eds), *Anzac Day Seventy Years On* (Sydney: Collins, 1986), 13–19, 16.
58. Catriona Elder, '"I spit on your stone": National identity, Women Against Rape and the cult of Anzac in Australia', in Maja Mikula (ed.), *Women, Activism and Social Change* (London: Routledge, 2005), 75.
59. Lyn Ariel, SWARC: www.radicalfeministvoice.com/9SWARC.pdf> Joyce Stevens, 'Women mourn rape in war on Anzac Day – 175 arrested', *Tribune* (Sydney), April 1983. Stevens' article is featured alongside several images of the armbands worn by some participants at the Sydney 1983 march.
60. *Canberra Times*, 23 April 1981.
61. Deborah Tyler, 'Making nations, making men: Feminists and the Anzac tradition', *Melbourne Historical Journal* 16 (1984), 24–33, 28.
62. Kathy Jones, *Media Images of Anzac* (Sydney: New South Wales Department of Education, 1983), 26a– 27a; with the caveat that the rapists were American rather than Australian soldiers. Doyle, 'Dismembering the Anzac legend', 118–20.
63. *Canberra Times*, 25 April 1981.
64. Ibid.
65. Ibid.
66. *Canberra Times*, 26 April 1980. ACT Judge T.D. Nicholl, a former RSL member, was the presiding judge and subsequently received enormous criticism for the decision.
67. Sara Dowse and Patricia Giles, 'Australia: Women in a warrior society', in Robin Morgan (ed.), *Sisterhood is Global: The international women's movement anthology* (Garden City, NY: Anchor Press/Doubleday, 1984), 111–16.
68. *New Zealand Herald*, 26 April 1978.
69. *Auckland Star*, 26 April 1978.
70. Adrian Howe, 'Anzac mythology and the feminist challenge', in Joy Damousi and Marilyn Lake (eds), *Gender and War: Australians at war in the twentieth century* (Cambridge: Cambridge University Press, 1995), 302–10.
71. *Age*, 25 April 1985. A series of stickers produced by the Melbourne Anti-Anzac Day Collective in 1986, 'Subject File – Anzac Day', State Library of Victoria, Melbourne. For

images of these protests see Jan Bassett, 'Women and Anzac Day, Melbourne', in Michael McKernan and Peter Stanley (eds), *Anzac Day Seventy Years On* (Sydney: Collins, 1986).

72. *Evening Post*, 26 April 1980.
73. Ibid.
74. Ibid.
75. Elder, '"I spit on your stone"', 81.
76. K.S. Inglis, *Sacred Places: War memorials in the Australian landscape* (Melbourne: Melbourne University Press, 1998), 466. The WAR actions in Canberra from 1980 to 1983 have since been the subject of a exhibition at the Canberra Museum and Gallery. See Gail Radford, 'Women Against Rape in War', Canberra Museum and Gallery, 9 October 2019: www.cmag.com.au/blog/women-against-rape-in-war
77. Women Against Rape, 'Press release from Women Against Rape', 2 38/29/01, 1976; see also 2 38/36/01, 1977–1979; Victorian Women's Liberation and Lesbian Feminist Archives (VWLLFA), 38, UMA; *Reveille* (Sydney), September/October 1981, 23; Ken Inglis, 'Men, women and war memorials: Anzac Australia', *Daedalus*, 116, 4 (1987), 35–59, 37, 119.
78. *New Zealand Herald*, 24 April 1984.
79. Peter Hobbins, 'Protest as paradox: Hegemony and Anzac Day, 1977–87', BA (Hons) essay, University of Sydney, 2008, 23; Stanley, 'Anzac Day as it was reported', 17; Clem Lloyd and Jacqui Rees, *The Last Shilling: A history of repatriation in Australia* (Melbourne: Melbourne University Press, 1994), 353.
80. Stephen Garton, *The Cost of War: Australians return* (Melbourne: Thomas Nelson, 1996), 239; Lloyd and Rees, *The Last Shilling*, 359–60.
81. 'Anzacs under fire again', *Sun*, 26 April 1984; 'Defiant women plan own anti-Anzac action', *Age*, 25 April 1984.
82. 'Subject File – Anzac Day, 1981–1986', State Library of Victoria (SLV), Melbourne. See for example, *WOMB Women of Melbourne Broadsheet*, 1 38/07/03, 1983–1984; *Women's Liberation Newsletter*, 1 38/07/03, 1979; VWLLFA 38, UMA, Melbourne; and *Worker's Newsletter* (New Zealand), for a New Zealand comparison, 1 38/14b/04, 1982-1983, UMA, Melbourne.
83. *Reveille*, July/August 1983, 6.
84. Peter Cooke, *All Formed Up: A history of Wellington Returned & Services' Association, 1916–2007* (Wellington: Ngaio Press, 2008), 130. The greater inclusion of women was in part out of necessity; women members increasingly acted as office bearers in the late 1970s as fewer and fewer volunteers committed to the association.
85. Philip Briant and Phil Thomson, *Warriors, Welfare and Eternal Vigilance*, Broadcast: May 1982, two sound cassettes: a series of four radio documentaries that examines the history and role of the RSL in Australian life.
86. *Age*, 25 April 1986.
87. Garton, *The Cost of War*, 236.
88. Lloyd and Rees, *The Last Shilling*, 359–60; Doyle, 'Dismembering the Anzac legend', 113–15. See also William Nagle, *The Odd Angry Shot* (Sydney: Angus & Robertson, 1975). The film of the same name was directed by Tom Jeffrey. Redgum, 'I Was Only 19', 1983: www.youtube.com/watch?v=Urtiyp-G6jY
89. Garton, *The Cost of War*, 230–31.

CHAPTER THREE

1. See Megan McMurchy and Jennifer Stott, *Signs of Independents: Ten years of the Creative Development Fund* (Sydney: Australian Film Commission, 1988).
2. The richness of this period is captured by Trisha Dunleavy and Hester Joyce in *New Zealand Film and Television: Institution, industry and cultural change* (Bristol and Chicago: Intellect, 2011).
3. Brian McFarlane, 'The film of the book: Adaptation and the Australian cinema', *Metro Magazine*, 49 (2017), 52–59. See also James Bennett and Rebecca Beirne, *Making Film and Television Histories: Australia and New Zealand* (London: I.B. Tauris, 2012), xx.
4. Jan Assmann and Aleida Assmann, 'Collective memory and cultural identity', *New German Critique*, 65 (1995), 125–33.
5. Marcia Landy, *Cinematic Uses of the Past* (Minneapolis; London: University of Minnesota Press, 1996).
6. Jeremy Payne, *Kaleidoscope*, TVNZ, 1982.
7. Ibid.; *Age*, 12 August 1981.
8. David Stratton, *The Avocado Plantation: Boom and bust in the Australian film industry* (Sydney: Pan Macmillan, 1990), 22–24.
9. For example, M. Haltof, 'Gallipoli, mateship, and the construction of Australian national identity', *Journal of Popular Film & Television*, 21, 1 (2004), 27–36; R. Morris, 'Growing up Australian: Renegotiating mateship, masculinity and "Australianness" in Hsu-Ming Teo *Behind the Moon*', *Journal of Intercultural Studies*, 27, 1–2 (2006), 155–66; Graham Seal, 'Anzac: The sacred in the secular', *Journal of Australian Studies*, 91 (2007), 135–44; Daniel Reynaud, *Celluloid Anzacs: The Great War through Australian cinema* (Melbourne: Victoria Australian Scholarly Publishing, 2007).
10. Bill Gammage, 'Re-thinking Anzac', Ministry of Culture and Heritage Panel, National Gallery of Australia, 7 May 2013.
11. *Peter Weir's Film of Gallipoli: Film study guide*, Melbourne: Education Department of Victoria, 1981.
12. 'Peter Weir on Gallipoli: "I felt somehow I was really touching history"', *Literature/Film Quarterly*, 9, 4 (1981): www.peterweircave.com/articles/articlej.html
13. *The Anzac Story*, ABC, 1965.
14. Reynaud, *Celluloid Anzacs*, 148.
15. *Report from Gallipoli*, ABC, 1977.
16. 'Peter Weir on Gallipoli'.
17. Ibid.
18. As C.E.W. Bean, *The Story of Anzac from the Outbreak of War to the End of the First Phase of the Gallipoli Campaign, May 4, 1915* (Brisbane: University of Queensland Press, 1981).
19. 'Peter Weir on Gallipoli'.
20. As discussed in Mark Halof, 'Gallipoli, mateship, and the construction of Australian national identity', *Journal of Popular Film and Television*, 2, 1 (1993), 27. Interestingly, Anthony Asquith's *Tell England* (1931), later released in the United States as *The Battle of Gallipoli*, also cleaves closely to the storyline of Rolfe's film.
21. The film's storyline also suggests the influence of Roger McDonald's novel *1915* (Brisbane: Queensland University Press, 1979), published in the same year as the final script was

completed, which follows the fortunes of two young Western Australians who join the Light Horse and fight in Gallipoli.

22. L.L. Robson, 'Voices from the trenches', *Meanjin*, 4 (1974), 320–22.
23. Bill Gammage, 'The broken years: A study of the diaries and letters of Australian soldiers in the Great War, 1914–18' (PhD thesis, Australian National University, 1970), iv–v.
24. These key phrases were repeated in glowing newspaper reviews of the book. See for example, *Canberra Times*, 21 June 1974.
25. Patsy Adam-Smith, *The Anzacs* (Sydney: Thomas Nelson, 1978). Adam-Smith's work, along with Gammage's, would have a second life of sorts with the boom in interest around Anzac Day in the 1990s. See *Canberra Times*, 26 October 1991; *Canberra Times*, 17 April 1982.
26. Lisa J. Del Pizzo, 'Not guilty – but not innocent: An analysis of the acquittal of John Demjanjuk and its impact on the future of Nazi war crimes trials', *Law Review* 137, 18 (1995).
27. Patrick O'Farrell, 'Oral history: Facts and fiction', *Quadrant*, 23, 148 (1979), 4–8.
28. Les Carlyon, *Gallipoli* (Sydney: Macmillan, 2001); Jonathan King, *Gallipoli Diaries* (Sydney: Kangaroo Press, 2003).
29. 'Peter Weir on Gallipoli'.
30. E.g. *Canberra Times*, 8 August 1981; *Sydney Morning Herald*, 8 August 1981.
31. 'The birth of a nation: An interview with Peter Weir', *Cineaste*, 11, 4 (1982), 42.
32. Ibid.
33. Ibid.
34. C.E.W. Bean, *The Official History of Australia in the War of 1914–1918, Volume 2*, 1941, 618.
35. Graeme Turner, *Film as Social Practice* (London and New York: Routledge, 1988), 178.
36. 'The birth of a nation'.
37. Jane Freebury, 'Screening Australia. *Gallipoli*: A study of nationalism on film', *Media International Australia*, 43, 1 (1987), 5–8 (5).
38. *Weekend Australian Magazine*, 14 August 1981.
39. *Age*, 22 August 1981.
40. *Sydney Morning Herald,* 11 July 1981.
41. Sylvia Lawson, 'Gallipoli: Picnic at the pyramids', *Filmnews*, November–December (1981), 11.
42. John Carroll, *Age Monthly Review*, 1, 7 (1981), 8.
43. Inga Clendinnen, 'The history question: Who owns the past?', *Quarterly Essay*, 23 (2006), 1.
44. Quoted in Haltof, 'Gallipoli', 34
45. *National Times*, 2 August 1981.
46. 'The birth of a nation'.
47. Bill Gammage, *The Story of Gallipoli* (Ringwood, Vic.: Penguin, 1981).
48. Peter Weir, Preface, in Gammage, *The Story of Gallipoli*, 6.
49. Anthony I. Ginnane & Philip Adams, 'Two views', *Cinema Papers*, 44/45 (1984), 71.
50. *TV Listener*, 9 July 1981; *Movie*, 3 May 1981.
51. Alistair Thomson, *Anzac Memories* (rev. edn), (Melbourne: Monash University Publishing, 2013).
52. *Evening Post*, 26 April 1983.
53. *Australian*, 10 August 1981.
54. *Weekend Australian*, 8 August 1981; *Sydney Morning Herald*, 8 August 1981.
55. *Evening Post*, 22 April 1982.
56. As quoted in the opening epigram of Gammage, *The Broken Years.*
57. *Auckland Institute and Museum News*, March 1982.

58. *Evening Post*, 22 April 1982.
59. Murray Gadd, 'A bibliography of Maurice Shadbolt: 1956–1980', *Journal of New Zealand Literature*, 2 (1984), 75–96.
60. For an overview of the August offensive see Ashley Ekins, *Gallipoli: A ridge too far* (Canberra: Exile Publishing, 2013), and Rhys Crawley, 'The myths of August at Gallipoli', in Craig Stockings (ed.), *Zombie Myths of Australian Military History* (Sydney: New South Press, 2010), 50–69.
61. Jeremy Payne, *Kaleidoscope*, TVNZ, 1982.
62. Michael Neil, Introduction in Maurice Shadbolt, *Once on Chunuk Bair* (Auckland: Hodder & Stoughton, 1982).
63. Ormond Burton, *The Silent Division: New Zealanders at the Front, 1914–1919* (Sydney: Angus & Robertson, 1935), 99.
64. Ibid., 120.
65. Maurice Shadbolt, *Voices of Gallipoli* (3rd edn) (Auckland: David Ling Publishing, 2014), 9–10.
66. James Bennett, 'Man alone and men together: Maurice Shadbolt, William Malone and Chunuk Bair', *Journal of New Zealand Studies*, 13 (2012): https://ojs.victoria.ac.nz/jnzs/article/view/1189
67. Shadbolt, *Voices of Gallipoli*, 8–9.
68. From Shadbolt's introduction to the play's opening-night programme, quoted in Philip Mann, 'Maurice Shadbolt the dramatist: On the dramaturgy of *Once on Chunuk Bair*', in Ralph Crane (ed.), *Ending the Silences: Critical essays on the works of Maurice Shadbolt* (Auckland: Hodder Moa Beckett, 1995), 130–46, 131.
69. Shadbolt, *Once on Chunuk Bair*, 83.
70. Robert James Rhodes, *Gallipoli* (New York: Macmillan, 1965).
71. What Jenny Macleod called 'superb but doubtful history' – Jenny Macleod, *Reconsidering Gallipoli* (London: Manchester University Press, 2014), 218.
72. Mann, 'Maurice Shadbolt the dramatist', 132.
73. Ian Mune, *Mune: An autobiography* (Nelson: Craig Potton Publishing, 2010), 225.
74. Quoted in Mann, 'Maurice Shadbolt the dramatist', 133.
75. J.M. Wilson, '"Colonize, pioneer. Bash and slash": *Once on Chunuk Bair* and the Anzac myth', *Journal of New Zealand Studies*, 34, 1 (2016), 27–53, 40.
76. In an interview with Philip Mann, 'The first production of *Once on Chunuk Bair*', *Illusion*, 11 (1989), 15.
77. Santanu Das, Introduction, in S. Das (ed.), *Race, Empire and First World War Writing* (Cambridge: Cambridge University Press, 2014), 4. See also Toby Haggith and Richard Smith, 'Sons of our empire: Shifting ideas of race and the cinematic representation of imperial troops in the World War', in Lee Grieveson and Colin MacCabe (eds), *Empire and Film* (London: Bloomsbury, 2011), 35–53.
78. Quoted in Mann, 'Maurice Shadbolt the dramatist', 133.
79. Jeremy Payne, *Kaleidoscope*, TVNZ, 1982.
80. This flattering contrast has been endorsed by Jock Phillips, James Bennett and Christopher Pugsley: see Jock Phillips, *To the Memory: New Zealand's war memorials* (Nelson: Potton & Burton, 2016); Bennett, 'Man alone and men together'; and Christopher Pugsley, *The Anzacs at Gallipoli: A story for Anzac Day* (Reed: Auckland, 1999).
81. Shadbolt had access to the diaries and letters of Malone over the 1980s, before the Malone

family papers were deposited with the National Library in 2008 (Shadbolt, *Voices of Gallipoli*). Much of this material was represented by Chris Pugsley and Charles Ferrall in *Remembering Gallipoli* (Wellington: Victoria University Press, 2015).

82. *Gallipoli: The New Zealand story*, TVNZ, 1984.
83. Chris Pugsley, 'Military advisor's perspective', *NZ On Screen*, April 2009: www.nzonscreen.com/title/gallipoli-the-new-zealand-story-1984/background
84. *Gallipoli: The New Zealand story*, TVNZ, 1984.
85. 'Christopher Pugsley on military history', RNZ: www.rnz.co.nz/national/programmes/writers/audio/20144937/christopher-pugsley-on-military-history
86. Chris Pugsley, *Gallipoli: The New Zealand story* (Auckland: Hodder & Stoughton, 1984), 1.
87. See also Chris Pugsley, *The Anzac Experience: New Zealand, Australia, and Empire in the First World War* (Auckland: Reed New Zealand, 2001).
88. Pugsley, *Gallipoli*, 14–15.
89. Promotional material, Eph-D-MUSEUM-1984-01, 1984/1985, National Army Museum (NZNAM), Waiōuru.
90. *Evening Post*, 24 April 1984.
91. Hodge to Wilson, 30 March 1983, Eph-D-MUSEUM-1984-01, 1984/1985, NZNAM, Waiōuru.
92. See 'The New Zealand story', ibid.
93. Stretton to Banner, 26 August 1982, ibid.
94. *New Zealand Herald*, 14 April 1982; press release, TVNZ, 22 March 1982. See also *Timaru Herald*, 30 March 1982.
95. 'The New Zealand story', Eph-D-MUSEUM-1984-01, 1984/1985, NZNAM, Waiōuru.
96. I.J. Robinson to TVNZ, 13 February 1983; C. Hodge to I.J. Robinson, 23 February 1983, Eph-D-MUSEUM-1984-01, 1984/1985, NZNAM, Waiōuru.
97. 'Gallipoli – research notes', 4, ibid.
98. K.S. Inglis, 'The Unknown Australian Soldier', *Journal of Australian Studies*, 23 (1999), 8–17, 15. A similar observation was made by Jock Phillips as he contemplated the relationship between state institutions, history and national identity: see Jock Phillips, 'Our history, our selves: The historian and national identity', *New Zealand Journal of History*, 30, 2 (2001), 107–23, 114.
99. K.S. Inglis, *Sacred Places: War memorials in the Australian landscape* (Melbourne: Melbourne University Press, 1998), 63, 250.
100. Talbot to TVNZ, 14 April 1982; Hodge to Talbot, 6 May 1982; Eph-D-MUSEUM-1984-01, 1984/1985, NZNAM, Waiōuru.
101. This was first intimated by Pugsley in *Gallipoli: The New Zealand story*, then reiterated in subsequent works, with the author advocating for legislative change over the 1990s: see 356; the introduction to *The Anzac Experience*; and 'Papers relating to Chunuk Bair Day', MS-Papers-11408-30, 1990-2012, Alexander Turnbull Library, Wellington.
102. Pugsley, *Gallipoli*, 355.
103. Ibid., 356. The 'loss of innocence' became an enduring theme of Pugsley's work. In 1992 he collaborated in the curating of the exhibition *A Loss of Innocence* through the National Archive Collection, Wellington, which exhibited paintings, photographs and other material from various archive collections. See 'A loss of innocence', *Bulletin*, no. 78, May/June 1992, 2.
104. *New Zealand Herald*, 27 April 1984.
105. Even Ian Mune, the play's original director and an accomplished filmmaker, saw the limits of

such an adaptation; see Mune, *Mune*, 228; *Chunuk Bair*, Daybreak Pictures, 1992; Bennett, 'Man alone and men together', 56.

106. See Annabel Cooper, *Filming the Colonial Past: The New Zealand wars on screen* (Dunedin: Otago University Press, 2018).
107. For an example of a distinct historiographical project by Pākehā historians in response to this Māori cultural 'revival', see Michael King, *Being Pākehā: An encounter with New Zealand and the Māori renaissance 1945–2004* (Auckland: Hodder & Stoughton, 1985).

CHAPTER FOUR

1. George Steinmetz, 'Culture and the state', in George Steinmetz (ed.), *State/Culture: State-formation after the cultural turn* (Ithaca: Cornell University Press, 1999), 8–9.
2. The exception to this is Jock Phillips' chapter '75 years since Gallipoli', in Atholl Anderson et al. (eds), *Towards 1990: Seven leading historians examine significant aspects of New Zealand history* (Wellington: GP Books, 1988), 103–08.
3. *Age*, 2 February 1990. This was amid the possibility that he would announce the date for the next federal election shortly afterwards and thus land the 75th in the middle of an election campaign. The poll would eventually be called for 28 March. Hawke was leading in approval polls over Andrew Peacock by 40–50 percent at the time; *Canberra Times*, 15 February 1990.
4. Speech by Prime Minister Robert Hawke, dawn service, Gallipoli, 25 April 1990.
5. 'Interview with Ed Attridge', Series 316 – Transcripts and cassette tapes of interviews with senior public servants, Australian National University Archives (ANUA), 316–80.
6. Cabinet submission 6589, NAA: A14039, 6589, 8.
7. 'Bob Hawke regarding the meetings he has had with Mrs Thatcher in the United Kingdom', 1989, NAA: M3658, 1324305, NAA, Canberra.
8. 'Gallipoli 1990: Anzac Day ceremonies', 01/09/89, 814, AAAC 7873 W5084/19, ANZ, Wellington.
9. 'Co-ordination – unveiling of memorials – Ataturk', 1990/1/6/3, AAAC 7873 W5084/19 1990/1/6/3, ANZ, Wellington; *Canberra Times*, 26 April 1985.
10. 'Agriculture memorandum of understanding between New Zealand and Turkey', 3 April 1990, AAAC 7873 W5084/19 1990/1/6/3, ANZ, Wellington.
11. Memo, joint Trade and Defence ministerial delegation in April 1989, 23 February 1989, Ministry of Defence; Quigley to Boag, 3 March 1989, AAAC 7873 W5084/18 1990/1/1/2/1, ANZ, Wellington.
12. See Burcu Cevik-Compiegne, '"We were not, they could not be": Anzac and Turkish diasporic politics of memory', *History Australia*, 15, 2 (2018), 306–22.
13. Brad West, 'Dialogical memorialization, international travel and the public sphere: A cultural sociology of commemoration and tourism at the First World War Gallipoli battlefields', *Tourist Studies*, 10, 3 (2011), 209–25.
14. *Tuggerong Valley View*, 7 February 1990; *Western Advocate*, 4 January 1990.
15. *Geraldton Guardian*, 16 January 1990.
16. 'News release', Ben Humphreys, Ministry of Veterans Affairs, 29 June 1989, file 89/41, M3850, 204, NAA, Canberra.
17. *Canberra Times*, 13 February 1990. Death and ill-health reduced the final number to 57. There were no applicants from the Australian territories.

18. 'Artists to join Gallipoli pilgrimage', press release, Department of Veterans' Affairs, 18 January 1990, file 89/41, M3850, 204, NAA, Canberra.
19. Ben Humphreys, 'Gallipoli', Department of Veterans' Affairs, January 1990, M3850, 204, NAA, Canberra.
20. *South East Advertiser*, 24 January 1990.
21. *Age*, 25 April 1990.
22. For a contemporary record see 'The Indian Army at Gallipoli', RNZ: www.rnz.co.nz/national/programmes/anzacday/galleries/the-indian-army-at-gallipoli
23. 'Assault on the Gallipoli myth', *Reader's Digest* (date unknown) 1990.
24. Ibid.
25. *Canberra Times*, 16 December 1989.
26. *Daily Telegraph*, 14 February 1990; *Melbourne Sun*, 14 February 1990.
27. 'Gallipoli 1990: Second report [based on trip to Europe 13–31 October 1990]', Attridge and Quinn, M3850, 204, NAA, Canberra.
28. 'Meeting on Friday; 10 March 1990', file 89/41, M3850, 204, NAA, Canberra.
29. *Vetaffairs*, Gallipoli 1990 Commemorative Edition, 1990), 1–3.
30. *Courier Mail*, (date unknown) 1990.
31. *Melbourne Herald*, 9 February 1990; *Courier Mail*, 12 February 1990.
32. 'Sentimental journey back to "hell"', *Melbourne Herald*, (date unknown) 1990.
33. *Melbourne Herald*, 9 February 1990.
34. *Vetaffairs*, 1 December 1990.
35. Steve Levitt, articles in the *Age*, March 1990.
36. *Canberra Times*, 24 April 1990.
37. *Advertiser*, 10 February 1990.
38. *Vetaffairs*, 1 December 1990, 4.
39. 'Interview with the Hon John Brown', Radio 2UE, 17 December 1990: https://parlinfo.aph.gov.au/sites/default/files/original/00008236.pdf
40. *Canberra Times*, (date unknown) 1990.
41. *Daily Telegraph*, 16 February 1990.
42. *Sydney Morning Herald*, 18 February 1990.
43. *Age*, 26 April 1990.
44. LT PT 13/1905; 1/3/4/1 Gallipoli 1990, General Administration, Organisation and Management, ABFK 7560 W5130/6 1113/2/2 1, ANZ, Wellington.
45. Ross J. Bastiaan, *Images of Gallipoli: Photographs from the collection of Ross J. Bastiaan* (Oxford: Oxford University Press, 1988), 204.
46. 'The unveiling of a plaque at Lone Pine', Hollway to Bastiaan, 29 January 1990, NAA: M3850, 204, NAA, Canberra.
47. 'Gallipoli plaque at Chunuk Bair', 16 March 1990, CBA 1599, TORW 15/03/90, AAAC 7873 W5084/19, ANZ, Wellington.
48. 'Gallipoli: Plaque at Chunuk Bair', 20 March 1990, 20/0258Z GLC, AAAC 7873 W5084/19, ANZ, Wellington.
49. 'Chunuk Bair – Gallipoli: Plaque', 23 March 1990, AAAC 7873 W5084/19, ANZ, Wellington.
50. Geoffrey Palmer to Bob Hawke, 15 December 1989, 1/6/3, ABLD W3778/133 139, ANZ, Wellington.
51. 'About the Waitangi Tribunal': https://waitangitribunal.govt.nz/about-waitangi-tribunal/
52. *New Zealand Herald*, 1 December 1987.

53. Michael Bassett, Minister of Internal Affairs, media statement, 17 May 1989, AAAC 7873 W5084/19, ANZ, Wellington.
54. Ibid.
55. 2YA *Checkpoint*, 12 May 1989, ABLD W3778/26, ANZ, Wellington. *Hauraki Herald*, 10 June 1989. The celebrated horticulturalist Sam McGredy bred a special rose, 'Aotearoa–New Zealand', to be presented to the Queen at Waitangi: *Northern Advocate*, 2 December 1989.
56. 'Project update, NZ 1990 Te Wero: The Challenge', Michael Bassett, further papers, 2008-199 Series-4604, ATL, Wellington.
57. *Te Iwi*, April 1989; *Te Iwi*, May 1989.
58. *Evening Post*, 18 February 1989.
59. 2YA *Checkpoint*, 12 May 1989, ABLD W3778/26, ANZ, Wellington.
60. Media release, 'Schools' activity encouraged for NZ 1990', 24 July 1989, ABLD W3778/26, ANZ, Wellington.
61. *Belonging Here – Toi Taketake*, Michael Bassett, further papers, 2008-199 Series-4604, ATL, Wellington.
62. 'Te Taumata Rangatahi Mo Te Tiriti o Waitangi Youth Treaty Summit Panui', Michael Bassett, further papers, 2008-199 Series-4604, ATL, Wellington.
63. Claudia Orange, *The Treaty of Waitangi* (2nd edn) (Wellington: Bridget Williams Books, 2011), 320.
64. *New Zealand Herald*, 8 December 1989.
65. *New Zealand Herald*, 18 December 1989.
66. *Bay of Plenty Times*, 16 December 1989.
67. Memo from Peking to Wellington, 24/3/7/9 – 20/07052, GCEC, ABLD W3778/26, ANZ, Wellington.
68. 'Treasuring the obscure', *Evening Post*, 16 December 1989.
69. 'Miscellaneous – media clippings', ABLD W3778/26, ANZ, Wellington.
70. 'Minutes of the 1990 Coalition meeting 30 August 1988', 2, ABLD W3778/26, ANZ, Wellington.
71. Media release, New Zealand 1990, 18 May 1989, ABLD W3778/26, ANZ, Wellington.
72. *New Zealand Herald*, 15 May 1989.
73. *NZ Listener*, 5 February 1990.
74. 'Miscellaneous – media clippings', ABLD W3778/26, ANZ, Wellington.
75. '1990 waka transportation', 28 November 1990, 1/4/2/1, ABLD W3778/8, ANZ, Wellington.
76. *Auckland Star*, 8 June 1989.
77. For various iwi see *Northland Age*, 26 April 1989; *Dominion*, 24 May 1989; *New Zealand Herald*, 16 May 1989; *Hawke's Bay Tribune*, 15 May 1989; *Otago Daily Times*, 10 April 1989.
78. *Herald Tribune*, 15 August 1989; *Hawke's Bay Tribune*, 22 August 1989.
79. *Nelson Evening Mail*, 1 August 1989.
80. *Nelson Evening Mail*, 9 August 1989.
81. *Hawkes Bay Tribune*, 11 June 1989.
82. 'Miscellaneous – media clippings', ABLD W3778/26, ANZ, Wellington.
83. 2YA radio, 31 August 1989, ABLD W3778/26, ANZ, Wellington.
84. *Daily News*, 15 August 1989.
85. Helen Robinson, 'Making a New Zealand Day: The creation and context of a national holiday', *New Zealand Journal of History*, 46, 1 (2012), 37–51 (44).

86. *Northern Advocate*, 8 June 1989.
87. *Northern Advocate*, 21 August 1989; *Chronicle*, 21 August 1989.
88. *Newsletter: Project Waitangi – Pākehā debate the Treaty*, February/March 1989, 1.
89. Duncan Ivison, Paul Patton and Will Sanders, Introduction, in Duncan Ivison (ed.), *Political Theory and the Rights of Indigenous Peoples* (Cambridge: Cambridge University Press, 2000), 3–10.
90. *New Zealand Herald*, 3 August 1989.
91. *Metro*, August 1989.
92. Ibid.
93. *Metro*, March 1989.
94. Ibid.
95. *Ashburton Guardian*, 29 December 1988.
96. *New Zealand Herald*, 3 August 1989.
97. *Te Iwi*, May 1989.
98. *New Zealand Herald*, 3 August 1989.
99. *Whakatane Beacon*, 25 July 1989.
100. *Press*, 5 June 1989.
101. 2YA, *Insight*, 18 June 1989, ABLD W3778/26, ANZ, Wellington.
102. 2YA, *Checkpoint*, 8 May 1989, ABLD W3778/26, ANZ, Wellington.
103. *Times Literary Supplement*, 2 February 1990; as he had argued in *NZJH* in 1971.
104. 2YA, *Checkpoint*, 8 May 1989; 2YA, 12 May 1989, ABLD W3778/26, ANZ, Wellington.
105. 2YA, 12 May 1989, ABLD W3778/26, ANZ, Wellington.
106. *Checkpoint*, 15 May 1989, ABLD W3778/26, ANZ, Wellington.
107. Claudia Orange, *The Treaty of Waitangi* (2nd edn) (Wellington: Bridget Williams Books, 2011), 228.
108. *Te Iwi*, May 1989.
109. *Evening Post*, 18 July 1989.
110. 'Minutes of meeting Tuesday 11 October 1988', 3, Michael Bassett, further papers, 2008-199 Series-4604, ATL, Wellington.
111. Orange, *The Treaty of Waitangi*, 228.
112. 'RSA wants Anzac Day kept as it is', *New Zealand Herald*, 2 May 1996; 'Anzac Day to stay as is says Bolger', *Evening Post*, 26 April 1996.

CHAPTER FIVE

1. Prime Minister Hon Paul Keating MP, 'Remembrance Day 1993: Commemorative address', 1993: www.awm.gov.au/commemoration/speeches/keating-remembrance-day-1993; Prime Minister Hon Helen Clark MP, 'Address by the Prime Minister at the St Paul's Cathedral Memorial Service for the Unknown Warrior', 2004: http://rsa.org.nz/about/nws2004sep/Unknown_Warrior.htm
2. William Davies, *The Limits of Neo-Liberalism: Authority, sovereignty and the logic of competition* (London: University of London Press, 2016); Jonathan Derbyshire, 'Actually existing neo-liberalism: Notes on William Davies' Limits of Neo-Liberalism', *Renewal: A journal of social democracy*: www.renewal.org.uk/articles/the-limits-of-neo-liberalism
3. See Henry Atkinson, 'Meaning and values of repatriation', in Paul Turnbull and Michael

Pickering (eds), *The Long Way Home : The meanings and values of repatriation* (New York: Berghahn Books, 2010), 15–19.

4. Statement by the Prime Minister, The Hon P.J. Keating MP, Canberra, 18 October 1993, PM 115/94, NAA, Canberra; *Australian*, 17 December 2013.
5. This is cognisant with Tony Ballantyne's analysis of the archive and the need for historians to 'turn' to the historical formation of these institutions. See 'Archives, public memory and the work of history: The 2015 Hocken lecture', Hocken Collections Uare Taoka o Hākena, University of Otago, Dunedin, 2015.
6. Bart Ziino, 'Mourning and commemoration in Australia: The case of Sir W.T. Bridges and the Unknown Australian Soldier', *History Australia*, 4, 2 (2007), 40.1–40.17, 40.1.
7. *Newcastle Morning Herald*, 23 August 1933.
8. Martin A. Crotty, '25 April 1915, Australian troops land at Gallipoli: Trial, trauma and the "birth of the nation"', in Martin A. Crotty and David Andrew Roberts (eds), *Turning Points in Australian History* (Sydney: University of New South Wales Press, 2009), 100–14; RSL papers NL MS 6609/2655B, NLA, Canberra.
9. 'Burial of unknown warrior: Background', Australian War Memorial, Proposal for the creation of a Tomb of the Unknown Soldier, AWM371, 93/1219, AWM, Canberra. See also 'Unknown warrior burial of an "Australian"', Australian War Memorial, A431, 1947/138, NAA, Canberra.
10. 'Burial of unknown warrior – brief notes', February 1973, AWM publications relating to the Tomb of the Unknown Soldier, 1993, AWM371 93/1733, NAA, Canberra.
11. See the Australian War Memorial guidebooks 1941–59; for example, *Guide to Australian War Memorial* (Sydney: Hastead Press, 1941).
12. Cited in K.S. Inglis, *Sacred Places: War memorials in the Australian landscape* (Melbourne: Melbourne University Press, 1998), 320–22.
13. When the design for the Canberra memorial was made public in 1938, via a large model erected in the Melbourne Exhibition Hall, media noted the remarkable basilican dome and the four niches in the design intended to hold statues. Amid speculation as to whose statues would sit in these niches, Treloar made no mention of the fact that the design had left the hall under the dome empty for the possibility of a future tomb. *Smith's Weekly*, 8 January 1938. Also see note in AWM371, 93/1219, NAA, Canberra.
14. Daniel Marc Segesser, 'Strong and friendly bonds … out of shared tragedy?': The Gallipoli/Canakkale battles in Canberra's City Planning and Architecture of Memory', in Hans-Lukas Kieser, Pearl Nunn and Thomas Schmutz (eds), *Remembering the Great War in the Middle East: From Turkey and Armenia to Australia and New Zealand* (London: I.B. Tauris, 2021), 157–76.
15. Charles Bean to George Foster Pearce, March 1918, quoted in Michael McKernan, *Here Is Their Spirit: A history of the Australian War Memorial 1917–1990* (St Lucia: University of Queensland Press, 1991), 58.
16. Museums Australia, 'Report of the Committee of Inquiry on Museums and National Collections including the report of the planning committee on the Gallery of Aboriginal Australia', Watson Ferguson & Co, Brisbane, 1975.
17. K.S. Inglis, 'The Unknown Australian Soldier', *Journal of Australian Studies*, 23 (1999), 15.
18. Australian War Memorial Act 1980, Commonwealth Consolidated Acts (AustLII), 1 January 1980.
19. *Canberra Times*, 31 January 1985.

20. The war memorial was awarded a substantial increase of $2m, together with an increase of some 30 staff, in the Malcolm Fraser Liberal government's 1982 budget. *Canberra Times*, 16 July 1991.
21. Michael McKernan, 'Writing about war', in M. McKernan and M. Browne (eds), *Australia: Two centuries of war and peace* (Canberra: Unwin Australia, 1988), 1–24, 19.
22. Ashley Ekins, 'Proposal', 6 June 1991, Proposal for the creation of a Tomb of the Unknown Soldier, AWM371 93/1161, NAA, Canberra.
23. Bill Gammage, 'Anzac's influence on Turkey and Australia', *Journal of the Australian War Memorial*, 18 (1991), 19.
24. K.S. Inglis, 'A sacred place: The making of the Australian War Memorial', *War & Society*, 3, 2 (1985), 100.
25. McKernan, *Here Is Their Spirit.*
26. Ekins, 'Proposal'.
27. Ibid.
28. Inglis, 'The Unknown Australian Soldier', 15.
29. Bill Gammage, 'Anzac's influence on Turkey and Australia', *Journal of the Australian War Memorial*, 18 (1991), 19.
30. Inglis, 'The Unknown Australian Soldier', 15.
31. *Canberra Times*, 23 April 1994.
32. Richard Reid to Alan E. Heggen, 19 January 1993, 'Directing Group', AWM371 93/1219, NAA, Canberra.
33. See also Ken Inglis papers, File 162, bundle of three indexed subject files titled: 'Anzac Day', 1990s – Acc98.147, NLA, Canberra.
34. 'Briefing notes: Inglis, Unknown Soldier', 24 February 1993, AWM 93/3/1583; Richard Reid to Brendan Kelson and Michael McKernan, 29 January 1993, AWM371 93/1219, NAA, Canberra.
35. McKernan to Kelson, Proposal for the creation of a Tomb of the Unknown Soldier, AWM371 92/1780, NAA, Canberra.
36. Report of the Directing Group meeting, 18 May 1993, AWM371 93/1219, NAA, Canberra.
37. Ibid.
38. Report of the Directing Group meeting, 14 September 1993, 3b, AWM371 93/1219, NAA, Canberra; Notes from meeting with Professor Ken Inglis ANU, 2 March 1993, 'Directing Group', AWM371 93/1219, NAA, Canberra.
39. Reid to McMahon, AHC, London, 28 July 1993, Negotiations with Commonwealth War Graves Commission, AWM371 93/1222, NAA, Canberra.
40. Ibid.
41. Alan Jones interview with Minister of Veterans' Affairs Ben Humphreys, 4 March 1993, 20E (transcript), Tomb of the Unknown Soldier – Media and community involvement, AWM371 93/2021, NAA, Canberra.
42. *Australian*, 7 October 1995.
43. Faulkner to Jorgenson, Chatswood RSL, AWM371 93/1219, AWM, Canberra.
44. Freeman to Kelson, 16 September 1993, AWM371 93/1219, AWM, Canberra.
45. Kelson to Garland, 25 November 1992, AWM371 93/1219, AWM, Canberra.
46. Smith to Kelson, 17 September 1992, AWM 87/0604, AWM371 93/1222, AWM, Canberra.
47. CWGC to Alan E. Heggen, 15 July 1992, P133/1 REC 15, Tomb of the Unknown Soldier – Negotiations with CWGC, AWM371 93/1222, NAA, Canberra.

48. The trip to Israel was significant: as well as meeting Jewish museum representatives, Kelson was interested in the Israeli government's failed project to repatriate Palestinian Jews who fought and died in Italy during the war.
49. Interview with Michael McKernan, 17 May 1993, 2CN, Tomb of the Unknown Soldier – Media and community involvement, AWM371 93/2021, NAA, Canberra.
50. Michael McKernan, 'Talking points', 18 May 1993, AWM371 93/2021, NAA, Canberra.
51. *Melbourne Herald*, 12 April 1993; *Canberra Times*, 6 March 1993.
52. *Canberra Times*, 22 October 1993.
53. Report of the Directing Group meeting, 14 September 1993; Latimer to Kelson, 26 July 1993, AWM371, 93/1219, NAA, Canberra. When the war memorial commissioned a special postcard to be sold in the lead-up to the entombment, the designer was contacted by the Naval Association and informed that the text could be changed from 'soldier' to 'warrior'. 'Telephone enquiries' (transcript), 8 September 1993, AWM371 93/2021, NAA, Canberra.
54. 'Official pallbearers', Garland to Prime Minister Paul Keating, 11 November 1993, AWM371 93/1608, NAA, Canberra.
55. Hall to Beaurepaire, chair of the Australian War Memorial Council, 5 September 1993, AWM371 93/1608, NAA, Canberra; Kelson to Hall, 16 September 1993, AWM371 93/1608, NAA, Canberra.
56. Healy to Kelson, 8 September 1993. Kelson cited the 'tight schedule': Kelson to Healy, 20 September 1993, AWM371 93/1608, NAA, Canberra.
57. Cullen to Kelson, 15 August 1993; reply 23 August 1993, AWM371 93/1645, NAA, Canberra.
58. RSL to Paul Keating, 28 June 1993, AWM371 93/1645, NAA, Canberra.
59. Kelson to Keys, 12 August 1993; Keys to Kelson, 5 August 1993, AWM371 93/1369, NAA, Canberra.
60. Thompson to Llewellyn, 2 July 1993, AWM371 93/113 271 2840; Garce to RSL, 28 June 1993, AWM371, 93/1068; Australian Heritage Commission Report, 3 June 1993; Memo to Brendan Kelson, 8 October 1993, Directing Group, 1993, AWM371, 93/1219, NAA, Canberra.
61. Kelson to Beaurepaire, 16 May 1993; Beaurepaire to Miller, 26 May 1993, AWM371 93/1369, NAA, Canberra.
62. Witheridge to Latimer, 20 July 1993, AWM371 93/1369, NAA, Canberra.
63. David M. Kennedy, *Freedom from Fear: The American people in depression and war, 1929–1945* (Oxford: Oxford University Press, 1999), 427–34.
64. www.awm.gov.au/visit/visitor-information/features/hall-of-memory/tomb
65. Tonkin Zulaikha Harford to Raffety, 'Tomb slab inscription', AWM371 93/1369, NAA, Canberra.
66. *Canberra Times*, 18 September 1993.
67. The governor-general would instead be named 'chief mourner': Report of the Directing Group meeting, 27 July 1993, AWM371 93/1219, NAA, Canberra.
68. Ibid.
69. *Canberra Times*, 12 November 1993.
70. Elizabeth M. Reed, *Bigger Than Gallipoli: War, history and memory in Australia* (Perth: University of Western Australia Press, 2004), 39.
71. *ABC News*, 11 November 2011.
72. *Guardian*, 29 October 2013
73. 'Remembrance Day commemorative address', AWM, November 11: www.awm.gov.au/commemoration/speeches/commemorative-address-11-november-2013

74. *New Zealand Parliamentary Debates* (*NZPD*), 1921, 192, 213.
75. Gareth Phipps, 'Bringing our boy home: The tomb of the unknown warrior and contemporary war remembrance', *Journal of New Zealand Studies*, 10 (2011), 159–84, 161.
76. *Auckland Star*, 6 January 1930.
77. Dominion Executive Council Records, New Zealand Returned and Services Association (NZRSA), Wellington.
78. E.g. *Ashburton Guardian*, 12 November1921, and *Evening Post*, 14 November 1921.
79. Phipps, 'Bringing our boy home', 181.
80. Conal McCarthy, *Te Papa: Reinventing New Zealand's national museum, 1998–2018* (Wellington: Te Papa Press, 2018), 70.
81. Newsletter, Nov–Dec, 1993, Papers of Dame Miriam Patricia Dell, ATL MS-Group-024.
82. *Evening Post*, 19 October 1999.
83. Graham Hucker, 'A determination to remember: Helen Clark and New Zealand's military heritage', *Journal of Arts Management, Law, and Society*, 40, 2 (2010), 105–18, 110.
84. Jonathan Boston, *Left Turn: The New Zealand general election of 1999* (Wellington: Victoria University Press, 2000); Brian Edwards, *Helen: Portrait of a prime minister* (Auckland: Exisle Publishing, 2001).
85. Michael Volkerling, 'The Helen Clark years: Cultural policy in New Zealand 1999–2008', *Journal of Arts Management, Law, and Society*, 40, 2 (2010), 95–104.
86. *New Zealand Herald*, 2 December 2003.
87. McGibbon to Acting General Manager, Heritage Group, 11 November 1999, Department of Internal Affairs, Ministry of Culture and Heritage (MCH), Wellington.
88. Ian McGibbon, *New Zealand Battlefields and Memorials of the Western Front* (Auckland: Penguin Books, 2001); Phipps, 'Bringing our boy home', 162.
89. The first conference was held in 1995 on the theme of 'New Zealand in the Second World War', followed by another on 'New Zealand in the South African War' in 1999. The 'Zealandia's Great War: New Zealand and the First World War' conference was to be held in July in the lead-up to the unknown interment, with keynotes from a range of academics, including Annette Becker, esteemed historian of the French Tomb of the Unknown Soldier.
90. Press release, 25 April 2002, MCH.
91. *Evening Post*, 25 April 2002.
92. 'Tomb of the Unknown Soldier, minutes – final copy', 13 September 2002, MCH, Wellington.
93. 'Tomb of the Unknown New Zealand Warrior', BR2002/142, 7 May 2002, Minister for Culture and Heritage, Wellington, MCH, Wellington.
94. Briefing to Clark, 11 December 2001, 3, MCH, Wellington.
95. Stubbs to Gower, MG 4/7, MCH, Wellington.
96. New Zealand's application to request the repatriation was more or less identical to the Canadian formula, C08939/BRU, 20 January 2004; REC 15/2, 21 October 1998. Also, the Canadians had copied Australia: Jean-Yves Bronze to AWM, 7 April 1997, MCH, Wellington.
97. The Canadian context is especially interesting as the NWM Carillon was intended as a sister instrument to the Peace Tower Carillon at the Parliament Buildings, Ottawa, Canada. See *The Tomb of the Unknown NZ Warrior: Conditions for the design selection process*, Ministry of Culture and Heritage, Wellington, 2003, 4, MCH, Wellington.
98. C00159/PAR, FRA/NZ/2/7/1 – 27 November 2002, MCH, Wellington.
99. 'Tomb of the Unknown Soldier – handover ceremony' (email), 2 December 2002, MCH, Wellington.

100. Statement by Prime Minister, The Hon Helen Clark MP, December 2002, MCH, Wellington. The selection panel comprised Andrew Renton-Green, chair of the war memorial; Studio Pacific architect Evzen Novak; a representative of the Defence Force; and one Māori and one non-Māori artist or curator.
101. OCS 3E, 'Winning design unveiled for Tomb of the Unknown Warrior', 14 April 2003, MCH, Wellington.
102. Ibid.
103. 'The Tomb of the Unknown NZ Warrior, conditions for the design selection process', 4, MCH, Wellington.
104. Tony Nightingale, 'Not so sacred ground: The National War Memorial', *Phanzine*, 9, 1 (2003), 4–5.
105. Minutes, 30 April 2003, MCH. Vincent O'Sullivan composed a poem, 'Homecoming – Te Hokinga Mai', to be read at the interment ceremony: www.mch.govt.nz/pukeahu/park/national-war-memorial/tomb/homecoming
106. E.g. the press release from Massey University: www.massey.ac.nz/~wwpubafs/2003/press_releases/15_05_03.html
107. *Mana*, June–July 2000; Peter Moehu, 'Hikoi ki Te Waipounamu', *Historic Places*, 78 (2000), 12–13. The memorial has become a pilgrimage site for Taranaki Māori and other communities: see Deena Coster, 'Peace hikoi to Parihaka presents new possibilities for partnership between Maori and Pakeha', *Stuff*, 2016: www.stuff.co.nz/taranaki-daily-news/80694456/peace-hikoi-to-parihaka-presents-new-possibilities-for-partnership-between-maori-and-pakeha
108. John-Paul Powely, *Kaitiaki o te Pō* (Wellington: Seraph Press, 2018).
109. Rachel Buchanan, 'Naming the Unknown Warrior': http://pukeahuanthology.org/stories/contesting-histories/naming-the-unknown-warrior/
110. Stubbs to Clark, 18 November 2003, 2, MCH, Wellington.
111. Others objected to 'warrior' on the basis that it evoked the rugby league team of the same name, and was more aggressive than 'soldier', which might have included medical corps personnel. Warrior was also deemed too grand for New Zealand's 'down to earth' character. The ministry supported the RSA view, internally ('Tomb of the Unknown Soldier, Minutes – Final copy', 13 December 2002, MCH, Wellington). For critical analysis of this imagery, see Brendan Hokowhitu, 'History and masculinity', in J. O'Brien and C. Anderson (eds), *Sources and Methods in Indigenous Studies* (London: Routledge, 2017), 195–204. For a history of the use of 'warrior' in commemorative language see Vincent O'Malley, *The Great War for New Zealand: Waikato 1800–2000* (Wellington: Bridget Williams Books, 2016), especially chapters 1 and 2.
112. Baird would publish his own reflections on the repatriation in 2020; see Kingsley Baird, 'The past we harvest that was yours': The rhetoric of national identity and the legacy of the Unknown Warrior in New Zealand memory, *Bulletin of the Auckland Museum*, 21 (2020), 19–26.
113. Kingsley Baird, 'Tomb of the Unknown Warrior – Te Toma o Te Toa Matangaro': www.kingsleybaird.com/artwork/tomb-of-the-unknown-warrior
114. Commonwealth War Graves Commission policy was not to allow non-CWGC staff at exhumations.
115. Helen Clark, 'Address at memorial service for Unknown Warrior', 11 November 2004: http://rsa.org.nz/about/nws2004sep/Unknown_Warrior.html

116. Mark McKenna, 'Keeping in step: The Anzac "resurgence" and "military heritage" in Australia and New Zealand', in S. Sumartojo and B. Wellings (eds), *Nation, Memory and Great War Commemoration: Mobilizing the past in Europe, Australia and New Zealand* (Oxford: Peter Lang, 2014), 151–67, 133.
117. *ABC News*, 11 November 2013.
118. The problems of the Australian War Memorial omitting reference to Australian colonial violence remains a contested issue in Australia. See Paul Daley, 'Why does the Australian War Memorial ignore the frontier war?', *Guardian*, 12 September 2013: www.theguardian.com/world/2013/sep/12/australian-war-memorial-ignores-frontier-war
119. McKernan, *Here Is Their Spirit.*

CHAPTER SIX

1. Quoted in Mark McKenna, 'When did Anzac become our national day?', in Henry Reynolds and Marilyn Lake (eds), *What's Wrong with Anzac?* (Sydney: New South Books, 2010), 110–34.
2. Nick Dyrenfurth, 'Mateship: Secular Australia's religion and how John Howard hijacked it', *Sydney Morning Herald*, 25 December 2014: www.smh.com.au/national/mateship-secular-australias-religion-and-how-john-howard-hijacked-it-20141217-129c7t.html
3. Karl James, 'Before the Anzac dawn: A military history of Australia to 1915', *Journal of Australian Studies*, 38, 3 (2014), 364–66.
4. For an example of this language in 2015, see 'The Australian Boer War Memorial': www.bwm.org.au/boer_war_day/Boer_War_Day2015.php
5. Jeff Hopkins-Weise, *Blood Brothers:The Anzac genesis* (Kent Town: Wakefield Press, 2009).
6. As quoted in Stuart McMillan, 'Defending the realm', in Philippa Mein Smith, Peter J. Hempenstall and Shaun Goldfinch (eds), *Remaking the Tasman World* (Christchurch: Canterbury University Press, 2008), 233–66, 261.
7. Graham Hucker, 'A determination to remember: Helen Clark and New Zealand's military heritage', *Journal of Arts Management, Law, and Society*, 40, 2 (2010), 105–18, 111.
8. Michael Bassett, *New Zealand's Prime Ministers: From Dick Seddon to John Key* (Auckland: David Ling, 2017), 465.
9. 'New Zealand memorial a tribute to the Anzac relationship, says PM', 24 April 2001: www.beehive.govt.nz/node/10309. The sculptor was Kingsley Baird who, three years later, would step into the breach of the failed Unknown Warrior tomb design.
10. Helen Clark, Prime Minister of New Zealand, 'Dedication of the New Zealand memorial, Anzac Parade, Canberra', 24 April 2001: www.beehive.govt.nz/node/10506
11. As quoted in Kathryn Hunter, 'States of mind: Remembering the Australian–New Zealand relationship', *Journal of the Australian War Memorial*, 36 (2001): www.awm.gov.au/articles/journal/j36/nzmemorial
12. John Howard, '"Australians at War" Address, Australia House, London', 10 November 2003: https://pmtranscripts.pmc.gov.au/release/transcript-20994
13. 'Transcript of the Prime Minister The Hon John Howard MP, address at official luncheon Parliament Buildings Wellington, New Zealand', 17 February 1997: https://pmtranscripts.pmc.gov.au/release/transcript-10245
14. Ibid.

15. Matt McDonald, '"Lest we forget": The politics of memory and Australian military intervention', *International Political Sociology*, 4, 3 (2010), 287–302.
16. 'Reflections on East Timor', 16 September 2015, *ANU* News: http://sdsc.bellschool.anu.edu.au/news-events/stories/3401/reflections-east-timor
17. John Howard, 'Radio interview with Mike Carlton, Radio 2UE', 9 September 1999: https://pmtranscripts.pmc.gov.au/release/transcript-11222
18. Ibid.
19. Ibid.
20. John Howard, 'Official visit by New Zealand Prime Minister', 2 March 2000: https://pmtranscripts.pmc.gov.au/release/transcript-11582
21. John Howard, 'Joint press conference with the Rt Hon Helen Clark MP Wellington, New Zealand', 26 February 2001: https://pmtranscripts.pmc.gov.au/release/transcript-11978
22. Published as *Defence 2000: Our future defence force*, Parliament of Australia, 2000.
23. Damien Fenton, 'Has New Zealand let down the Anzac tradition?', *New Zealand International Review* (2001), 19–22; see also Helen Clark, 'New Zealand foreign policy: Pushing the big ideas', *New Zealand International Review* (1999), 2–4; 'New Zealand's Clark government creates a strategic vacuum in the Pacific', *Defence and Foreign Affairs Strategic Policy*, 29, 4/5/ (2001), 10–11.
24. Quoted in Fenton, ibid., 19.
25. 'Transcript of the Prime Minister The Hon John Howard MP joint press conference with the Rt Hon Helen Clark Prime Minister of New Zealand', 2 March 2000: https://pmtranscripts.pmc.gov.au/release/transcript-11485
26. John Howard, 'Dawn service, Gallipoli, Turkey', 25 April 2000: https://pmtranscripts.pmc.gov.au/release/transcript-22688
27. John Howard, 'Turkish international service at Mehmetcik Abide', 25 April 2000: https://pmtranscripts.pmc.gov.au/release/transcript-22690
28. Phil Goff, Minister of Foreign Affairs and Trade, 'Anzac dawn service speech – Gallipoli', 25 April 2001: www.beehive.govt.nz/node/10329
29. 'Goff speech to Turkish international service at Mehmetcik Abide', *Scoop*, 25 April 2001: www.scoop.co.nz/stories/PA0104/S00376/turkish-international-service-at-mehmetcik-abide.htm
30. John Howard, 'Joint press conference with The Rt Hon Helen Clark MP, Prime Minister of New Zealand, Kirribilli House, Sydney', 28 September 2000: https://pmtranscripts.pmc.gov.au/release/transcript-22887
31. John Howard, 'Joint press conference with the Rt Hon Helen Clark MP Wellington, New Zealand', 26 February 2001: https://pmtranscripts.pmc.gov.au/release/transcript-11978
32. Ibid. For the New Zealand press reaction to the use of 'bludger' language, see *New Zealand Herald*, 25 April 2001.
33. John Howard, 'Joint doorstop with Prime Minister of New Zealand, The Rt Hon Helen Clark MP, Auckland', 24 February 2001: https://pmtranscripts.pmc.gov.au/release/transcript-11957
34. Hugh White, as quoted in McMillan, 'Defending the realm'.
35. For background on Howard's 'double feint' see Jack Holland, 'Howard's war on terror: A conceivable, communicable and coercive foreign policy discourse', *Australian Journal of Political Science*, 45, 4 (2010), 643–61.
36. Macmillan, 'Defending the realm', 233.
37. John Howard, 'Address at luncheon given by Rt Hon Helen Clark MP and Professor Peter Davis, Wellington', 26 February 2001: https://pmtranscripts.pmc.gov.au/release/transcript-12376

38. Ibid.
39. Ibid.
40. Greg Ansley, 'War brings New Zealand and Australia together and sets us apart', *New Zealand Herald*, 20 April 2001: www.nzherald.co.nz/nz/news/article.cfm?c_id=1&objectid=183936
41. Helen Clark, 'Dedication of the New Zealand Memorial, Anzac Parade, Canberra'. For contemporary reactions see 'Dedication day underlines spirit of Anzac mateship', 25 April 2001: www.nzherald.co.nz/nz/news/article.cfm?c_id=1&objectid=184628
42. John Howard, 'Speech at the National RSL Congress Melbourne', 5 September 2001: https://pmtranscripts.pmc.gov.au/release/transcript-12422
43. For a contemporary critique see Tony Wright, 'Rescuing the truth (about the *Tampa* crisis)', *Bulletin*, 120, 6313 (2002), 20–21. For a broader context see Anthony Burke, *Fear of Security: Australia's invasion anxiety* (Melbourne: Cambridge University Press, 2008).
44. John Howard, 'Television interview with Barrie Cassidy – Insiders ABC', 2 September 2001: https://pmtranscripts.pmc.gov.au/release/transcript-11908
45. John Howard, 'Joint press conference with the Prime Minister of New Zealand The Right Hon Helen Clark MP, Port Moresby, Papua New Guinea', 25 October 2005: https://pmtranscripts.pmc.gov.au/release/transcript-22004
46. *Dominion Post*, 6 November 2010.
47. John Howard, 'Anzac Day 2002', 25 April 2002: https://pmtranscripts.pmc.gov.au/release/transcript-12819
48. Clark reflected on this decision in 2006: Helen Clark, 'Iraq and Afghanistan', *Presidents & Prime Ministers*, 12, 3 (2003), 21, 36.
49. John Howard, 'Visit to Australia by the Right Hon Helen Clark MP Prime Minister of New Zealand', 15 February 2002: https://pmtranscripts.pmc.gov.au/release/transcript-12789; Bassett, *New Zealand's Prime Ministers*, 485.
50. 'PM will attend Queen Mother's funeral', *New Zealand Herald*, 2 April 2002: www.nzherald.co.nz/nz/news/article.cfm?c_id=1&objectid=1292774
51. 'Private Alec Campbell', *Monument Australia*: www.monumentaustralia.org.au/themes/people/military/display/100621-private-alec-campbell
52. Press Office – Governor-General of Australia, December 1997.
53. Campbell's statement has been frequently cited since; see for example, *New Zealand Herald*, 19 April 2015.
54. John Meyers and Bryn Dolan, 'Alec Campbell, the last sentinel of Gallipoli', *Sabretache*, 43, 4 (2002), 39–41.
55. John Howard, 'Address at the State Funeral Service of Alec William Campbell, the Cathedral Church of St David, Hobart', 24 May 2002: https://pmtranscripts.pmc.gov.au/release/transcript-12946
56. This 'epideictic' use of the Anzac legend was noted by Jason Flanagan, in J. Flanagan, 'John Howard's "use" of the Anzac Legend: Applying an epideictic lens', *Australian Journal of Politics and History*, 64, 1 (2018), 98–111.
57. John Howard, 'Radio interview with John Laws, 2UE', 14 October 2002: https://pmtranscripts.pmc.gov.au/release/transcript-12503
58. John Howard, 'Transcript of the Prime Minister the Hon John Howard MP joint doorstop interview with the Prime Minister of New Zealand, The Right Hon Helen Clark, Los Cabos, Mexico', 25 October 2002: https://pmtranscripts.pmc.gov.au/release/transcript-12638
59. John Howard, 'Transcript of the Prime Minister the Hon John Howard MP Press conference

on departure for London Sydney International Airport', 7 April 2002: https://pmtranscripts.pmc.gov.au/release/transcript-10673; John Howard, 'Transcript of The Prime Minister The Hon John Howard MP address to joint meeting of the US Congress', 12 June 2002: https://pmtranscripts.pmc.gov.au/release/transcript-12906

60. Ibid.
61. John Howard, 'Transcript of the Prime Minister the Hon John Howard MP interview with Steve Liebmann, *Today Show*', 15 August 2002: https://pmtranscripts.pmc.gov.au/release/transcript-12510/
62. Ibid.
63. John Howard, 'Joint press conference with New Zealand Prime Minister Helen Clark, Sheraton Hotel, Auckland', 9 March 2003: https://pmtranscripts.pmc.gov.au/release/transcript-20713
64. John Howard, 'Joint press conference with New Zealand Prime Minister Helen Clark Wellington, New Zealand', 10 March 2003: https://pmtranscripts.pmc.gov.au/release/transcript-20717; 'Who do you think you are kidding, Mr Howard?', *Australian Politics*, 9 March 2003: www.australianpolitics.com/news/2003/03/03-03-09a.shtml
65. John Howard, 'Address to official luncheon banquet hall, Parliament House Wellington, New Zealand', 10 March 2003: https://pmtranscripts.pmc.gov.au/release/transcript-20527
66. John Howard, 'Address at the launch of the distinctively Australian Chowder Bay Heritage Area, Mosman', 18 December 2003: https://pmtranscripts.pmc.gov.au/release/transcript-21053
67. Ibid.
68. Ibid.
69. John Howard, 'Doorstop interview, Sydney Airport', 1 May 2003: https://pmtranscripts.pmc.gov.au/release/transcript-20712
70. John Howard, 'Joint press conference with Prime Minister of New Zealand, Helen Clark, Parliament House, Canberra', 3 March 2004: https://pmtranscripts.pmc.gov.au/release/transcript-21139
71. Bassett, *New Zealand's Prime Ministers*, 470.
72. John Howard, 'Doorstop interview, Iraq', 25 April 2004: https://pmtranscripts.pmc.gov.au/release/transcript-21232
73. 'PM commemorates Anzac Day in Iraq', *ABC News*, 25 April 2004: www.abc.net.au/news/2004-04-25/pm-commemorates-anzac-day-in-iraq/175550
74. Ibid.
75. Ibid.
76. For contemporary responses, see *Why the War Was Wrong*, review, *Sydney Morning Herald*, 6 December 2003: www.smh.com.au/entertainment/books/why-the-war-was-wrong-20031206-gdhxbd.html
77. *Bulletin with Newsweek*, 121, 6361 (2003). For a contemporary interview with the protesters see Sylvia Lawson, 'Desecration and defacement: Criminalizing dissent in a time of war', *Overland* 182 (2006), 20–27.
78. *Bulletin with Newsweek*, 12121, 6361 (2003).
79. *New Zealand Parliamentary Debates*, 2004, 621, 16865.
80. Brian Edwards, *Helen: Portrait of a prime minister* (Auckland: Exisle Publishing, 2001); 'Anzac rain pays moving tribute', *Dominion Post*, quoted in Hucker, 'A determination to remember', 107.

81. Helen Clark, 'Address – Mt Albert Anzac Day service', *Scoop*, 25 April 2006: www.scoop.co.nz/stories/PA0604/S00360.htm
82. '30 years later, an apology to Vietnam vets', *Stuff*, 31 January 2009: www.stuff.co.nz/national/politics/461111/30-years-later-an-apology-to-Vietnam-vets
83. Michael Bassett, *The Mother of All Departments: The history of the Department of Internal Affairs* (Auckland: Auckland University Press, 1997), 252–57.
84. See Michael Volkerling, 'The Helen Clark years: Cultural policy in New Zealand 1999–2008', *Journal of Arts Management, Law, and Society*, 40, 2 (2010), 95–104.
85. 'Tears as Helen Clark barred from speaking at Waitangi', *1 News*, 6 February 2015: www.tvnz.co.nz/one-news/new-zealand/back-in-the-day-tears-as-helen-clark-barred-from-speaking-at-waitangi-6229227
86. 'Clark closes ugly chapter at Waitangi', *New Zealand Herald*, 6 February 2004: www.nzherald.co.nz/nz/news/article.cfm?c_id=1&objectid=888612
87. Ibid.
88. Tom Bennion, 'Lands under the sea: Foreshore and seabed', in Michael Belgrave, Merata Kawharu and David Williams (eds), *Waitangi Revisited: Perspectives on the Treaty of Waitangi* (Melbourne: Oxford University Press, 2004), 233–47.
89. 'Clark's no-show at Waitangi a political risk', *Stuff*, 15 December 2009: http://i.stuff.co.nz/national/blogs/on-the-house/1877816/Clarks-no-show-at-Waitangi-a-political-risk
90. *Telegraph* (UK), 12 November 2003.
91. A specially dedicated Australian memorial in London had been mooted in the interwar period. Bruce Scates, Frank Bongiorno, Rebecca Wheatley and Laura James, '"Such a great space of water between us": Anzac Day in Britain, 1916–39', *Australian Historical Studies*, 45, 2 (2014), 220–41, 236.
92. Robert Hill, Minister for Defence, 'Green light for Australian memorial in London', 11 January 2003: https://parlinfo.aph.gov.au/parlInfo/download/media/pressrel/QMA86/upload_binary/qma863.pdf;fileType=application%2Fpdf#search=%22media/pressrel/QMA86%22
93. Quoted in Paul Walker, 'Australian war memorial', *Architecture AU*, 1 September 2003: https://architectureau.com/articles/australian-war-memorial/
94. 'AWM London design competition', Office of Australian War Graves, NZ2350.G7 A82 2002.
95. 'About the wall', *AWM London*: www.awmlondon.gov.au/about-the-wall; 'Australian War Memorial London', Tonkin-Zulaikha-Greer Architects: www.tzg.com.au/project/aus-war-memorial/
96. 'Australian War Memorial London', Tonkin-Zulaikha-Greer Architects: www.tzg.com.au/project/aus-war-memorial/
97. 'Commemorative mission', CML2003 NLA 3424490.
98. John Howard, 'Address at the dedication of the Australian War Memorial, Hyde Park Corner, London', 11 November 2003: https://pmtranscripts.pmc.gov.au/release/transcript-20997
99. John Howard, 'Joint press conference with the Rt Hon Helen Clark, Prime Minister of New Zealand Parliament House, Wellington, New Zealand', 21 February 2005: https://pmtranscripts.pmc.gov.au/release/transcript-21625
100. 'You're not the voice, try and understand it', *Sydney Morning Herald*, 18 February 2005: www.smh.com.au/national/youre-not-the-voice-try-and-understand-it-20050218-gdkral.html; John Howard, 'Joint press conference with the Rt Hon Helen Clark Prime Minister of New

Zealand, Langham Hotel, New Zealand', 20 February 2005: https://pmtranscripts.pmc.gov.au/release/transcript-21620

101. John Howard, 'Address at a reception hosted by the Rt Hon Helen Clark Prime Minister of New Zealand, Langham Hotel, Auckland', 20 February 2005: https://pmtranscripts.pmc.gov.au/release/transcript-21621
102. Ibid.
103. As argued in the book of that title: Keith Sinclair, *A Destiny Apart: New Zealand's search for a national identity* (Auckland: Unwin Port Nicholson Press, 1986).
104. Helen Clark, 'Address at dawn service, Anzac day', 26 April 2005: www.beehive.govt.nz/speech/address-dawn-service-anzac-day
105. John Howard, 'Press conference Istanbul, Turkey', 26 April 2005: https://pmtranscripts.pmc.gov.au/release/transcript-21721
106. Grant Rodwell, *Moral Panics and School Educational Policy* (Melbourne: Routledge, 2018), 93.
107. 'Values for Australian Schooling': www.curriculum.edu.au/verve/_resources/9_point_values_with_flag_only.pdf; for context see 'National Framework for Values Education in Australian Schools', Australian Government: www.curriculum.edu.au/values/val_national_framework_for_values_education,8757.html
108. Helen Clark, 'Address to the Returned Services Association', 12 July 2005: www.beehive.govt.nz/node/23643
109. See 'Design for NZ memorial in Hyde Park, London': https://mch.govt.nz/nz-identity-heritage/national-monuments-war-graves/new-zealand-memorial-london
110. Judith Tizard, 'Speech delivered to NZ veterans and contingent travelling to the dedication of the NZ Memorial in London', 6 November 2006: www.beehive.govt.nz/speech/speech-delivered-nz-veterans-and-contingent-travelling-dedication-nz-memorial-london
111. 'Queen, Blair, Clark at opening of NZ memorial', *New Zealand Herald*, 12 November 2006: www.nzherald.co.nz/nz/news/article.cfm?c_id=1&objectid=10410356
112. 'NZ war memorial marks a "special bond"', *BBC*, 16 September 2006: http://news.bbc.co.uk/2/hi/uk_news/5350868.stm
113. 'PM: Address to the NZ memorial dedication ceremony', *Scoop*, 13 November 2006: www.scoop.co.nz/stories/PA0611/S00215/pm-address-to-the-nz-memorial-dedication-ceremony.htm
114. IPD/PD/L, 14 November 2006, MCH.
115. UK/NZ 2/4/1 Clark, 14 November 2006, MCH.
116. Helen Clark, 'Dominion Day reception', 27 September 2007: www.beehive.govt.nz/speech/dominion-day-reception
117. Bassett, *New Zealand's Prime Ministers*, 491.
118. 'Ministry for Culture and Heritage: Concepts of nationhood: Marking 100 years since the proclamation of Dominion status for New Zealand, 1907–2007', [Pamphlet folder. 2007] Eph-B-HISTORY-2007-01, ATL, Wellington.
119. Helen Clark, 'Prime Minister welcomes Australian commitment to Anzac Memorial', 10 May 2007: www.beehive.govt.nz/release/prime-minister-welcomes-australian-commitment-anzac-memorial
120. Helen Clark, 'The trans-Tasman relationship', 16 June 2008: www.beehive.govt.nz/speech/trans-tasman-relationship
121. John Howard, 'Transcript of the Prime Minister the Hon John Howard MP address at official luncheon Parliament Buildings, Wellington, New Zealand', 17 February 1997: https://pmtranscripts.pmc.gov.au/release/transcript-10245

CHAPTER SEVEN

1. Department of Aboriginal Affairs, *Out of the Silent Land* (Canberra: Australian Government Publishing Service, 1984); Elliott Johnston, *Royal Commission into Aboriginal Deaths in Custody: National report* (Canberra: Australian Government Publishing Service, 1991): www.austlii.edu.au/au/other/IndigLRes/rciadic/; Waitangi Tribunal, *Report of the Waitangi Tribunal on the Te Reo Maori Claim* (Wai 11), April 1986: https://forms.justice.govt.nz/search/Documents/WT/wt_DOC_68482156/Report
2. Tim Rowse, 'Indigenous cultural capital: An inescapably political concept', public lecture, Australian National University, 28 October 2019.
3. James Bennett, 'Lest we forget Black Diggers: Recovering Aboriginal Anzacs on television', *Journal of Australian Studies*, 38, 4 (2014), 457–75, 458; William Guynn, *Writing History in Film* (New York: Routledge, 2006), 178.
4. John Hartley and Alan McKee, *The Indigenous Public Sphere: The reporting and reception of Indigenous issues in the Australian media, 1994–1997* (Oxford: Oxford University Press, 2000), 31.
5. *Holmes*, 25 April 1991; *One News at 6*, Television New Zealand, 2004.
6. 'Briefing to the incoming ministers of Māori affairs and finance'; Māori Television, 2008: www.tpk.govt.nz/documents/download/182/tpk-mtsbim-2008-en.pdf; 'Māori Television marks fifth on-air anniversary', *Throng*, 13 April 2009: www.throng.co.nz/2009/03/Māori-television-marks-fifth-on-air-anniversary/
7. '*Tama Tū* press kit', 2006: http://tamatu.co.nz/media/2006+Press+kit+Tama+Tu.doc
8. The NITV news bulletin started in February 2008, initially with five minutes of news, later expanded to a 15-minute and finally a half-hour bulletin.
9. These conflicts include WWI and WWII, the Vietnam and Korean wars. When WWI began, Indigenous military men and women were not permitted to enlist on the grounds of their race: www.sbs.com.au/nitv/explainer/who-were-black-diggers
10. 'Black Diggers Anzac Day march on NITV', *Deadly Vibe*, 24 April 2008: www.deadlyvibe.com.au/2008/04/black-diggers-anzac-day-march-on-nitv/
11. *The Forgotten* (2003): www.creativespirits.info/resources/movies/the-forgotten
12. Lisanne Gibson and Joanna Besley, *Monumental Queensland: Signposts on a cultural landscape* (Brisbane: University of Queensland Press, 2004), 51–54.
13. *Koori Mail*, 21 May 2008.
14. *Koori Mail*, 8 December 2005; *National Indigenous Times*, December 2005.
15. Glen Stasiuk, 'Warriors then … warriors still: Aboriginal soldiers in the 20th century', in Andrew Gunstone (ed.), *History, Politics & Knowledge: Essays in Australian Indigenous studies* (Melbourne: Australian Scholarly Publishing, 2008), 191–205; 191–92.
16. Ibid., 195.
17. 'Director's reflections', *NZ on Screen Iwi Whitiāhua*, 2 September 2013: www.nzonscreen.com/title/maori-battalion-march-to-victory-1990/background/tainui-stephens
18. 'A perspective', *NZ on Screen Iwi Whitiāhua*, 19 August 2008: www.nzonscreen.com/title/maori-battalion-march-to-victory-1990/background/mihi-murray
19. These documentaries appeared alongside earlier documentaries that promoted alternative readings of the wars, such as *War Stories Our Mothers Never Told Us*, Gaylene Preston Productions, 1995.
20. 'RSA launches new national association', RSA, 5 October 2014: http://rsa.org.nz/News/RSA-launches-new-National-Association

21. 'NITV: Launch Day', *TV Tonight*, 5 December 2012: http://tvtonight.com.au/2012/12/nitv-launch-day.html; Tim Bradley, 'NITV free to air promo': www.youtube.com/watch?v=YAkOY3_RUJk
22. *Living Black*, 'Anzac Harry Allie', NITV, 2011.
23. This would become an important part of Denning Orman's tenure as channel manager. See 'Tanya Orman-Denning: 'It is vital that Aboriginal and Torres Strait Islander people see themselves positively reflected in the media', SBS, 18 October 2017: www.sbs.com.au/nitv/article/2017/10/13/tanya-orman-denning-it-vital-aboriginal-and-torres-strait-islander-people-see
24. 'Profile – Tanya Denning Orman', NITV: www.nitv.org.au/fx-story.cfm?sid=EA03540F-B96B-4736-E539CA3FB0D96160
25. *Living Black*, 'A Spirit Returns', NITV, 2012; *Awaken*, 'Anzac Legend and Legacy', NITV, 2012.
26. The Australian Reconciliation Barometer aims to identify the attitudes Indigenous and non-Indigenous Australians hold about one another, and about reconciliation. It also attempts to shed some light on opportunities for moving the relationship forward, towards a greater reconciled, shared unity. *Reconciliation Australia Annual Review 2012–13,* Reconciliation Australia, Canberra, 2013.
27. As quoted in the special episode of *Living Black* series, 23 April 2013, SBS.
28. NITV, *Anzac Day 2013*, SBS, 2013.
29. NITV, 'NITV commemorates Anzac Day', 25 April 2013: www.facebook.com/NITVAustralia/
30. For an example of how this narrative strategy has influenced non-Indigenous media coverage of Indigenous military experience, see 'Indigenous soldiers who hid their identity to serve: The untold story', ABC Local Radio PM programme, 31 December 2014: https://www.abc.net.au/radio/programs/pm/indigenous-soldiers-who-hid-their-identity-to/5994284
31. *Anzacs: Remembering our heroes – The forgotten warriors*, SBS, 2014.
32. *Koori Mail*, 30 April 2005.
33. *Koori Mail*, 7 May 2001.
34. Luke Briscoe, *NITV Anzac focus*, SBS, 24 June 2015: www.sbs.com.au/nitv/article/2015/04/06/nitv-anzac-focus
35. This was part of a comment thread on Māori Television's Facebook page: www.facebook.com/maoritv.nz/
36. Sue Abel, 'Māori Television, Anzac Day, and constructing "nationhood"', in Brendan Hokowhitu and Vijay Devadas (eds), *The Fourth Eye: Māori media in Aotearoa New Zealand* (Minnesota: University of Minnesota Press, 2013), 201–15.
37. Danny Keenan, 'We came of age on battlefields of New Zealand', *New Zealand Herald*, 20 April 2006: www.nzherald.co.nz/nz/news/article.cfm?c_id=1&objectid=10378631
38. *Ngā Morehu Hoia o Te Rua Tekau mā Waru*, Māori Television, 2010; *Hitler and the Gumdiggers*, Māori Television, 2010.
39. *Ngā Uri o Ruku te Kapa,* Māori Television, 2014.
40. *Te Marutuna o te Tangata: The Commanders*, Māori Television, 2014.
41. *The Final Hui: 28th Battalion Association,* Māori Television, 2013.
42. NZ officials debated whether Samoan recruits could make up a platoon within the contingent, which places their numbers around 50 men. See Mataia Louise, '"Odd men from the Pacific": The participation of Pacific Island men in the 28 (Maori) Battalion in the Second World War' (MA thesis, University of Otago, 2007), 49–50.
43. *Ngā Toa o Te Moana-Nui-A-Kiwa: Warriors of the Pacific: Solomon Islands*, Māori Television, 2011.

44. *Our Pacific*, Māori Television, 2010.
45. *Amoiha Te Mauri*, Māori Television, 2010.
46. Arapeta Awatere, *Awatere: A soldier's story* (ed. Hinemoa Awatere) (Wellington: Huia Press, 2002).
47. *The Black Legacy*, Māori Television, 2015.
48. *Ngarimu VC*, TVNZ, 1993; *Anzac Day 2013*, Māori Television, 2013; *London Gazette*, 1 June 1943.
49. *Ngārimu VC: The whanau remembers*, Maori Television, 2013.
50. Jerry Mateparae, 'Battle of Gate Pā commemorations', 29 April 2014: https://gg.govt.nz/publications/battle-gate-pa-commemorations
51. *Ngā Rā o Hune: The Days of June*, Māori Television, 2015; *Shovels and Guns*, Māori Television, 2015.
52. This is a recurring theme of Hokowhitu's work; see Brendan Hokowhitu and Tiffany Page, 'Postcolonial peace', *Junctures*, 14 (2011): https://junctures.org/index.php/junctures/article/view/195/280
53. 'S1Ep0: Exploring the gaps between us and the past', History Labs, 28 May 2018: https://historylab.net/s1ep0-exploring-the-gaps/
54. 'NITV journalist intimidated by Canberra police on Anzac Day', *Sydney Morning Herald*, 30 April 2015. NITV complained about the intimidation by police officers: 'NITV makes formal complaint against ACT police over alleged intimidation of journalist at Anzac Day protest march', *ABC*, 29 April 2015: www.abc.net.au/news/2015-04-29/nitv-to-make-formal-complaint-after-journalist-harrassed/6431536
55. Geoffrey White, *Memorializing Pearl Harbor: Unfinished histories and the work of remembrance* (Durham: Duke University Press, 2016).

CHAPTER EIGHT

1. James Brown, *Anzac's Long Shadow: The cost of our national obsession* (Sydney: Black Inc., 2014), 10; WW100, 'New Zealand's First World War Centenary Programme: The programme overview July 2014': ww100.govt.nz/sites/default/files/files/WW100
2. *Vetaffairs*, Gallipoli 1990 Commemorative Edition, 1990, 5.
3. 'Anzac Centenary: 100 years in the making', Anzac Centenary Advisory Board, January 2013: www.anzaccentenary.gov.au/sites/default/files/documents/acab_report.doc. See also 'How Australia may commemorate the Anzac Centenary', National Commission on the Commemoration of the Anzac Centenary, March 2011; and the Australian government's response to the Advisory Board report, published April 2013: http://centenaire.org/sites/default/files/references-files/govt_response.pdf
4. Brown, *Anzac's Long Shadow*, 10–13. Factoring in estimated private and corporate donations, that sum rises to $500m.
5. 'Anzac Centenary: 100 years in the making'.
6. 'Govt spends $20m on WWI arts and culture', *Stuff*, 19 April 2015: www.stuff.co.nz/national/last-post-first-light/67781872/govt-spends-20m-on-wwi-arts-and-culture
7. Ibid.
8. Carolyn Holbrook, 'Making sense of the Great War Centenary', in Carolyn Holbrook and Keir Reeves (eds), *The Great War: Aftermath and commemoration* (Sydney: New South Press, 2019), 244–48, 244.

9. To highlight Inglis' contribution in the centenary period, *Inside Story* republished his original despatches from the 1965 pilgrimage as an online article on the eve of Anzac Day: https://insidestory.org.au/letters-from-a-pilgrimage/
10. *Australian*, 26 April 2013.
11. Australian Historical Association, 'Foundational Histories: Australian Historical Association Conference 2015 – Conference Abstracts', University of Sydney, 2015: www.sydney.edu.au/arts/history/docs/aha2015/AHA_2015_conference_abstracts.pdf
12. Peter Mandler, 'The "crisis in the humanities" in comparative perspective', Australian Historical Conference 2015, University of Sydney, 2015.
13. 'Final 2015 NZHA conference schedule', New Zealand Historical Association: https://nzha.org.nz/2015/11/30/re-final-2015-nzha-conference-schedule/
14. 'Change to Anzac Day march declared out of order', *Age*, 25 February 2016: www.theage.com.au/national/victoria/change-to-anzac-day-march-declared-out-of-order-20160222-gn0do9.html
15. 'Anzac Day 2016: Alternate march held in Melbourne to protest against RSL rule change', *ABC News*, 25 April 2016: www.abc.net.au/news/2016-04-25/alternate-anzac-march-held-in-melbourne-protest-rsl-rule-change/7355320
16. '"Give me strength": Anzac protest boy's full barrage', *Newshub*, 26 April 2017: www.newshub.co.nz/home/new-zealand/2017/04/give-me-strength-anzac-protest-boy-s-full-barrage.html
17. Ibid.
18. 'Te Papa and Weta Workshop open ground-breaking Gallipoli exhibition', April 2015: www.tepapa.govt.nz/about/press-and-media/press-releases/2015-news-and-media-releases/te-papa-and-weta-workshop-open
19. For a lengthier discussion of this shift in authority see Nicholas Haig, 'Once more, with feeling: An enquiry into the Museum of New Zealand Te Papa Tongarewa's exhibition Gallipoli: The scale of our war' (MA thesis, Massey University, 2016), 49.
20. 'Te Papa and Weta Workshop open ground-breaking Gallipoli exhibition'; Jay Winter, *War Beyond Words* (Cambridge: Cambridge University Press, 2017), 3–5.
21. See for example the depiction of Anzac Cove at night, an image that aligns with Weir's famous 'Crossing the River Styx' scene in the 1981 film: www.tepapa.govt.nz/visit/exhibitions/gallipoli-scale-our-war
22. Technically, the war relics collection, distributed around museums in New Zealand by the Defence Department from 1919 to 1922, was a 'national war collection'. For a broader discussion around imperial war relic collecting, see Jennifer Wellington, *Exhibiting War: The Great War, museums, and memory in Britain, Canada and Australia* (Cambridge: Cambridge University Press, 2017), 1–12.
23. Chris Pugsley, *Gallipoli: The New Zealand story* (Auckland: Hodder & Stoughton, 1984), 11, 12, 27.
24. 'Te Papa and Weta Workshop open ground-breaking Gallipoli exhibition'.
25. Diego Bonelli, Thierry Jutel and Alfio Leotta, '"Selling the creative city": Wellington tourism film in the neoliberal era', *Studies in Australasian Cinema*, 13, 2–3 (2019), 32–50.
26. *Metro*, 1 March 2016.
27. 'Te Papa marks a record year for Gallipoli: The scale of our war', Te Papa, 25 April 2016: www.tepapa.govt.nz/about/press-and-media/press-releases/2016-news-and-media-releases/te-papa-marks-record-year-for

28. Puawai Cairns, 'The wait and the fight: Telling Māori WW1 histories and the search for alternative platforms', *Te Pouhere Kōrero*, 2016.
29. *Spirit of Anzac Centenary Experience*, Australian War Memorial: www.awm.gov.au/about/our-work/projects/spirit-anzac-centenary-experience
30. 'Coalition to spend half a billion dollars on Australian War Memorial project', *Guardian*, 31 October 2018: https://www.theguardian.com/australia-news/2018/nov/01/coalition-to-spend-half-a-billion-dollars-on-australian-war-memorial-project
31. 'Waitangi 175 ledger of events June 2016', D-0666522, MCH: https://mch.govt.nz/sites/default/files/Waitangi%20175%20ledger%20of%20events%20June%202016%20(D-0666522).PDF#overlay-context=waitangi175; 'History in the making at Mangungu Mission', *Scoop*, 29 January 2015: www.scoop.co.nz/stories/PO1501/S00111/history-in-the-making-at-mangungu-mission.htm
32. 'Governor-General of New Zealand: Waitangi Day speech', *Scoop*, 6 February 2015: www.scoop.co.nz/stories/PA1502/S00062/governor-general-of-new-zealand-waitangi-day-speech.htm
33. 'Te Hiku Media provide online live video stream of Waitangi', *Te Hiku*, 3 February 2015: https://tehiku.nz/te-hiku-tv/waitangi-175/217/te-hiku-media-provide-online-live-video-stream-of-waitangi
34. '175th anniversary of Waitangi Treaty', *Stuff*, 3 February 2015: www.stuff.co.nz/auckland/local-news/northland/northern-news/65713733/175th-anniversary-of-waitangi-treaty
35. John Key, 'Dedication of Australian memorial in Pukeahu National War Memorial Park', 20 April 2015: www.beehive.govt.nz/speech/dedication-australian-memorial-pukeahu-national-war-memorial-park
36. Ibid.
37. 'War memorial's "Australian" heart is made in India', *Stuff*, 21 April 2015: www.stuff.co.nz/national/67881452/war-memorials-australian-heart-is-made-in-india
38. 'War memorial haste is unseemly', *Stuff*, 27 September 2012: http://www.stuff.co.nz/dominion-post/comment/7732947/War-memorial-haste-is-unseemly
39. Ibid.
40. Ibid.
41. Tony Abbott, 'Remarks at unveiling of the Sir John Monash Centre winning design, Villers-Bretonneux', 26 April 2015: https://pmtranscripts.pmc.gov.au/release/transcript-24400
42. 'Submissions', Parliament of Australia: www.aph.gov.au/Parliamentary_Business/Committees/Joint/Public_Works/Sir_John_Monash_Centre/Submissions
43. David Stephens, 'Money, Monash and motive: Analysing a project in France', *Honest History*: http://honesthistory.net.au/wp/money-monash-and-motive-analysing-a-project-in-france-i/
44. As quoted by Romain Fathi, '"Look at me! Look at me!" The Sir John Monash Centre at Villers-Bretonneux: A Frenchman's reflection on his visit', 12 March 2019: http://honesthistory.net.au/wp/fathi-romain-look-at-me-look-at-me-the-sir-john-monash-centre-at-villers-bretonneux-a-frenchmans-reflection-on-his-visit/
45. David Ellery, 'Monash Centre: The new front in history wars', *Canberra Times*, 7 July 2018: www.canberratimes.com.au/story/6015151/monash-centre-the-new-front-in-history-wars/
46. 'The maintenance of memory: Sir John Monash Centre', *Architecture AU*, 28 May 2019: https://architectureau.com/articles/sir-john-monash-centre-aa/
47. Ibid.
48. 'Following in their footsteps – the making of Ngā Tapuwae', WW100: https://ww100.govt.nz/following-in-their-footsteps-the-making-of-nga-tapuwae

49. 'NZ war memorial museum on Western Front project to be unveiled', *RNZ*, 2 November 2018: www.rnz.co.nz/news/national/370090/nz-war-memorial-museum-on-western-front-project-to-be-unveiled
50. 'Tony Abbott: NZ "splendid sons" of Anzac in Isis fight', *New Zealand Herald*, 20 April 2015: www.nzherald.co.nz/nz/news/article.cfm?c_id=1&objectid=11435429
51. Tony Abbott, 'Interview with Scott Bevan, *ABC News*', 24 April 2015: https://pmtranscripts.pmc.gov.au/release/transcript-24392; 'Joint Statement by Prime Ministers Hon Tony Abbott and Rt Hon John Key', 1 March 2015: www.beehive.govt.nz/release/joint-statement-prime-ministers-hon-tony-abbott-and-rt-hon-john-key
52. Tony Abbott, '2015 Gallipoli dawn service', 25 April 2015: www.aph.gov.au/About_Parliament/Parliamentary_Departments/Parliamentary_Library/pubs/AnzacDay2016/Speeches
53. John Blaxland, 'Daesh and the unintended consequences of a modern Anzac force', *WA Today*, 4 March 2015: www.watoday.com.au/comment/daesh-and-the-unintended-consequences-of-a-modern-anzac-force-20150304-13un71.html
54. 'Indigenous Australians mark Anzac Day', SBS, 2015: www.sbs.com.au/news/indigenous-australians-mark-anzac-day
55. Andrew Stephens, 'Black Diggers: The untold story of our Indigenous soldiers', *Sydney Morning Herald*, 3 April 2015: www.smh.com.au/entertainment/black-diggers-the-untold-story-of-our-indigenous-soldiers-20150328-1m9pme.html
56. 'Indigenous soldiers who hid their identity to serve: The untold story', *ABC News*, 31 December 2014: www.abc.net.au/pm/content/2014/s4156077.htm
57. One of the project's leading researchers, Noah Riseman, has benefited from the expanding inclusionary narrative of Anzac as a scholar of LGBT military service and remembrance.
58. *For Country, For Nation*, Australian War Memorial: www.awm.gov.au/visit/exhibitions/for-country-for-nation
59. See Emily Gallagher's review, 'The first war for country, for nation', *Inside Story*, 18 May 2017: https://insidestory.org.au/the-first-war-for-country-for-nation/
60. Ibid.
61. Federica Caso, 'Representing indigenous soldiers at the Australian War Memorial: A political analysis of the art exhibition *For Country, For Nation*', *Australian Journal of Political Science*, 55, 4 (2020), 345–61, 346.
62. 'March of respect keeps growing', *Central*, 29 April 2015, 9.
63. 'NITV, Natalie Whyte, Redfern Anzac Day 2015', YouTube: www.youtube.com/watch?v=SptcqyNiHFw
64. 'March of respect keeps growing'.
65. 'Māori Television recreates past, bringing together New Zealanders to celebrate Anzac Day', Māori Television, 27 April 2018: http://stoppress.co.nz/news/Māori-television-recreates-past-bringing-together-new-zealanders-celebrate-anzac-day
66. 'Uluru Statement from the Heart': https://ulurustatement.org
67. Henry Reynolds, *Truth-Telling: History, sovereignty, and the Uluru Statement* (Sydney: New South Press, 2021).
68. 'Final report November 2018', Commonwealth of Australia, 2018: www.aph.gov.au/Parliamentary_Business/Committees/Joint/Former_Committees/Constitutional_Recognition_2018/ConstRecognition/Final_Report

69. A theme taken up by Mark McKenna in his essay, 'Moment of truth: History and Australia's future', *Quarterly Essay*, 69 (2018).
70. Vincent O'Malley, *The Great War for New Zealand: Waikato, 1800–2000* (Wellington: Bridget Williams Books, 2016), 16.
71. 'Students prepare to take NZ Land Wars petition to Parliament', *New Zealand Herald*, 7 December 2015: www.nzherald.co.nz/nz/students-prepare-to-take-nz-land-wars-petition-to-parliament
72. Jerry Mateparae, 'Battle of Ōrākau', 1 April 2014: https://gg.govt.nz/publications/battle ōrākau
73. 'Rā Maumahara – The journey to a national commemoration', Te Puni Kōkiri: www.tpk.govt.nz/en/whakamahia/te-putake-o-te-riri-wars-and-conflicts-in-new-zeal/ra-maumahara-the-journey-to-a-national-commemoration
74. Joan Beaumont, 'Commemoration in Australia: A memory orgy?', *Australian Journal of Political Science*, 50, 3 (2015), 536–44.
75. The observation was also made by Romain Fathi, 'Crowds at dawn services have plummeted in recent years. It's time to reinvent Anzac Day', *The Conversation*, 21 April 2021: https://theconversation.com/crowds-at-dawn-services-have-plummeted-in-recent-years-its-time-to-reinvent-anzac-day-157313
76. *Daily Telegraph*, 23 January 2018.
77. 'DVA Annual Report 2018–2019': www.transparency.gov.au/annual-reports/department-veterans-affairs/reporting-year/2018-2019-19
78. WW100 Final Report, April 2019: ww100.govt.nz/final-report
79. Holbrook, 'Making sense of the Great War Centenary', 248.
80. Jay Winter, 'Historical remembrance in the twenty-first century', *The Annals of the American Academy of Political and Social Science*, 617 (2008), 6–13, 12.

Bibliography

ARCHIVES

ANU Australian National University, Canberra
ANZ Archives New Zealand, Wellington
ATL Alexander Turnbull Library, Wellington
AWM Australian War Memorial, Canberra
MBL Macmillan Brown Library, Christchurch
MCH Ministry of Culture and Heritage, Wellington
NAA National Archives of Australia, Canberra
NLA National Library Australia, Canberra
NLNZ National Library of New Zealand, Wellington
NZNAM National Army Museum, Waiōuru
NZPD New Zealand Parliamentary Debates, Wellington
NZRSA New Zealand Returned Services Association, Wellington
OAWG Office of Australian War Graves, Canberra
SLV State Library of Victoria, Melbourne
UAL University of Auckland Library, Auckland
UMA University of Melbourne Archive, Melbourne

BOOKS

Adam-Smith, Patsy, *The Anzacs* (Sydney: Thomas Nelson, 1978)

Awatere, Arapeta, *Awatere: A soldier's story* (ed. Hinemoa Awatere) (Wellington: Huia Press, 2002)

Ballantyne, Tony, *Webs of Empire: Locating New Zealand's colonial past* (Wellington: Bridget Williams Books, 2012)

Bassett, Michael, *New Zealand's Prime Ministers: From Dick Seddon to John Key* (Auckland: David Ling, 2017)

Bassett, Michael, *The Mother of All Departments: The history of the Department of Internal Affairs* (Auckland: Auckland University Press, 1997)

Bastiaan, Ross J., *Images of Gallipoli: Photographs from the collection of Ross J. Bastiaan* (Oxford: Oxford University Press, 1988)

Bean, C.E.W., *The Official History of Australia in the War of 1914–1918* (vols I–VI) (Canberra: Australian War Memorial, 1941)

Bean, C.E.W., *The Story of Anzac from the Outbreak of War to the End of the First Phase of the Gallipoli Campaign, May 4, 1915* (Brisbane: University of Queensland Press, 1981)

Beaumont, Joan, *Broken Nation: Australians in the Great War* (Sydney: Allen & Unwin, 2014)

Belgrave, Michael, *Historical Frictions: Māori claims and reinvented histories* (Auckland: Auckland University Press, 2005)

Bennett, James and Rebecca Beirne, *Making Film and Television Histories: Australia and New Zealand* (London: I.B. Tauris, 2012)

Boston, Jonathan, *Left Turn: The New Zealand general election of 1999* (Wellington: Victoria University Press, 2000)

Brown, James, *Anzac's Long Shadow: The cost of our national obsession* (Sydney: Black Inc., 2014)

Burke, Anthony, *Fear of Security: Australia's invasion anxiety* (Melbourne: Cambridge University Press, 2008)

Burton, Ormond, *The Silent Division: New Zealanders at the Front, 1914–1919* (Sydney: Angus & Robertson, 1935)

Byrnes, Giselle, *The Waitangi Tribunal and New Zealand History* (Oxford: Oxford University Press, 2004)

Carlyon, Les, *Gallipoli* (Sydney: Macmillan, 2001)

Carlyon, Jenny and Diana Morrow, *Changing Times: New Zealand since 1945* (Auckland: Auckland University Press, 2014)

Clark, Manning, *A History of Australia: The old dead tree and the young tree green, 1916–1935* (vol. 6) (Melbourne: Melbourne University Press, 1987)

Clarke, Stephen, *After the War: The RSA in New Zealand* (Auckland: Penguin, 2016)

Cleave, Peter, *Making Sense of a Small State: The body of memory and the ritual of acknowledgement in Aotearoa-New Zealand* (Palmerston North: Campus Press, 2015)

Clements, Kevin, *Back from the Brink: The creation of a nuclear-free New Zealand* (Wellington: Allen & Unwin, 1988)

Cooke, Peter, *All Formed Up: A history of Wellington Returned & Services' Association, 1916–2007* (Wellington: Ngaio Press, 2008)

Cooper, Annabel, *Filming the Colonial Past: The New Zealand Wars on screen* (Dunedin: Otago University Press, 2018)

Coutts, Brent and Nicholas Fitness, *Protest in New Zealand* (Auckland: Pearson Press, 2013)

Curran, James and Stuart Ward, *The Unknown Nation: Australia after empire* (Melbourne: Melbourne University Press, 2006)

Damousi, Joy, *The Labour of Loss: Mourning, memory, and wartime bereavement in Australia* (Cambridge: Cambridge University Press, 1999)

Davies, William, *The Limits of Neo-Liberalism: Authority, sovereignty and the logic of competition* (London: University of London Press, 2016)

Department of Aboriginal Affairs, *Out of the Silent Land* (Canberra: Australian Government Publishing Service, 1984)

Doyle, Jeff, Jeffrey Grey and Peter Pierce, *Australia's Vietnam War* (Austin: University of Texas, 2002)

Dunleavy, Trisha and Hester Joyce, *New Zealand Film and Television: Institution, industry and cultural change* (Bristol and Chicago: Intellect, 2011)

Easton, Brian, *The Whimpering of the State: Policy after MMP* (Auckland: Auckland University Press, 1999)

Edwards, Brian, *Helen: Portrait of a prime minister* (Auckland: Exisle Publishing, 2001)

Ekins, Ashley, *Gallipoli: A ridge too far* (Canberra: Exisle Publishing, 2013)

Else, Anne, *Women Together: A history of women's organisations in New Zealand – Ngā Rōpū Wāhine o te Motu* (Wellington: Daphne Brasell Associates Press and Historical Branch, Department of Internal Affairs, 1993)

Ferrall, Charles and Harry Ricketts, *How We Remember: New Zealanders and the First World War* (Wellington: Victoria University Press, 2014)

Fousek, John, *To Lead the Free World: American nationalism and the cultural roots of the Cold War* (Chapel Hill, NC: University of North Carolina Press, 2000)

Fussell, Paul, *The Great War and Modern Memory* (New York: Oxford University Press, 1975)

Gammage, Bill, *The Story of Gallipoli* (Ringwood, Vic.: Penguin, 1981)
Garton, Stephen, *The Cost of War: Australians return* (Melbourne: Thomas Nelson, 1996)
Gibson, Lisanne and Joanna Besley, *Monumental Queensland: Signposts on a cultural landscape* (Brisbane: University of Queensland Press, 2004)
Graves, Matthew, *Memorial Diplomacy: The international politics of the past* (London: Palgrave Macmillan, 2018)
Guynn, William, *Writing History in Film* (New York: Routledge, 2006)
Hagopian, Patrick, *The Vietnam War in American Memory: Veterans, memorials, and the politics of healing* (Amherst: University of Massachusetts Press, 2009)
Hartley, John and Alan McKee, *The Indigenous Public Sphere: The reporting and reception of Indigenous issues in the Australian media, 1994–1997* (Oxford: Oxford University Press, 2000)
Haultain-Gall, Matthew, *The Battlefield of Imperishable Memory: Passchendaele and the Australian legend* (Melbourne: Monash University Press, 2021)
Hawkins, Jo, *Consuming Anzac: The history of Australia's most powerful brand* (Perth: UWA Publishing, 2018)
Hocking, Jenny, *The Dismissal Dossier. The Palace Connection: Everything you were never meant to know about November 1975* (Melbourne: Melbourne University Press, 2017)
Holbrook, Carolyn, *Anzac: The unauthorised biography* (Sydney: New South Books, 2014)
Hope, Stanton, *Gallipoli Revisited: An account of the* Duchess of Richmond *pilgrimage-cruise* (London: W.W. Stanton Hope, 1934)
Hopkins-Weise, Jeff, *Blood Brothers: The Anzac genesis* (Kent Town: Wakefield Press, 2009)
Inglis, K.S., *Sacred Places: War memorials in the Australian landscape* (Melbourne: Melbourne University Press, 1998)
Johnston, Elliott, *Royal Commission into Aboriginal Deaths in Custody: National report* (Canberra: Australian Government Publishing Service, 1991)
Jones, Kathy, *Media Images of Anzac* (Sydney: New South Wales Department of Education, 1983)
Kennedy, David M., *Freedom from Fear: The American people in depression and war, 1929–1945* (Oxford: Oxford University Press, 1999)
King, Jonathan, *Gallipoli Diaries* (Sydney: Kangaroo Press, 2003)
King, Michael, *Being Pākehā: An encounter with New Zealand and the Māori renaissance 1945–2004* (Auckland: Hodder & Stoughton, 1985)
Koopman-Boyden, Peggy and Claudia D. Scott, *The Family and Government Policy in New Zealand* (Sydney: Allen & Unwin, 1984)
Lack, John, K.S. Inglis and Jay Winter, *Anzac Remembered: Selected writings by K.S. Inglis* (Melbourne: Melbourne University Press, 1998)
Laidlaw, Chris, *Rites of Passage: Beyond the New Zealand identity crisis* (Auckland: Hodder Moa Beckett, 1999)
Landy, Marcia, *Cinematic Uses of the Past* (Minneapolis; London: University of Minnesota Press, 1996)
Leonard, Richard, *The Mystical Gaze of the Cinema: The films of Peter Weir* (Melbourne: Melbourne University Press, 2009)
Lincoln, Bruce, *Between History and Myth: Stories of Harald Fairhair and the founding of the state* (Chicago: Chicago University Press, 2014)
Lloyd, Clem and Jacqui Rees, *The Last Shilling: A history of repatriation in Australia* (Melbourne: Melbourne University Press, 1994)
Locke, Elsie, *Peace People: A history of peace activities in New Zealand* (Christchurch: Hazard Press, 1992)

McCarthy, Conal, *Te Papa: Reinventing New Zealand's national museum, 1998–2018* (Wellington: Te Papa Press, 2018)

Macdonald, Lyn, *1915* (Brisbane: Queensland University Press, 1979)

Macintyre, Stuart, *A Concise History of Australia* (Cambridge: Cambridge University Press, 2004)

Maclean, Chris and Jock Phillips, *The Sorrow and the Pride: New Zealand war memorials* (Wellington: Historical Publications Branch, 1990)

Macleod, Jenny, *Reconsidering Gallipoli* (London: Manchester University Press, 2014)

Margalit, Avishai, *The Ethics of Memory* (Cambridge, Mass.; London: Harvard University Press, 2004)

McGibbon, Ian, *New Zealand's Vietnam War: A history of combat, commitment, and controversy* (Auckland: Exisle Publishing, 2010)

McGibbon, Ian, *New Zealand Battlefields and Memorials of the Western Front* (Auckland: Penguin Press, 2001)

McGibbon, Ian, *The Oxford Companion to New Zealand Military History* (Melbourne: Oxford University Press, 2000)

McKernan, Michael, *Here Is Their Spirit: A history of the Australian War Memorial 1917–1990* (St Lucia: University of Queensland Press, 1991)

McMurchy, Megan and Jennifer Stott, *Signs of Independents: Ten years of the Creative Development Fund* (Sydney: Australian Film Commission, 1988)

Moorehead, Alan, *Gallipoli* (Ware, Hertfordshire: Wordsworth Editions, 1997) (first published 1956)

Moses, John Anthony and George F. Davis, *Anzac Day Origins: Canon DJ Garland and trans-Tasman commemoration* (Sydney: Barton Books, 2013)

Mune, Ian, *Mune: An autobiography* (Nelson: Craig Potton Publishing, 2010)

Murphy, John, *A Harvest of Fear: A history of Australia's Vietnam War* (Sydney: Allen & Unwin, 1993)

Museums Australia, *Report of the Committee of Inquiry on Museums and National Collections including the report of the planning committee on the Gallery of Aboriginal Australia* (Brisbane: Watson Ferguson & Co., 1975)

Nagle, William, *The Odd Angry Shot* (Sydney: Angus & Robertson, 1975)

Napper, Lawrence, *The Great War in Popular British Cinema of the 1920s* (London: Palgrave Macmillan, 2015)

O'Malley, Vincent, *The Great War for New Zealand: Waikato 1800–2000* (Wellington: Bridget Williams Books, 2016)

Orange, Claudia, *The Treaty of Waitangi* (2nd edn) (Wellington: Bridget Williams Books, 2011)

Orange, Claudia, *The Treaty of Waitangi | Te Tiriti o Waitangi: An illustrated history* (Wellington: Bridget Williams Books, 2021)

Peter Weir's Film of Gallipoli: Film study guide, (Melbourne: Education Department of Victoria, 1981)

Phillips, Jock, *To the Memory: New Zealand's war memorials* (Nelson: Potton & Burton, 2016)

Poweley, John-Paul, *Kaitiaki o te Pō* (Wellington: Seraph Press, 2018)

Pugsley, Chris, *The Anzac Experience: New Zealand, Australia, and Empire in the First World War* (Auckland: Reed, 2001)

Pugsley, Christopher, *The Anzacs at Gallipoli: A story for Anzac Day* (Auckland: Reed, 1999)

Pugsley, Chris, *Gallipoli: The New Zealand story* (Auckland: Hodder & Stoughton, 1984)

Pugsley, Chris and Charles Ferrall, *Remembering Gallipoli* (Wellington: Victoria University Press, 2015)

Rabel, Roberto, *New Zealand and the Vietnam War: Politics and diplomacy* (Auckland: Auckland University Press, 2005)

Reed, Liz, *Bigger Than Gallipoli: War, history and memory in Australia* (Perth: University of Western Australia Press, 2004)

Reynaud, Daniel, *Celluloid Anzacs: The Great War through Australian cinema* (Melbourne: Victoria Australian Scholarly Publishing, 2007)

Reynolds, Henry, *Truth-telling: History, sovereignty, and the Uluru Statement* (Sydney: New South Press, 2021)

Reynolds, Henry, *Dispossession: Black Australians and white invaders* (Sydney: Allen & Unwin, 1989)

Reynolds, Henry, *Aborigines and Settlers: The Australian experience, 1788–1939* (Melbourne: Cassell Australia, 1972)

Rhodes, Robert James, *Gallipoli* (New York: Macmillan, 1965)

Rodwell, Grant, *Moral Panics and School Educational Policy* (Melbourne: Routledge, 2018)

Russell, Marcia, *Revolution: New Zealand from fortress to free market* (Auckland: Hodder Moa Beckett, 1996)

Scates, Bruce, *Return to Gallipoli: Walking the battlefields of the Great War* (Cambridge: Cambridge University Press, 2009)

Schwarz, Bill, *The White Man's World* (Oxford, New York: Oxford University Press, 2011)

Shadbolt, Maurice, *Voices of Gallipoli* (3rd edn) (Auckland: David Ling Publishing, 2014)

Shadbolt, Maurice, *Voices of Gallipoli* (Auckland: Hodder & Stoughton, 1988)

Sinclair, Keith, *A Destiny Apart: New Zealand's search for a national identity* (Auckland: Unwin Port Nicholson Press, 1986)

Smith, Philippa Mein, *A Concise History of New Zealand* (Melbourne: Cambridge University Press, 2011)

Sparrow, James T., *Warfare State* (Oxford: Oxford University Press, 2011)

Stratton, David, *The Avocado Plantation: Boom and bust in the Australian film industry* (Sydney: Pan Macmillan, 1990)

Thomson, Alistair, *Anzac Memories* (rev. edn), (Melbourne: Monash University Publishing, 2013)

Thomson, Alistair, *Anzac Memories: Living with the legend* (Oxford: Oxford University Press, 1994)

Turner, Graeme, *Film as Social Practice* (London and New York: Routledge, 1988)

Webber, N.P., *The First Fifty Years of the New Zealand Returned Services Association 1916 to 1966* (Wellington: New Zealand Returned and Services Association, 1966)

Ward, Stuart, 'A war memorial in celluloid: The Gallipoli legend in Australian cinema, 1940s–1980s', in Jenny Macleod (ed.), *Gallipoli: Making history* (London: Frank Cass, 2004), 59–72

Wellings, Ben, *English Nationalism and Euroscepticism: Losing the peace* (London: Peter Lang, 2012)

Wellington, Jennifer, *Exhibiting War: The Great War, museums, and memory in Britain, Canada and Australia* (Cambridge: Cambridge University Press, 2017)

White, Geoffrey, *Memorializing Pearl Harbor: Unfinished histories and the work of remembrance* (Durham: Duke University Press, 2016)

Wilson, Margaret, *The Struggle for Sovereignty: New Zealand and twenty-first century statehood* (Wellington: Bridget Williams Books, 2015)

Winegard, Timothy, *Indigenous Peoples of the British Dominions and the First World War* (New York: Cambridge University Press, 2011)

BOOK CHAPTERS

Abel, Sue, 'Māori Television, Anzac Day, and constructing "nationhood"', in Brendan Hokowhitu and Vijay Devadas (eds), *The Fourth Eye: Māori media in Aotearoa New Zealand* (Minneapolis: University of Minnesota Press, 2013), 201–15

Ashton, Paul and Paula Hamilton, '"Unfinished business": Public history in a postcolonial nation', in Daniel Walkowitz and Lisa Maya Knauer (eds), *Contested Histories in Public Places* (Durham: Duke University Press, 2009), 71–98

Atkinson, Henry, 'Meaning and values of repatriation', in Paul Turnbull and Michael Pickering (eds), *The Long Way Home: The meanings and values of repatriation* (New York: Berghahn Books, 2010), 15–19

Bassett, Jan, 'Women and Anzac Day, Melbourne', in Michael McKernan and Peter Stanley (eds), *Anzac Day Seventy Years On* (Sydney: Collins, 1986), 114–34.

Bongiorno, Frank, 'Anzac and the politics of inclusion', in Shanti Sumartojo and Ben Wellings (eds), *Nation, Memory and Great War Commemoration* (Bern: Peter Lang, 2014), 81–97

Crawley, Rhys, 'The myths of August at Gallipoli', in Craig Stockings (ed.), *Zombie Myths of Australian Military History* (Sydney: New South Press, 2010), 50–69

Crotty, Martin A., '25 April 1915, Australian troops land at Gallipoli: Trial, trauma and the "birth of the nation"', in Martin A. Crotty and David Andrew Roberts (eds), *Turning Points in Australian History* (Sydney: University of New South Wales Press, 2009), 100–14

Curthoys, Ann, 'Losing our way after the imperial turn: Charting academic uses of the postcolonial', in Antoinette Burton, *After the Imperial Turn: Thinking with and through the nation* (Durham, NC: Duke University Press, 2003), 90–101

Das, Santanu, 'Introduction', in Santanu Das (ed.), *Race, Empire and First World War Writing* (Cambridge: Cambridge University Press, 2014), 1–32

Devadas, Vijay, 'Governing indigenous sovereignty: Biopolitics and the "terror raids" in New Zealand', in Brendan Hokowhitu and Vijay Devadas (eds), *The Fourth Eye: Maori media in Aotearoa New Zealand* (Minneapolis: University of Minnesota Press, 2013), 3–24

Dowse, Sara and Patricia Giles, 'Australia: Women in a warrior society', in Robin Morgan (ed.), *Sisterhood is Global: The international women's movement anthology* (Garden City, NY: Anchor Press/Doubleday, 1984)

Elder, Catriona, '"I spit on your stone": National identity, Women Against Rape and the cult of Anzac in Australia', in Maja Mikula (ed.), *Women, Activism and Social Change* (London: Routledge, 2005), 71–81

Haggith, Toby and Richard Smith, 'Sons of our empire: Shifting ideas of race and the cinematic representation of imperial troops in the World War', in Lee Grieveson and Colin MacCabe (eds), *Empire and Film* (London: British Film Institute, 2011), 35–53

Hall, Stuart, 'The West and the rest: Discourse and power', in Stuart Hall and Bram Gieben (eds), *Formations of Modernity* (Cambridge: Cambridge University Press, 1994), 222–37

Hokowhitu, Brendan, 'History and masculinity', in J. O'Brien and C. Anderson (eds), *Sources and Methods in Indigenous Studies* (London: Routledge, 2017), 195–204

Holbrook, Carolyn, 'Making sense of the Great War Centenary', in Carolyn Holbrook and Keir Reeves (eds), *The Great War: Aftermath and commemoration* (Sydney: New South Press, 2019), 244–48.

Howe, Adrian, 'Anzac mythology and the feminist challenge', in Joy Damousi and Marilyn Lake (eds), *Gender and War: Australians at war in the twentieth century* (Cambridge: Cambridge University Press, 1995), 302–10

Ivison, Duncan, Paul Patton and Will Sanders, 'Introduction', in Duncan Ivison (ed.), *Political Theory and the Rights of Indigenous Peoples* (Cambridge: Cambridge University Press, 2000), 3–10

Macmillan, Stuart, 'Defending the realm', in Philippa Mein Smith, Peter J. Hempenstall and Shaun Goldfinch (eds), *Remaking the Tasman World* (Christchurch: Canterbury University Press, 2008), 233–66

Mann, Philip, 'Maurice Shadbolt the dramatist: On the dramaturgy of *Once on Chunuk Bair*', in Ralph Crane (ed.), *Ending the Silences. Critical essays on the works of Maurice Shadbolt* (Auckland: Hodder Moa Beckett, 1995), 130–46

McGibbon, Ian, 'In the footsteps of the New Zealanders: Gallipoli', in Kynan Gentry and Gavin McLean (eds), *Heartlands: New Zealand historians write about where history happened* (Auckland: Penguin, 2006), 90–106

McKenna, Mark, 'Keeping in step: The Anzac "resurgence and "military heritage" in Australia and New Zealand', in S. Sumartojo and B. Wellings (eds), *Nation, Memory and Great War Commemoration: Mobilizing the past in Europe, Australia and New Zealand* (Oxford: Peter Lang, 2014), 151–67

McKenna, Mark, 'The history anxiety', in Alison Bashford and Stuart Macintyre (eds), *The Cambridge History of Australia: Volume 2: The Commonwealth of Australia* (Cambridge–New York: Cambridge University Press, 2013), 561–80

McKenna, Mark, 'Anzac Day: How did it become Australia's national day?', in Henry Reynolds and Marilyn Lake (eds), *What's Wrong with Anzac?* (Sydney: New South Books, 2010), 110–34

McKernan, Michael, 'Writing about war', in Michael McKernan and Margaret Browne (eds), *Australia: Two centuries of war and peace* (Canberra: Unwin Australia, 1988), 1–24

Morris, Paul, 'Who are we? New Zealand identity and spirituality', in James H. Liu et al. (eds), *New Zealand Identities: Departures and destinations* (Wellington: Victoria University Press, 2005), 242–54

Neil, Michael, 'Introduction', in Maurice Shadbolt, *Once on Chunuk Bair* (Auckland: Hodder & Stoughton, 1982)

Phillips, Jock, 'New Zealand and the Anzus alliance: Changing national self-perceptions, 1945–88', in Richard Baker (ed.), *Australia, New Zealand, and the United States* (New York: Praegar, 1991), 189–201

Phillips, Jock, '75 years since Gallipoli', in Atholl Anderson et al. (eds), *Towards 1990: Seven leading historians examine significant aspects of New Zealand history* (Wellington: GP Books, 1988), 103–08

Segesser, Daniel Marc, 'Strong and friendly bonds … out of shared tragedy?: The Gallipoli/ Canakkale battles in Canberra's City Planning and Architecture of Memory', in Hans-Lukas Kieser, Pearl Nunn and Thomas Schmutz (eds), *Remembering the Great War in the Middle East: From Turkey and Armenia to Australia and New Zealand* (London: I.B. Tauris, 2021), 157–76

Stanley, Peter, 'Anzac Day as it was reported', in Michael McKernan and Peter Stanley (eds), *Anzac Day Seventy Years On* (Sydney: Collins, 1986), 13–19

Stasiuk, Glen, 'Warriors then … warriors still: Aboriginal soldiers in the 20th century', in Andrew Gunstone (ed.), *History, Politics & Knowledge: Essays in Australian Indigenous studies* (Melbourne: Australian Scholarly Publishing, 2008), 191–205

Steinmetz, George, 'Culture and the state', in George Steinmetz (ed.), *State/Culture: State-formation after the cultural turn* (Ithaca: Cornell University Press, 1999), 8–9

Wellings, Ben, 'Lest you forget: Australian nationalism in a global era', in Shanti Sumartojo and Ben Wellings (eds), *Nation, Memory and Great War Commemoration: Mobilizing the past in Europe, Australia and New Zealand* (Oxford: Peter Lang, 2014), 45–59

White, Richard, 'Inventing Australia revisited', in Geoffrey Curgenven Bolton and Wayne Hudson (eds), *Creating Australia: Changing Australian history* (St Leonards: Allen & Unwin, 1997), 13–26

JOURNAL ARTICLES

Assmann, Jan and Aleida Assmann, 'Collective memory and cultural identity', *New German Critique*, 65 (1995), 125–33

Baird, Kingsley, '"The past we harvest that was yours": The rhetoric of national identity and the legacy of the Unknown Warrior in New Zealand memory', *Bulletin of the Auckland Museum*, 21 (2020), 19–26

Beaumont, Joan, 'Commemoration in Australia: A memory orgy?', *Australian Journal of Political Science*, 50, 3, (2015), 536–44

Bennett, James, 'Lest we forget Black Diggers: Recovering Aboriginal Anzacs on television', *Journal of Australian Studies*, 38, 4, (2014), 457–75

Bennett, James, 'Man alone and men together: Maurice Shadbolt, William Malone and Chunuk Bair', *Journal of New Zealand Studies*, 13 (2012): https://ojs.victoria.ac.nz/jnzs/article/view/1189

Bonelli, Diego, Thierry Jutel and Alfio Leotta, '"Selling the creative city": Wellington tourism film in the neoliberal era', *Studies in Australasian Cinema*, 13, 2–3 (2019), 32–50

Cairns, Puawai, 'The wait and the fight: Telling Māori WWI histories and the search for alternative platforms', *Te Pouhere Kōrero* (2016), 1–8

Caso, Federica, 'Representing indigenous soldiers at the Australian War Memorial: A political analysis of the art exhibition *For Country, For Nation*', *Australian Journal of Political Science*, 55, 4 (2020), 345–61

Cevik-Compiegne, Burcu, '"We were not, they could not be": Anzac and Turkish diasporic politics of memory', *History Australia*, 15, 2, (2018), 306–22

Clark, Helen, 'Iraq and Afghanistan', *Presidents & Prime Ministers*, 12, 3, (2003), 21–36

Clark, Helen, 'New Zealand foreign policy: Pushing the big ideas', *New Zealand International Review* (1999), 2–4

Clendinnen, Inga, 'The history question: Who owns the past?', *Quarterly Essay*, 23 (2006), 1

Cocker, Alan, 'Malcolm Ross, journalist and photographer: The perfect war correspondent?', *Pacific Journalism Review*, 22, 1 (2016), 152–66

Davies, Susanne, 'Women, war, and the violence of history: An Australian perspective', *Violence Against Women*, 2, 4 (1996), 359–77

Del Pizzo, Lisa J., 'Not guilty – but not innocent: An analysis of the acquittal of John Demjanjuk and its impact on the future of Nazi war crimes trials', *Law Review*, 137, 18 (1995), 137–78

Doyle, Jeff, 'Dismembering the Anzac legend: Australian popular culture and the Vietnam War', *Vietnam Generation*, 3, 2 (1992), 109–25

Fenton, Damien, 'Has New Zealand let down the Anzac tradition?', *New Zealand International Review* (1999), 19–22

Flanagan, Jason, 'John Howard's "use" of the Anzac Legend: Applying an epideictic lens', *Australian Journal of Politics and History*, 64, 1 (2018), 98–111

Freebury, Jane, 'Screening Australia. *Gallipoli*: A study of nationalism on film', *Media International Australia*, 43, 1, (1987), 5–8

Gadd, Murray, 'A bibliography of Maurice Shadbolt: 1956–1980', *Journal of New Zealand Literature*, 2 (1984), 75–96

Gammage, Bill, 'Anzac's influence on Turkey and Australia', *Journal of the Australian War Memorial*, 18 (1991), 19

Goodger, Kay, 'Proceedings of the Women's Liberation Conference', *Socialist Action*, 4, 6 (1972), 1

Hall, Stuart, 'Thinking the diaspora: Home-thoughts from abroad', *Small Axe. A Caribbean Journal of Criticism*, 6, 1 (1999): 1–24

Haltof, Mark, 'Gallipoli, mateship, and the construction of Australian national identity', *Journal of Popular Film & Television*, 21, 1 (2004), 27–36

Hokowhitu, Brendan and Tiffany Page, 'Postcolonial Peace', *Junctures*, 14 (2011): https://junctures.org/index.php/junctures/article/view/195/280

Holbrook, Carolyn, 'Screening Anzac: Anzac-themed television in Australia and New Zealand during the First World War centenary', *Journal of Australian Studies*, 44, 4 (2020), 440–56

Holland, Jack, 'Howard's war on terror: A conceivable, communicable and coercive foreign policy discourse', *Australian Journal of Political Science*, 45, 4 (2010), 643–61

Hucker, Graham, 'A determination to remember: Helen Clark and New Zealand's military heritage', *Journal of Arts Management, Law, and Society*, 40, 2 (2010), 105–18

Hunter, Kathryn, 'States of mind: Remembering the Australian–New Zealand relationship', *Journal of the Australian War Memorial*, 36 (2001): www.awm.gov.au/articles/journal/j36/nzmemorial

Inglis, K.S., 'The Unknown Australian Soldier', *Journal of Australian Studies*, 23 (1999), 8–17

Inglis, K.S., 'Kapferer on Anzac and Australia', *Social Analysis*, 29 (1990), 67–73

Inglis, K.S., 'Men, women, and war memorials: Anzac Australia', *Daedalus*, 116, 4 (1987), 35–59.

Inglis, K.S., 'A sacred place: The making of the Australian War Memorial', *War & Society*, 3, 2 (1985), 100

Inglis, K.S., 'Return to Gallipoli', *Australian National University Historical Journal*, 3 (1966), 43–62

Inglis, K.S., 'The Anzac tradition', *Meanjin*, 24, 1 (1965), 25–44

Inglis, K.S. and Jock Phillips, 'War memorials in Australia and New Zealand: A comparative survey', *Australian Historical Studies*, 24, 96 (1991) 179–91

James, Karl, 'Before the Anzac dawn: A military history of Australia to 1915', *Journal of Australian Studies*, 38, 3 (2014), 364–66

Johnson, Miranda, 'Burdens of belonging: Indigeneity and the re-founding of Aotearoa New Zealand', *New Zealand Journal of History*, 45, 1 (2011), 102–12

Lawson, Sylvia, 'Desecration and defacement: Criminalizing dissent in a time of war', *Overland*, 182 (2006), 20–27

Loveridge, Stephen, 'Another great war?: New Zealand interpretations of the First World War towards and into the Second World War', *First World War Studies*, 7, 3 (2016), 303–25

Macleod, Jenny, 'The fall and rise of Anzac Day: 1965 and 1990 compared', *War & Society*, 20, 1 (2002), 149–68

Maddocks, Ian and Seumas Spark, '"Taim bilong uni": Ken Inglis at the University of Papua New Guinea', *History Australia*, 14, 4 (2017), 545–60

Mann, Philip, 'The first production of *Once on Chunuk Bair*', *Illusion*, 11 (1989), 15

McDonald, Matt, '"Lest we forget": The politics of memory and Australian military intervention', *International Political Sociology*, 4, 3 (2010), 287–302

McKenna, Mark, 'Moment of truth: History and Australia's future', *Quarterly Essay*, 69 (2018)

McKenna, Mark and Stuart Ward, '"It was really moving, mate": The Gallipoli pilgrimage and sentimental nationalism in Australia', *Australian Historical Studies*, 38, 129 (2007), 141–51

Meyers, John and Bryn Dolan, 'Alec Campbell: The last sentinel of Gallipoli', *Sabretache*, 43, 4 (2002), 39–41

Morris, R., 'Growing up Australian: Renegotiating mateship, masculinity and "Australianness" in Hsu-Ming Teo's *Behind the Moon*', *Journal of Intercultural Studies*, 27, 1–2 (2006), 155–66

Moeahu, Peter, 'Hikoi ki te Waipounamu', *Historic Places*, 78 (2000), 12–13

'New Zealand's Clark government creates a strategic vacuum in the Pacific', *Defence and Foreign Affairs Strategic Policy*, 29, 4/5 (2001), 10–11

Nightingale, Tony, 'Not so sacred ground: The National War Memorial', *Phanzine*, 9, 1 (2003), 4–5

O'Farrell, Patrick, 'Oral history: Facts and fiction', *Quadrant*, 23, 148 (1979), 4–8

Phillips, Jock, 'Our history, our selves: The historian and national identity', *New Zealand Journal of History*, 30, 2 (2001), 107–23

Phipps, Gareth, 'Bringing our boy home: The tomb of the unknown warrior and contemporary war remembrance', *Journal of New Zealand Studies*, 10 (2011), 159–84

Riseman, Noah, 'Evolving commemorations of Aboriginal and Torres Strait Islander military service', *Wicazo Sa Review*, 32, 1 (2017), 80–101

Robinson, Helen, 'Making a New Zealand Day: The creation and context of a national holiday', *New Zealand Journal of History*, 46, 1 (2012), 37–51

Robinson, Helen, 'Lest we forget?: The fading of New Zealand war commemorations, 1946–1966', *New Zealand Journal of History*, 44, 1 (2010), 76–91

Robson, L.L., 'Voices from the trenches', *Meanjin*, 4 (1974), 320–22

Roche, Michael, 'Failure deconstructed: Histories and geographies of soldier settlement in New Zealand circa 1917–39', *New Zealand Geographer*, 64, 1 (2008), 46–56

Scates, Bruce, 'Letters from a pilgrimage: Reflection on the 1965 return to Gallipoli', *History Australia*, 14, 4 (2017), 530–44

Scates, Bruce, Frank Bongiorno, Rebecca Wheatley and Laura James, '"Such a great space of water between us": Anzac Day in Britain, 1916–39', *Australian Historical Studies*, 45, 2 (2014), 220–41

Scott, Nick, 'Black-bans and black eyes: Implications of the 1971 Springbok rugby tour', *Labour History*, 108 (2015), 145–63

Seal, Graham, '"… and in the morning …": Adapting and adopting the dawn service', *Journal of Australian Studies* 35, 1 (2011), 49–63

Seal, Graham, 'Anzac: The sacred in the secular', *Journal of Australian Studies*, 91 (2007), 135–44

Smith, Philippa Mein, 'The "NZ" in Anzac: Different remembrance and meaning', *First World War Studies*, 7, 2 (2016), 193–211

Sumartojo, Shanti, 'Tweeting from the past: Commemorating the Anzac centenary @ ABCNews1915', *Memory Studies* (2017): https://doi.org/10.1177/1750698017709873

Twomey, Christina, 'Trauma and the reinvigoration of Anzac: An argument', *History Australia*, 10, 3 (2013), 85–108

Tyler, Deborah, 'Making nations, making men: Feminists and the Anzac tradition', *Melbourne Historical Journal*, 16 (1984), 24–33

Volkerling, Michael, 'The Helen Clark years: Cultural policy in New Zealand 1999–2008', *Journal of Arts Management, Law, and Society*, 40, 2 (2010), 95–104

West, Brad, 'Dialogical memorialization, international travel and the public sphere: A cultural sociology of commemoration and tourism at the First World War Gallipoli battlefields', *Tourist Studies*, 10, 3 (2011), 209–25

Willis, Freya, 'A reconciled nation? Mabo and the reimagining of Australia's national history', *Journal of Australian Studies* (2021): DOI: 10.1080/14443058.2021.1974922

Wilson, J.M., '"Colonize, pioneer. Bash and slash": *Once on Chunuk Bair* and the Anzac myth', *Journal of New Zealand Studies*, 34, 1 (2016), 27–53

Winter, Jay, 'Historical remembrance in the twenty-first century', *The Annals of the American Academy of Political and Social Science*, 617 (2008), 6–13

Winter, Jay, 'Migration, war and empire: The British case', *Les annales de démographie historique*, 103 (2002), 143–60

Wright, Tony, 'Rescuing the truth (about the *Tampa* crisis)', *Bulletin*, 120, 6313 (2002), 20–21

Ziino, Bart, '"A lasting gift to his descendants": Family memory and the Great War in Australia', *History and Memory*, 22, 2 (2010), 125–46

Ziino, Bart, 'Mourning and commemoration in Australia: The case of Sir W.T. Bridges and the Unknown Australian Soldier', *History Australia*, 4, 2 (2007), 40.1–40.17

MAGAZINES AND NEWSPAPERS

Advertiser (Adelaide)
Age (Melbourne)
Ashburton Guardian
Auckland Institute and Museum News
Auckland Star
Australian
Bay of Plenty Times
Bendigo Advertiser
Biz
Bulletin with Newsweek
Bulletin
Canberra Times
Central (Sydney)
Chronicle
Cineaste
Cinema Papers
Courier Mail
Daily News
Daily Telegraph
Dominion Post
Evening Post
Fairfield Broadcaster
Filmnews
Geraldton Guardian
Hauraki Herald
Hawke's Bay Tribune
Herald Tribune
Honi Soit
Journal of External Affairs

Katoomba Daily
Koori Mail
Literature/Film Quarterly
London Gazette
Mana
Melbourne Herald
Melbourne Sun
Metro
Mirror
Movie
National Indigenous Times
National Times
Nelson Evening Mail
New Zealand Herald
New Zealand Listener
Newcastle Morning Herald
Northern Advocate
Northland Age
Otago Daily Times
Press
Radio Listener
Reader's Digest
Reveille (Sydney)
Reveille (Canberra)
Salient
Smith's Weekly
South East Advertiser
Sun (Melbourne)
Sunday Telegraph
Sunraysia (Mildura)
Sydney Morning Herald
Te Iwi
Telegraph
Tharunka
Timaru Herald
Times Literary Supplement
Tribune (Sydney)
Tuggerong Valley View
TV Listener
Valley Hill Times
Vetaffairs
Walkabout
Weekend Australian
Weekly News
West Australian
Western Advocate

Western Herald
Whakatane Beacon
Zealandia

MUSIC, TELEVISION, FILM AND RADIO

ABC News, ABC, 1965
Amoiha Te Mauri, Māori Television, 2010
Anzac Day, Maori Television, 2010
Anzac Day 2013, Māori Television, 2013
Anzac Day 2013, NITV, 2013
Anzac Plus Fifty: People at war, NZBC, 1965
Anzacs: Remembering Our Heroes – The forgotten warriors, SBS, 2014
Awaken, 'Anzac Legend and Legacy', NITV, 2012
Bogle, Eric, 'And the Band Played Waltzing Matilda', Australia, Franklyn B. Paverty, 1979
Briant, Philip and Phil Thomson, *Warriors, Welfare and Eternal Vigilance*, RSL, 1982
Chunuk Bair, Daybreak Pictures, 1992
Gallipoli: The New Zealand story, TVNZ, 1984
Hitler and the Gumdiggers, Māori Television, 2010
Kaleidoscope, TVNZ, 1982
Living Black, 'A Spirit Returns', NITV, 2012
Living Black, NITV, 2013
Living Black, 'Anzac Harry Allie', NITV, 2011
Ngā Morehu Hoia o Te Rua Tekau mā Waru, Māori Television, 2010
Ngā Rā o Hune: The Days of June, Māori Television, 2015
Ngā Toa o Te Moana-Nui-a-Kiwa: Warriors of the Pacific: Solomon Islands, Māori Television, 2011
Ngā Uri o Ruku te Kapa, Māori Television, 2014
Ngarimu VC, TVNZ, 1993
Ngārimu VC: The whānau remembers, Māori Television, 2013
One News at 6, TVNZ, 2004
Our Pacific, Māori Television, 2010
Report from Gallipoli, ABC, 1977
Shovels and Guns, Māori Television, 2015
Te Marutuna o te Tangata: The Commanders, Māori Television, 2014
Te Reo o te Māori, NZBC, 1965
The Anzac Story, ABC, 1965
The Black Legacy, Māori Television, 2015
The Final Hui: 28th Battalion Association, Māori Television, 2013
War Stories Our Mothers Never Told Us, Gaylene Preston Productions, 1995

UNPUBLISHED DISSERTATIONS, THESES AND CONFERENCE PAPERS

Crotty, Martin A., 'Gallipoli 1965: The unhappy pilgrimage', Australian Historical Association Conference (Australian National University, 2018)

Montgomerie, Deborah, 'Anzac anthems, New Zealand history and the two world wars', Winter Lecture (University of Auckland, 2009)
Gammage, Bill, 'Re-thinking Anzac', Ministry of Culture and Heritage Panel (National Gallery of Australia, 2013)
Gammage, Bill, 'The broken years: A study of the diaries and letters of Australian soldiers in the Great War, 1914–18' (PhD thesis, Australian National University, 1970)
Haig, Nicholas, 'Once more, with feeling: An enquiry into the Museum of New Zealand Te Papa Tongarewa's exhibition *Gallipoli: The scale of our war*' (MA thesis, Massey University, 2016)
Hobbins, Peter, 'Protest as paradox: Hegemony and Anzac Day, 1977–87' (BA (Hons) essay, University of Sydney, 2008)
Inglis, Ken, 'C.E.W. Bean, Australian historian', The John Murtagh Macrossan lecture (University of Queensland, 1969)
Irving, Nick, 'Global thought, local action: Australian activism during the Vietnam War 1961–1972' (PhD thesis, University of Sydney, 2017)
Lee, Barry, 'Struggling to make the world a better place: Exploring some experiences of activists in the Auckland Progressive Youth Movement (1965–1977)' (PhD thesis, Auckland University of Technology, 2019)
Louise, Mataia, '"Odd men from the Pacific": The participation of Pacific Island men in the 28 (Maori) Battalion in the Second World War', (MA thesis, University of Otago, 2007)
Loveridge, Steven, '"Sentimental equipment": New Zealand, the Great War and cultural mobilisation' (PhD thesis, Victoria University of Wellington, 2013)
Mandler, Peter, 'The "crisis in the humanities" in comparative perspective', Australian Historical Conference 2015 (University of Sydney, 2015)
Rowse, Tim, 'Indigenous cultural capital: An inescapably political concept', Public lecture, (Australian National University, 28 October 2019)
Worthy, Scott, 'Communities of remembrance: The memory of the Great War in New Zealand, 1915–1939' (MA thesis, University of Auckland, 2001)

WEBSITES

'175th anniversary of Waitangi treaty', *Stuff*, 3 February 2015: www.stuff.co.nz/auckland/local-news/northland/northern-news/65713733/175th-anniversary-of-waitangi-treaty
'30 years later, an apology to Vietnam vets', *Stuff*, 31 January 2009: www.stuff.co.nz/national/politics/461111/30-years-later-an-apology-to-Vietnam-vets
'A perspective', *NZ on Screen Iwi Whitiāhua,* 19 August 2008: www.nzonscreen.com/title/maori-battalion-march-to-victory-1990/background/mihi-murray
Abbott, Tony, '2015 Gallipoli dawn service', *Australian Parliament House*, 25 April 2015: www.aph.gov.au/About_Parliament/Parliamentary_Departments/Parliamentary_Library/pubs/AnzacDay2016/Speeches
Abbott, Tony, 'Interview with Scott Bevan, *ABC News*', 24 April 2015: https://pmtranscripts.pmc.gov.au/release/transcript-24392
Abbott, Tony, 'Remarks at unveiling of the Sir John Monash Centre winning design, Villers-Bretonneux', 26 April 2015: https://pmtranscripts.pmc.gov.au/release/transcript-24400
ABC Local Radio PM programme, 'Indigenous soldiers who hid their identity to serve: The untold story', 31 December 2014: www.abc.net.au/radio/programs/pm/

indigenous-soldiers-who-hid-their-identity-to/5994284
'About the wall', *AWM London*: www.awmlondon.gov.au/about-the-wall
Ansley, Greg, 'War brings New Zealand and Australia together and sets us apart', *New Zealand Herald*, 20 April 2001: www.nzherald.co.nz/nz/news/article.cfm?c_id=1&objectid=183936
'Anzac Centenary: 100 years in the making', Anzac Centenary Advisory Board, January 2013: www.anzaccentenary.gov.au/sites/default/files/documents/acab_report.doc
'Anzac Day 2016: Alternate march held in Melbourne to protest against RSL rule change', *ABC News*, 25 April 2016: www.abc.net.au/news/2016-04-25/alternate-anzac-march-held-in-melbourne-protest-rsl-rule-change/7355320
Ariel, Lyn, *SWARC*: www.radicalfeministvoice.com/9SWARC.pdf&gt
'Australian War Memorial London', Tonkin Zulaikha Greer Architects: www.tzg.com.au/project/aus-war-memorial/
Baird, Kingsley, 'Tomb of the Unknown Warrior – Te Toma o Te Toa Matangaro': www.kingsleybaird.com/artwork/tomb-of-the-unknown-warrior
'Bali bombing: Kiwi victims to attend 10th anniversary', *New Zealand Herald*, 10 October 2012: www.nzherald.co.nz/nz/news/article.cfm?c_id=1&objectid=10839643
'Black Diggers Anzac Day march on NITV', *Deadly Vibe*, 24 April 2008: www.deadlyvibe.com.au/2008/04/black-diggers-anzac-day-march-on-nitv/
Blaxland, John, 'Daesh and the unintended consequences of a modern Anzac force', *WA Today*, 4 March 2015: www.watoday.com.au/comment/daesh-and-the-unintended-consequences-of-a-modern-anzac-force-20150304-13un71.html
Bradley, Tim, 'NITV free to air promo': www.youtube.com/watch?v=YAkOY3_RUJk
'Briefing to the incoming ministers of Māori affairs and finance', Māori Television, 2008: www.tpk.govt.nz/documents/download/182/tpk-mtsbim-2008-en.pdf
Briscoe, Luke, 'NITV Anzac focus', SBS, 24 June 2015: www.sbs.com.au/nitv/article/2015/04/06/nitv-anzac-focus
Buchanan, Rachel, 'Naming the Unknown Warrior', Pukeahu Anthology: http://pukeahuanthology.org/stories/contesting-histories/naming-the-unknown-warrior/
Burgmann, Meredith, 'The Women Against Rape in War Collective's protests against Anzac Day in Sydney, 1983 and 1984', University of Technology Sydney: https://epress.lib.uts.edu.au/journals/index.php/mcs/article/view/4222
'Change to Anzac Day march declared out of order', *Age*, 25 February 2016: www.theage.com.au/national/victoria/change-to-anzac-day-march-declared-out-of-order-20160222-gn0do9.html
'Christopher Pugsley on military history', RNZ: www.rnz.co.nz/national/programmes/writers/audio/20144937/christopher-pugsley-on-military-history
'Clark closes ugly chapter at Waitangi', *New Zealand Herald*, 6 February 2004: www.nzherald.co.nz/nz/news/article.cfm?c_id=1&objectid=888612
Clark, Helen, 'Address – Mt Albert Anzac Day service', *Scoop*, 25 April 2006: www.scoop.co.nz/stories/PA0604/S00360
Clark, Helen, 'Address at dawn service, Anzac Day', Beehive, 26 April 2005: www.beehive.govt.nz/speech/address-dawn-service-anzac-day
Clark, Helen, 'Address by the Prime Minister at the St Paul's Cathedral Memorial Service for the Unknown Warrior', RSA, 2004: http://rsa.org.nz/about/nws2004sep/Unknown_Warrior.html
Clark, Helen, 'Address to the Returned Services Association', Beehive, 12 July 2005: www.beehive.govt.nz/node/23643

Clark, Helen, 'Dedication of the New Zealand memorial, Anzac Parade, Canberra', Beehive, 24 April 2001: www.beehive.govt.nz/node/10506
Clark, Helen, 'Dominion Day reception', Beehive, 27 September 2007: www.beehive.govt.nz/speech/dominion-day-reception
Clark, Helen, 'New Zealand memorial a tribute to the Anzac relationship, says PM', Beehive, 24 April 2001: www.beehive.govt.nz/node/10309.
Clark, Helen, 'Prime Minister welcomes Australian commitment to Anzac Memorial', Beehive, 10 May 2007: www.beehive.govt.nz/release/prime-minister-welcomes-australian-commitment-anzac-memorial
Clark, Helen, 'The trans-Tasman relationship', Beehive, 16 June 2008: www.beehive.govt.nz/speech/trans-tasman-relationship
'Clark's no-show at Waitangi a political risk', *Stuff*, 15 December 2009: http://i.stuff.co.nz/national/blogs/on-the-house/1877816/Clarks-no-show-at-Waitangi-a-political-risk
'Coalition to spend half a billion dollars on Australian War Memorial project', *Guardian*, 31 October 2018: www.theguardian.com/australia-news/2018/nov/01/coalition-to-spend-half-a-billion-dollars-on-australian-war-memorial-project
Daley, Paul, 'Why does the Australian War Memorial ignore the frontier war?', *Guardian*, 12 September 2013: www.theguardian.com/world/2013/sep/12/australian-war-memorial-ignores-frontier-war
'Dedication day underlines spirit of Anzac mateship', *New Zealand Herald*, 25 April 2001: www.nzherald.co.nz/nz/news/article.cfm?c_id=1&objectid=184628
Denning Orman, Tanya, 'It is vital that Aboriginal and Torres Strait Islander people see themselves positively reflected in the media', SBS, 18 October 2017: www.sbs.com.au/nitv/article/2017/10/13/tanya-orman-denning-it-vital-aboriginal-and-torres-strait-islander-people-see
Derbyshire, Jonathan, 'Actually existing neo-liberalism: Notes on William Davies' *Limits of Neo-Liberalism*', *Renewal: A journal of social democracy*: www.renewal.org.uk/articles/the-limits-of-neo-liberalism
'Design for NZ memorial in Hyde Park, London', MCH: https://mch.govt.nz/nz-identity-heritage/national-monuments-war-graves/new-zealand-memorial-london
'Director's reflections', NZ on Screen Iwi Whitiāhua, 2 September 2013: www.nzonscreen.com/title/maori-battalion-march-to-victory-1990/background/tainui-stephens
'DVA Annual Report 2018–2019', Department of Veterans' Affairs: www.transparency.gov.au/annual-reports/department-veterans-affairs/reporting-year/2018-2019-19
Dyrenfurth, Nick, 'Mateship: Secular Australia's religion and how John Howard hijacked it', *Sydney Morning Herald*, 25 December 2014: www.smh.com.au/national/mateship-secular-australias-religion-and-how-john-howard-hijacked-it-20141217-129c7t.html
Ellery, David, 'Monash Centre: The new front in history wars', *Canberra Times*, 7 July 2018: www.canberratimes.com.au/story/6015151/monash-centre-the-new-front-in-history-wars/
'Ep0: Exploring the gaps between us and the past', *History Labs*, 28 May 2018: https://historylab.net/ep0-exploring-the-gaps
Fathi, Romain, 'Crowds at dawn services have plummeted in recent years. It's time to reinvent Anzac Day', *The Conversation*, 21 April 2021: https://theconversation.com/crowds-at-dawn-services-have-plummeted-in-recent-years-its-time-to-reinvent-anzac-day-157313
Fathi, Romain, '"Look at me! Look at me!" The Sir John Monash Centre at Villers-Bretonneux: A Frenchman's reflection on his visit', 12 March 2019: http://honesthistory.net.au/wp/

fathi-romain-look-at-me-look-at-me-the-sir-john-monash-centre-at-villers-bretonneux-a-frenchmans-reflection-on-his-visit/

'Final 2015 NZHA conference schedule', New Zealand Historical Association: https://nzha.org.nz/2015/11/30/re-final-2015-nzha-conference-schedule/

'Final report November 2018', Commonwealth of Australia, 2018: www.aph.gov.au/Parliamentary_Business/Committees/Joint/Former_Committees/Constitutional_Recognition_2018/ConstRecognition/Final_Report

'Following in their footsteps the making of Ngā Tapuwae', WW100: https://ww100.govt.nz/following-in-their-footsteps-the-making-of-nga-tapuwae

For Country, For Nation, Australian War Memorial: www.awm.gov.au/visit/exhibitions/for-country-for-nation

'Foundational Histories: Australian Historical Association Conference 2015 – Conference Abstracts', Australian Historical Association, University of Sydney, 2015: www.sydney.edu.au/arts/history/docs/aha2015/AHA_2015_conference_abstracts.pdf

Gallagher, Emily, 'The first war for country, for nation', *Inside Story*, 18 May 2017: https://insidestory.org.au/the-first-war-for-country-for-nation/

'"Give me strength": Anzac protest boy's full barrage', *Newshub*, 26 April 2017: www.newshub.co.nz/home/new-zealand/2017/04/give-me-strength-anzac-protest-boy-s-full-barrage.html

'Goff speech to Turkish international service at Mehmetcik Abide', *Scoop*, 25 April 2001: www.scoop.co.nz/stories/PA0104/S00376/turkish-international-service-at-mehmetcik-abide.htm

Goff, Phil, 'Anzac dawn service speech – Gallipoli', Beehive, 25 April 2001: www.beehive.govt.nz/node/10329

'Governor-General of New Zealand: Waitangi Day speech', *Scoop*, 6 February 2015: www.scoop.co.nz/stories/PA1502/S00062/governor-general-of-new-zealand-waitangi-day-speech.htm

'Govt spends $20m on WWI arts and culture', *Stuff*, 19 April 2015: www.stuff.co.nz/national/last-post-first-light/67781872/govt-spends-20m-on-wwi-arts-and-culture

Hawke, Bob, 'Speech by the prime minister at the handover ceremony of the Young Endeavour Sydney', PM Transcripts, 26 January 1988: https://pmtranscripts.pmc.gov.au/release/transcript-7279

Hill, Robert, 'Green light for Australian memorial in London', Parliament of Australia, 11 January 2003: https://parlinfo.aph.gov.au/parlInfo/download/media/pressrel/QMA86/upload_binary/qma863.pdf

'History in the making at Mangungu Mission', *Scoop*, 29 January 2015: www.scoop.co.nz/stories/PO1501/S00111/history-in-the-making-at-mangungu-mission.htm

Holt, Harold, 'Statement by the Prime Minister, the Rt. Hon. Harold Holt, in the House of Representatives: Commemorative medallion and badge', PM Transcripts, 16 March 1967: https://pmtranscripts.pmc.gov.au/sites/default/files/original/00001524.pdf

'Howard, John, 'Address to official luncheon banquet hall, Parliament House Wellington, New Zealand', PM Transcripts, 10 March 2003: https://pmtranscripts.pmc.gov.au/release/transcript-20527

Howard, John, '"Australians at War" Address Australia House, London', PM Transcripts, 10 November 2003: https://pmtranscripts.pmc.gov.au/release/transcript-20994

Howard, John, 'Address at a reception hosted by the Rt Hon Helen Clark Prime Minister of New Zealand, Langham Hotel, Auckland', PM Transcripts, 20 February 2005: https://pmtranscripts.pmc.gov.au/release/transcript-21621

Howard, John, 'Address at luncheon given by Rt Hon Helen Clark MP and Professor Peter Davis,

Wellington', PM Transcripts, 26 February 2001: https://pmtranscripts.pmc.gov.au/release/transcript-12376
Howard, John, 'Address at the dedication of the Australian War Memorial Hyde Park Corner, London', 11 November 2003: https://pmtranscripts.pmc.gov.au/release/transcript-20997
Howard, John, 'Address at the launch of the distinctively Australian Chowder Bay Heritage Area, Mosman', PM Transcripts, 18 December 2003: https://pmtranscripts.pmc.gov.au/release/transcript-21053
Howard, John, 'Address at the state funeral service of Alec William Campbell, the Cathedral Church of St David, Hobart', PM Transcripts, 24 May 2002: https://pmtranscripts.pmc.gov.au/release/transcript-12946
Howard, John, 'Anzac Day 2002', PM Transcripts, 25 April 2002: https://pmtranscripts.pmc.gov.au/release/transcript-12819
Howard, John, 'Dawn service, Gallipoli, Turkey', PM Transcripts, 25 April 2000: https://pmtranscripts.pmc.gov.au/release/transcript-22688
Howard, John, 'Doorstop interview, Iraq', PM Transcripts, 25 April 2004: https://pmtranscripts.pmc.gov.au/release/transcript-21232
Howard, John, 'Doorstop interview, Sydney Airport', PM Transcripts, 1 May 2003: https://pmtranscripts.pmc.gov.au/release/transcript-20712
Howard, John, 'Joint doorstop with Prime Minister of New Zealand, The Rt Hon Helen Clark MP, Auckland', PM Transcripts, 24 February 2001: https://pmtranscripts.pmc.gov.au/release/transcript-11957
Howard, John, 'Joint press conference with New Zealand Prime Minister Helen Clark, Sheraton Hotel, Auckland', PM Transcripts, 9 March 2003: https://pmtranscripts.pmc.gov.au/release/transcript-20713
Howard, John, 'Joint press conference with New Zealand Prime Minister Helen Clark, Wellington, New Zealand', PM Transcripts, 10 March 2003: https://pmtranscripts.pmc.gov.au/release/transcript-20717
Howard, John, 'Joint press conference with Prime Minister of New Zealand, Helen Clark, Parliament House, Canberra', PM Transcripts, 3 March 2004: https://pmtranscripts.pmc.gov.au/release/transcript-21139
Howard, John, 'Joint press conference with the Prime Minister of New Zealand The Hon Helen Clark MP, Port Moresby, Papua New Guinea', PM Transcripts, 25 October 2005: https://pmtranscripts.pmc.gov.au/release/transcript-22004
Howard, John, 'Joint press conference with the Rt Hon Helen Clark, Prime Minister of New Zealand, Parliament House, Wellington, New Zealand', PM Transcripts, 21 February 2005: https://pmtranscripts.pmc.gov.au/release/transcript-21625
Howard, John, 'Joint press conference with the Rt Hon Helen Clark Prime Minister of New Zealand, Langham Hotel, New Zealand', PM Transcripts, 20 February 2005: https://pmtranscripts.pmc.gov.au/release/transcript-21620
Howard, John, 'Joint press conference with The Rt Hon Helen Clark MP, Prime Minister of New Zealand, Kirribilli House, Sydney', PM Transcripts, 28 September 2000: https://pmtranscripts.pmc.gov.au/release/transcript-22887
Howard, John, 'Joint press conference with the Rt Hon Helen Clark MP, Wellington, New Zealand', PM Transcripts, 26 February 2001: https://pmtranscripts.pmc.gov.au/release/transcript-11978
Howard, John, 'Official visit by New Zealand Prime Minister', PM Transcripts, 2 March 2000: https://pmtranscripts.pmc.gov.au/release/transcript-11582

Howard, John, 'Press conference Istanbul, Turkey', PM Transcripts, 26 April 2005: https://pmtranscripts.pmc.gov.au/release/transcript-21721

Howard, John, 'Radio interview with John Laws, 2UE', PM Transcripts, 14 October 2002: https://pmtranscripts.pmc.gov.au/release/transcript-12503

Howard, John, 'Radio interview with Mike Carlton, Radio 2UE', PM Transcripts, 9 September 1999: https://pmtranscripts.pmc.gov.au/release/transcript-11222

Howard, John, 'Speech at the National RSL Congress Melbourne', PM Transcripts, 5 September 2001: https://pmtranscripts.pmc.gov.au/release/transcript-12422

Howard, John, 'Television interview with Barrie Cassidy – InsidersABC', PM Transcripts, 2 September 2001: https://pmtranscripts.pmc.gov.au/release/transcript-11908

Howard, John, 'Transcript of the Prime Minister the Hon John Howard MP address at official luncheon, Parliament Buildings Wellington, New Zealand', PM Transcripts, 17 February 1997: https://pmtranscripts.pmc.gov.au/release/transcript-10245

Howard, John, 'Transcript of the Prime Minister the Hon John Howard MP joint doorstop interview with the Prime Minister of New Zealand, The Right Hon Helen Clark, Los Cabos, Mexico', PM Transcripts, 25 October 2002: https://pmtranscripts.pmc.gov.au/release/transcript-12638

Howard, John, 'Transcript of the Prime Minister the Hon John Howard MP Press conference on departure for London Sydney International Airport', PM Transcripts, 7 April 2002: https://pmtranscripts.pmc.gov.au/release/transcript-10673

Howard, John, 'Transcript of The Prime Minister The Hon John Howard MP address to joint meeting of the US Congress', PM Transcripts, 12 June 2002: https://pmtranscripts.pmc.gov.au/release/transcript-12906

Howard, John, 'Transcript of the Prime Minister the Hon John Howard MP interview with Steve Liebmann, *Today Show*', PM Transcripts, 15 August 2002: https://pmtranscripts.pmc.gov.au/release/transcript-12510/

Howard, John, 'Transcript of the Prime Minister The Hon John Howard MP joint press conference with the Rt Hon Helen Clark Prime Minister of New Zealand', PM Transcripts, 2 March 2000: https://pmtranscripts.pmc.gov.au/release/transcript-11485

Howard, John, 'Turkish international service at Mehmetcik Abide', PM Transcripts, 25 April 2000: https://pmtranscripts.pmc.gov.au/release/transcript-22690

Howard, John, 'Visit to Australia by the Right Hon Helen Clark MP Prime Minister of New Zealand', PM Transcripts, 15 February 2002: https://pmtranscripts.pmc.gov.au/release/transcript-12789

'Indigenous Australians mark Anzac Day', SBS, 2015: www.sbs.com.au/news/indigenous-australians-mark-anzac-day

'Indigenous soldiers who hid their identity to serve: The untold story', *ABC News*, 31 December 2014: www.abc.net.au/pm/content/2014/s4156077.htm

Inglis, Ken, 'Letters from a pilgrimage: Ken Inglis' despatches from the Anzac tour to Gallipoli, April–May 1965', *Analysis & Policy Observatory*: http://apo.org.au/node/54313

'Interview with the Hon John Brown', Radio 2UE, 17 December 1990: https://parlinfo.aph.gov.au/parlInfo/search/display/display.w3p;query=Id%3A%22media%2Fpressrel%2FHPR03008231%22;src1=sm1

Keating, Paul, 'Remembrance Day 1993: Commemorative address', AWM, 1993: www.awm.gov.au/commemoration/speeches/keating-remembrance-day-1993

Keenan, Danny, 'We came of age on battlefields of New Zealand', *New Zealand Herald*, 20 April 2006: www.nzherald.co.nz/nz/news/article.cfm?c_id=1&objectid=10378631

Key, John, 'Speech at dawn service in Anzac Cove in Gallipoli', *Scoop*, 26 April 2015: www.scoop.co.nz/stories/PA1504/S00333/john-keys-speech-at-dawn-service-in-anzac-cove-in-gallipoli.html

Key, John, 'Dedication of Australian memorial in Pukeahu National War Memorial Park', 20 April 2015: www.beehive.govt.nz/speech/dedication-australian-memorial-pukeahu-national-war-memorial-park

'Māori Television marks fifth on-air anniversary', *Throng*, 13 April 2009: www.throng.co.nz/2009/03/Māori-television-marks-fifth-on-air-anniversary

'Māori Television recreates past, bringing together New Zealanders to celebrate Anzac Day', Māori Television, 27 April 2018: http://stoppress.co.nz/news/Māori-television-recreates-past-bringing-together-new-zealanders-celebrate-anzac-day

Mateparae, Jerry, 'Battle of Gate Pa Commemorations', 29 April 2014: https://gg.govt.nz/publications/battle-gate-pa-commemorations

Mateparae, Jerry, 'Battle of Ōrākau', 1 April 2014: https://gg.govt.nz/publications/battle-ōrākau

'National Framework for Values Education in Australian Schools', *Education Services Australia*: www.curriculum.edu.au/values/val_national_framework_for_values_education,8757

'New Zealand's First World War Centenary Programme: The programme overview July 2014', WW100: ww100.govt.nz/sites/default/files/files/WW100

'Ngā Tupuwae/New Zealand First World War Trails', *Ngā Tupuwae*: https://ngatapuwae.govt.nz

'NITV commemorates Anzac Day', NITV, 25 April 2013: www.facebook.com/NITVAustralia

'NITV, Natalie Whyte, Redfern Anzac Day 2015', YouTube: www.youtube.com/watch?v=SptcqyNiHFw

'NITV: Launch Day', *TV Tonight*, 5 December 2012: http://tvtonight.com.au/2012/12/nitv-launch-day.html

'NZ war memorial marks a "special bond"', BBC, 16 September 2006: http://news.bbc.co.uk/2/hi/uk_news/5350868.stm

'NZ war memorial museum on Western Front project to be unveiled', RNZ, 2 November 2018: www.rnz.co.nz/news/national/370090/nz-war-memorial-museum-on-western-front-project-to-be-unveiled

'PM commemorates Anzac Day in Iraq', *ABC News*, 25 April 2004: www.abc.net.au/news/2004-04-25/pm-commemorates-anzac-day-in-iraq/175550

'PM will attend Queen Mother's funeral', *New Zealand Herald*, 2 April 2002: www.nzherald.co.nz/nz/news/article.cfm?c_id=1&objectid=1292774

'PM: Address to the NZ memorial dedication ceremony', *Scoop*, 13 November 2006: www.scoop.co.nz/stories/PA0611/S00215/pm-address-to-the-nz-memorial-dedication-ceremony.htm

'Private Alec Campbell', Monument Australia: www.monumentaustralia.org.au/themes/people/military/display/100621-private-alec-campbell

'Profile – Tanya Denning Orman', NITV: www.nitv.org.au/fx-story.cfm?sid=EA03540F-B96B-4736-E539CA3FB0D96160

Pugsley, Chris, 'Military advisor's perspective', NZ On Screen, April 2009: www.nzonscreen.com/title/gallipoli-the-new-zealand-story-1984/background

'Queen, Blair, Clark at opening of NZ memorial', *New Zealand Herald*, 12 November 2006: www.nzherald.co.nz/nz/news/article.cfm?c_id=1&objectid=10410356

'Rā Maumahara – The journey to a national commemoration', Te Puni Kōkiri: www.tpk.govt.nz/en/

whakamahia/te-putake-o-te-riri-wars-and-conflicts-in-new-zeal/ra-maumahara-the-journey-to-a-national-commemoration

Radford, Gail, 'Women Against Rape in War', Canberra Museum and Gallery, 9 October 2019: www.cmag.com.au/blog/women-against-rape-in-war

Redgum, 'I Was Only 19 – 1983': www.youtube.com/watch?v=Urtiyp-G6jY

'Reflections on East Timor', *ANU News*, 16 September 2015: http://sdsc.bellschool.anu.edu.au/news-events/stories/3401/reflections-east-timor

'Remembrance Day commemorative address', AWM, November 2013. www.awm.gov.au/commemoration/speeches/commemorative-address-11-november-2013

'RSA launches new national association', RSA, 5 October 2014: http://rsa.org.nz/News/RSA-launches-new-National-Association

Spirit of Anzac Centenary Experience, Australian War Memorial: www.awm.gov.au/about/our-work/projects/spirit-anzac-centenary-experience

Stanley, Peter, 'Talking Turkey', Honest History: http://honesthistory.net.au/wp/talking-turkey

Stephens, Andrew, 'Black Diggers: The untold story of our Indigenous soldiers', *Sydney Morning Herald*, 3 April 2015: www.smh.com.au/entertainment/black-diggers-the-untold-story-of-our-indigenous-soldiers-20150328-1m9pme.html

Stephens, David, 'Money, Monash and motive: Analysing a project in France'http://honesthistory.net.au/wp/money-monash-and-motive-analysing-a-project-in-france-i/

Students prepare to take NZ Land Wars petition to Parliament', *New Zealand Herald*, 7 December 2015: www.nzherald.co.nz/nz/students-prepare-to-take-nz-land-wars-petition-to-parliament

'*Tama Tū* press kit', Tama Tū, 2006: http://tamatu.co.nz/media/2006+Press+kit+Tama+Tu.doc

'Te Hiku Media provide online live video stream of Waitangi', Te Hiku, 3 February 2015: https://tehiku.nz/te-hiku-tv/waitangi-175/217/te-hiku-media-provide-online-live-video-stream-of-waitangi

'Te Papa and Weta Workshop open ground-breaking Gallipoli exhibition', April 2015: www.tepapa.govt.nz/about/press-and-media/press-releases/2015-news-and-media-releases/te-papa-and-weta-workshop-open

'Te Papa marks a record year for *Gallipoli: The scale of our war*', Te Papa, 25 April 2016: www.tepapa.govt.nz/about/press-and-media/press-releases/2016-news-and-media-releases/te-papa-marks-record-year

'Tears as Helen Clark barred from speaking at Waitangi', *Newshub*, 6 February 2015: www.tvnz.co.nz/one-news/new-zealand/back-in-the-day-tears-as-helen-clark-barred-from-speaking-at-waitangi-6229227

'The Australian Boer War Memorial', Australian Boer War Memorial: www.bwm.org.au/boer_war_day/Boer_War_Day2015.php

'The Indian Army at Gallipoli', *RNZ:* www.rnz.co.nz/national/programmes/anzacday/galleries/the-indian-army-at-gallipoli

'The maintenance of memory: Sir John Monash Centre', *Architecture AU*, 28 May 2019: https://architectureau.com/articles/sir-john-monash-centre-aa/

Tizard, Judith, 'Speech delivered to NZ veterans and contingent travelling to the dedication of the NZ Memorial in London', Beehive, 6 November 2006: www.beehive.govt.nz/speech/speech-delivered-nz-veterans-and-contingent-travelling-dedication-nz-memorial-london

'Tony Abbott: NZ "splendid sons" of Anzac in Isis fight', *New Zealand Herald*, 20 April 2015: www.nzherald.co.nz/nz/news/article.cfm?c_id=1&objectid=11435429

'Transcript of the Prime Minister The Hon John Howard MP address at official luncheon

Parliament Buildings Wellington, New Zealand', PM Transcripts, 17 February 1997: https://pmtranscripts.pmc.gov.au/release/transcript-10245

Uluru Statement from the Heart: https://ulurustatement.org

'Values for Australian Schooling', Education Services Australia: www.curriculum.edu.au/verve/_resources/9_point_values_with_flag_only.pdf

'Waitangi 175 ledger of events June 2016', D-0666522, MCH: https://mch.govt.nz/sites/default/files/Waitangi%20175%20ledger%20of%20events%20June%202016%20(D-0666522).PDF#overlay-context=waitangi175

Walker, Paul, 'Australian war memorial', *Architecture AU*, 1 September 2003: https://architectureau.com/articles/australian-war-memorial

'War memorial haste is unseemly', *Stuff*, 27 September 2012: www.stuff.co.nz/dominion-post/comment/7732947/War-memorial-haste-is-unseemly

'War memorial's "Australian" heart is made in India', *Stuff*, 21 April 2015: www.stuff.co.nz/national/67881452/war-memorials-australian-heart-is-made-in-india

'Who do you think you are kidding, Mr Howard?', *Australian Politics*, 9 March 2003: www.australianpolitics.com/news/2003/03/03-03-09a.shtml

Why the War Was Wrong, review, *Sydney Morning Herald*, 6 December 2003: www.smh.com.au/entertainment/books/why-the-war-was-wrong-20031206-gdhxbd.html

WW100 Final Report, April 2019: ww100.govt.nz/final-report

'You're not the voice, try and understand it', *Sydney Morning Herald*, 18 February 2005: www.smh.com.au/national/youre-not-the-voice-try-and-understand-it-20050218-gdkral.html

Acknowledgements

I could not have completed *Anzac Nations* without the collaboration and support of many different people. First and foremost, ngā mihi to Otago University Press publisher Sue Wootton, editor Imogen Coxhead and designer Fiona Moffat for their professional care and attention in assisting with this author's first book publication. Thanks also to the reviewers who provided critical feedback on the manuscript.

I am grateful to family and friends who courageously read early drafts of various chapters, in particular Phillip Light and Danielle van Dalen, as well as my fellow writers at the Auckland Writer's Club. Special thanks to Michael Bassett and Chris Pugsley for taking time to answer questions about their roles in these histories. I also wish to acknowledge the hard work of my image researcher, Andrew McKay, and photographers Kevin Hawkins and Tanya Arya.

Behind all the necessary writing and editing is the considerable encouragement and friendship of my colleagues from the Department of History at the University of Canterbury, Maxim Institute, history staff and students at Waipapa Taumata Rau University of Auckland, and the human history team at Auckland War Memorial Museum Tāmaki Paenga Hira.

To friends, family and loved ones: thank you.

Index

Bold denotes illustrations